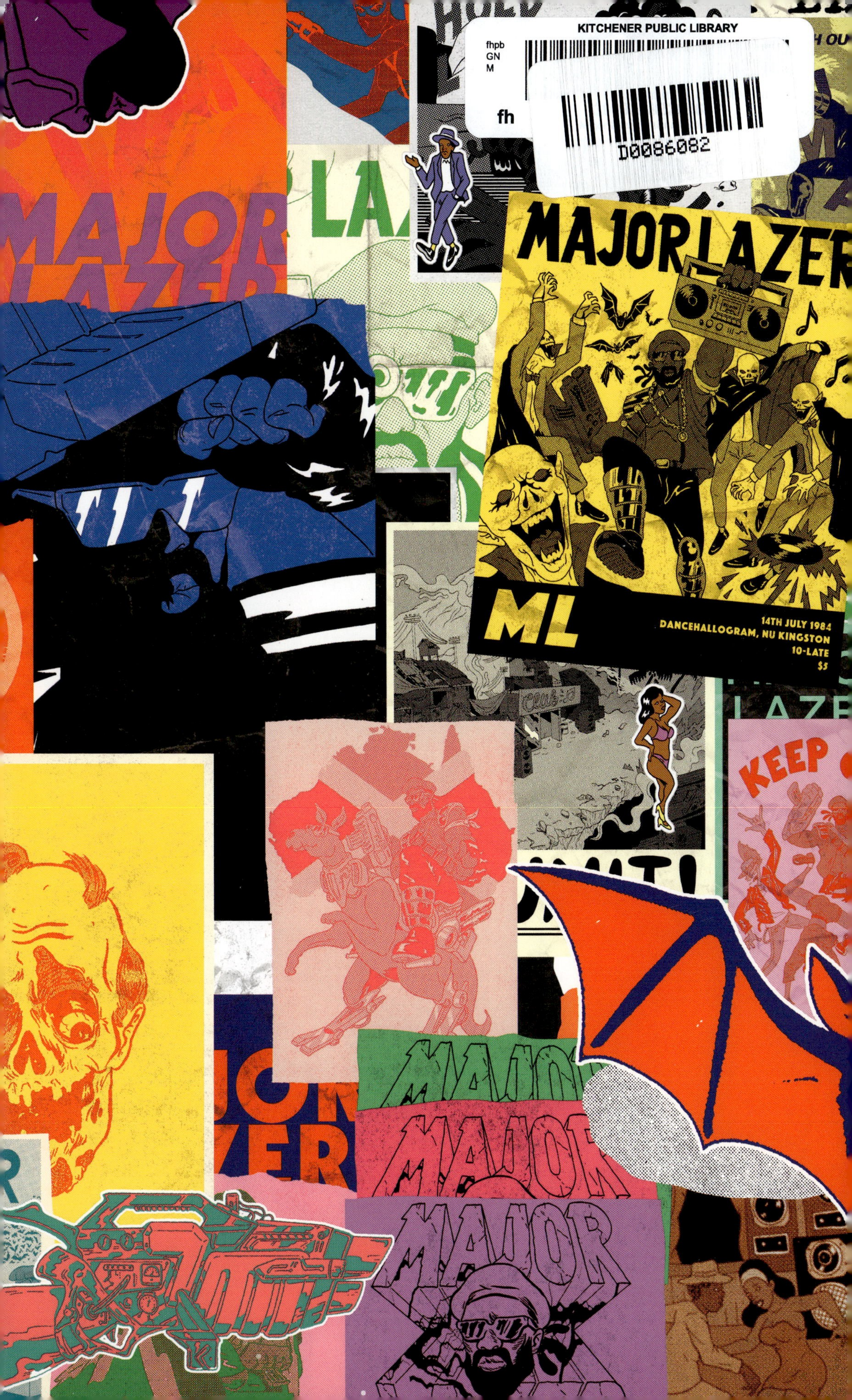
MAJOR
MAJORLAZER
ML
14TH JULY 1984
DANCEHALLOGRAM, NU KINGSTON
10-LATE
$5
KEEP
MAJOR
MAJOR
MAJOR

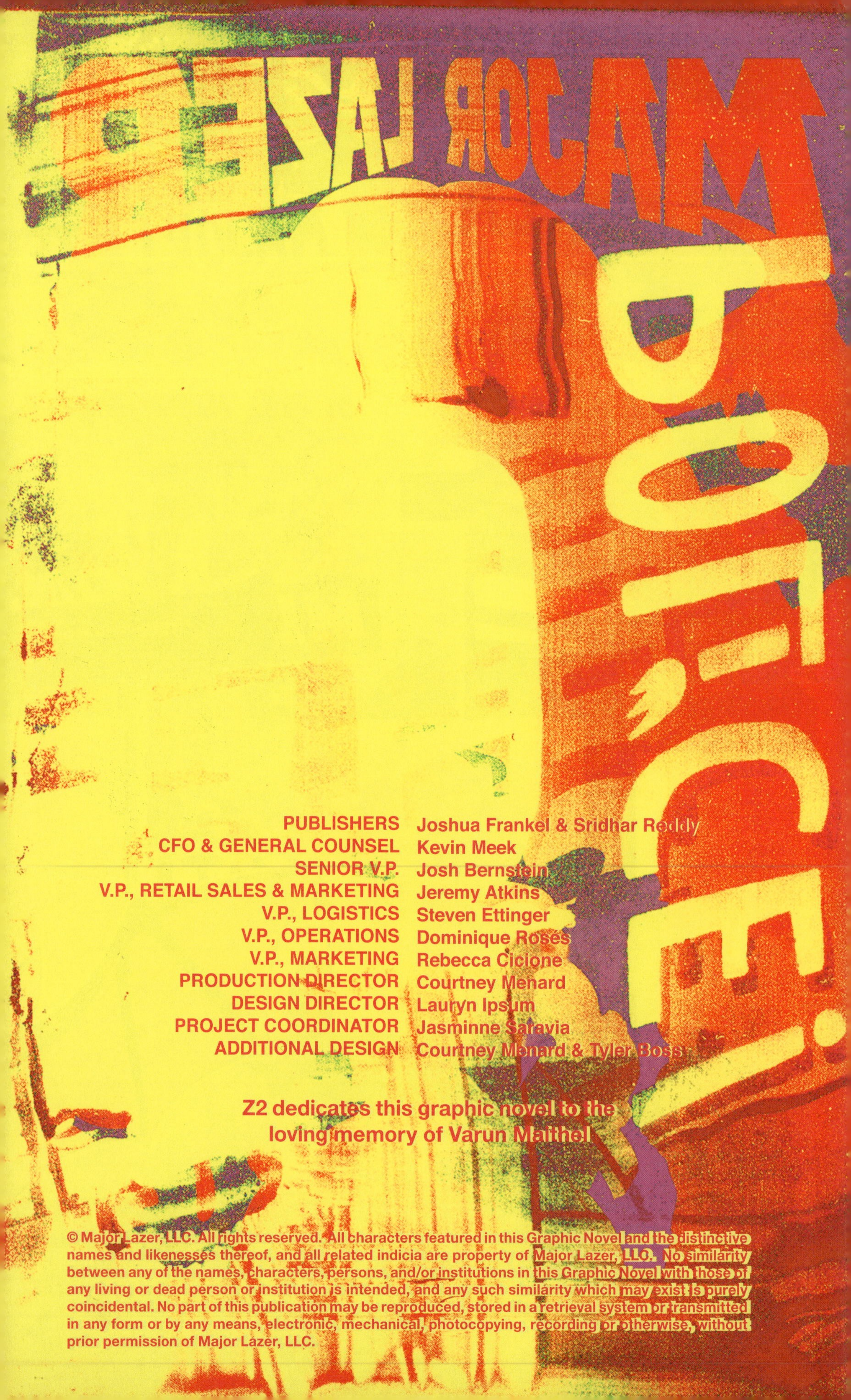

PUBLISHERS Joshua Frankel & Sridhar Reddy
CFO & GENERAL COUNSEL Kevin Meek
SENIOR V.P. Josh Bernstein
V.P., RETAIL SALES & MARKETING Jeremy Atkins
V.P., LOGISTICS Steven Ettinger
V.P., OPERATIONS Dominique Rosés
V.P., MARKETING Rebecca Cicione
PRODUCTION DIRECTOR Courtney Menard
DESIGN DIRECTOR Lauryn Ipsum
PROJECT COORDINATOR Jasminne Saravia
ADDITIONAL DESIGN Courtney Menard & Tyler Boss

Z2 dedicates this graphic novel to the loving memory of Varun Maithel

MAJOR LAZER
YEAR NEGATIVE ONE

Written & Illustrated by
Ferry Gouw

Edited by
Chris Robinson

Standard edition cover by
Ferry Gouw
Deluxe Edition cover by
Natacha Bustos

Special Thanks to
Jessica Moran & TMWRK MANAGEMENT

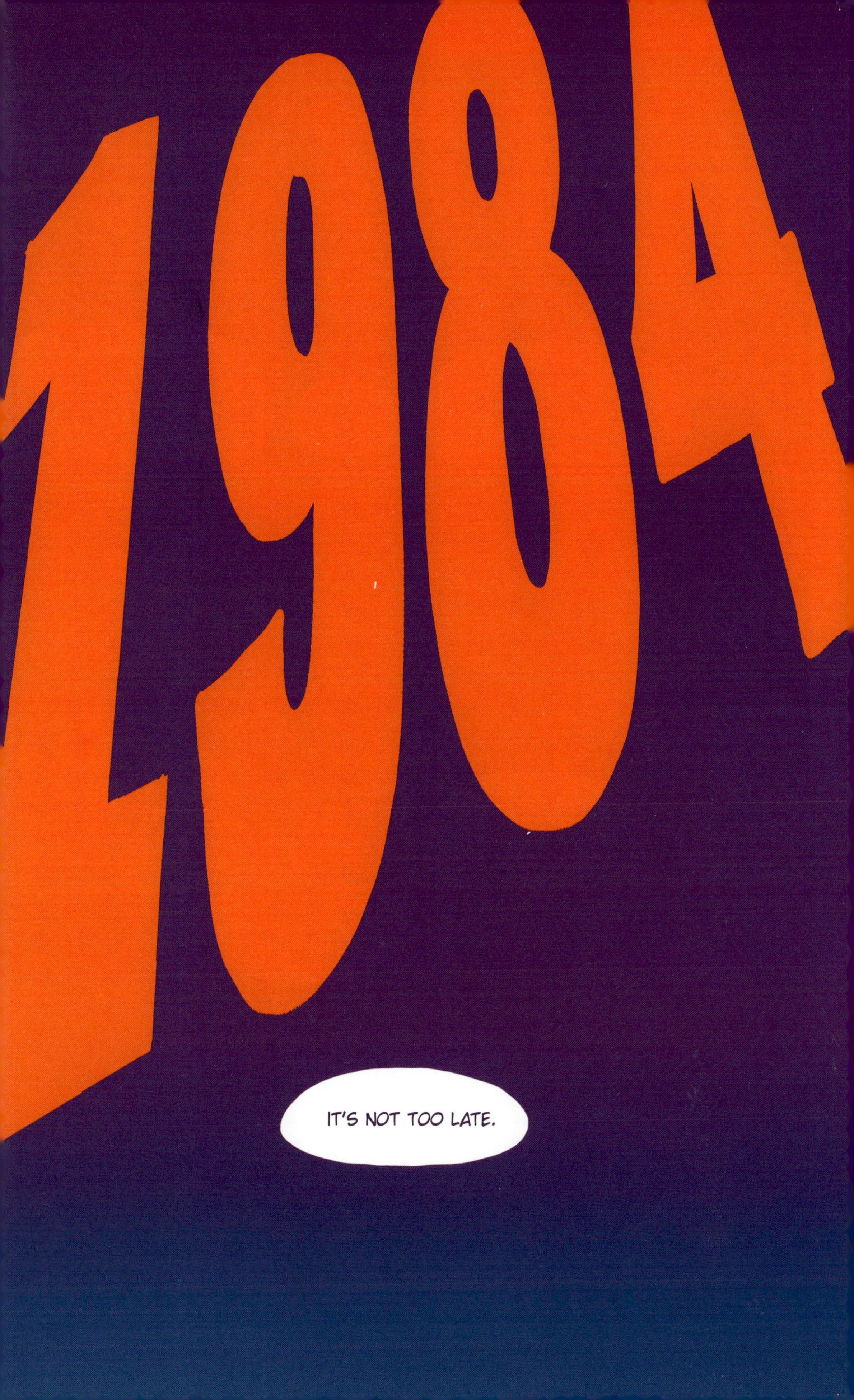
1984
IT'S NOT TOO LATE.

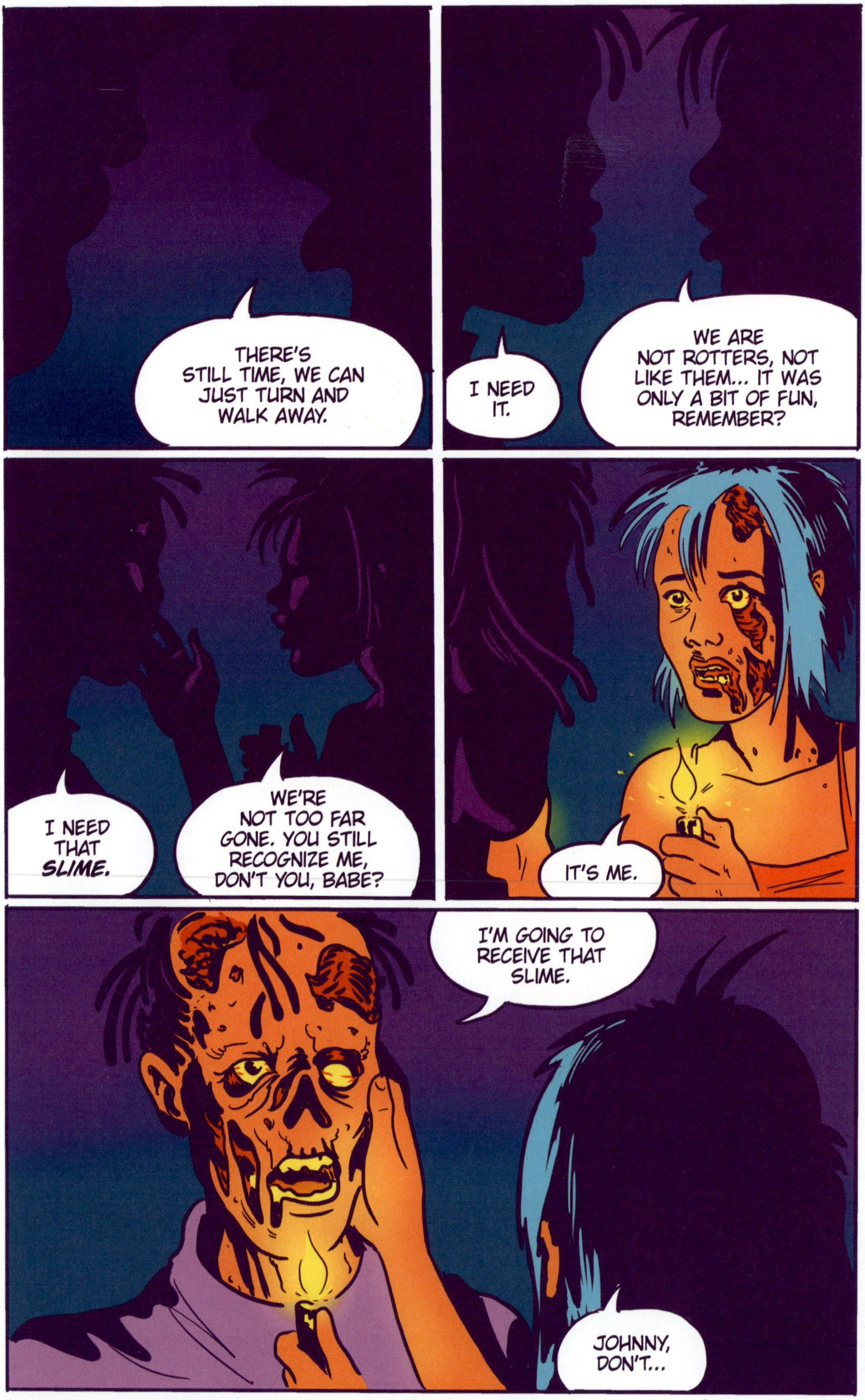
THERE'S STILL TIME, WE CAN JUST TURN AND WALK AWAY.
I NEED IT.
WE ARE NOT ROTTERS, NOT LIKE THEM... IT WAS ONLY A BIT OF FUN, REMEMBER?
I NEED THAT *SLIME.*
WE'RE NOT TOO FAR GONE. YOU STILL RECOGNIZE ME, DON'T YOU, BABE?
IT'S ME.
I'M GOING TO RECEIVE THAT SLIME.
JOHNNY, DON'T...

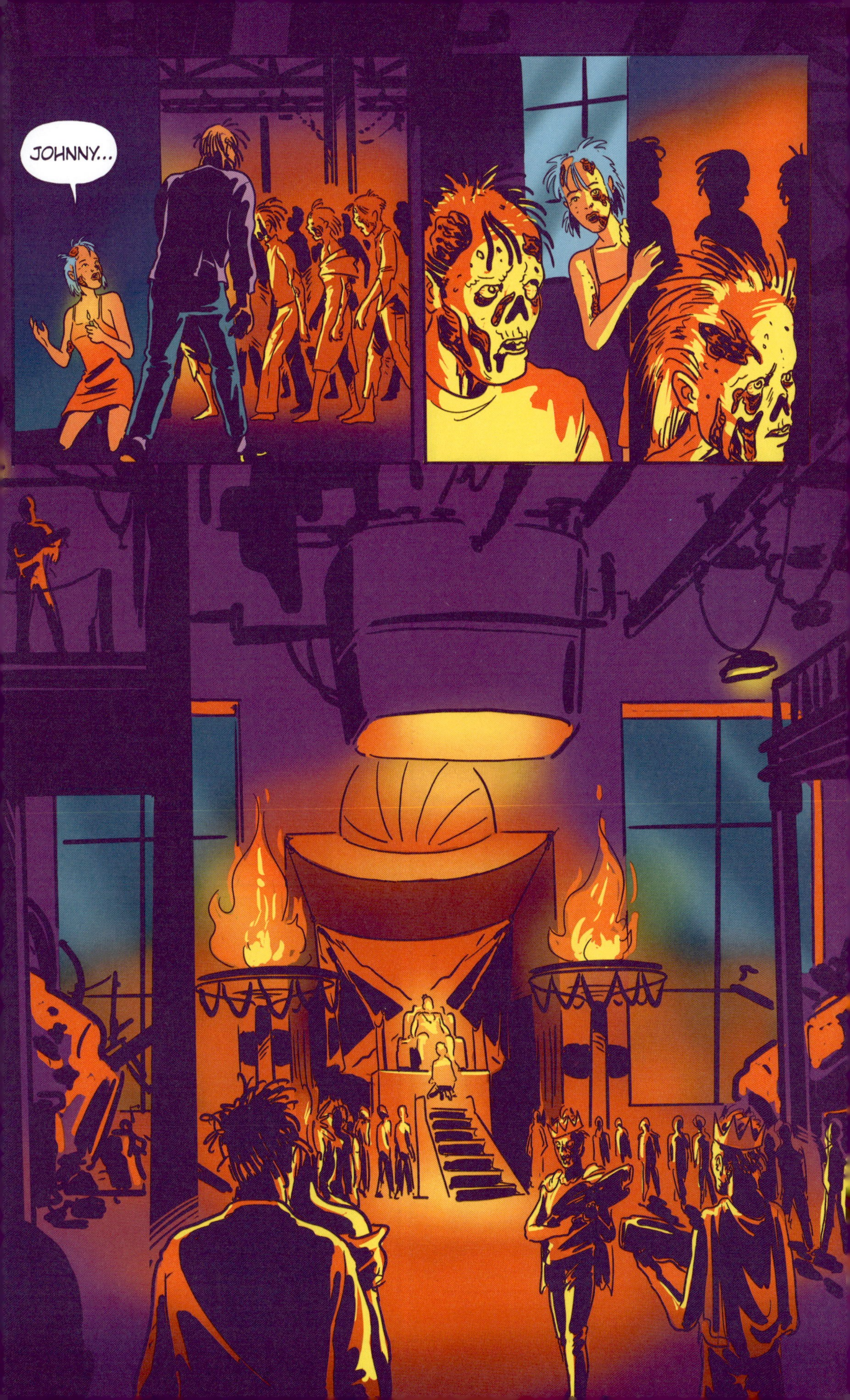
JOHNNY...

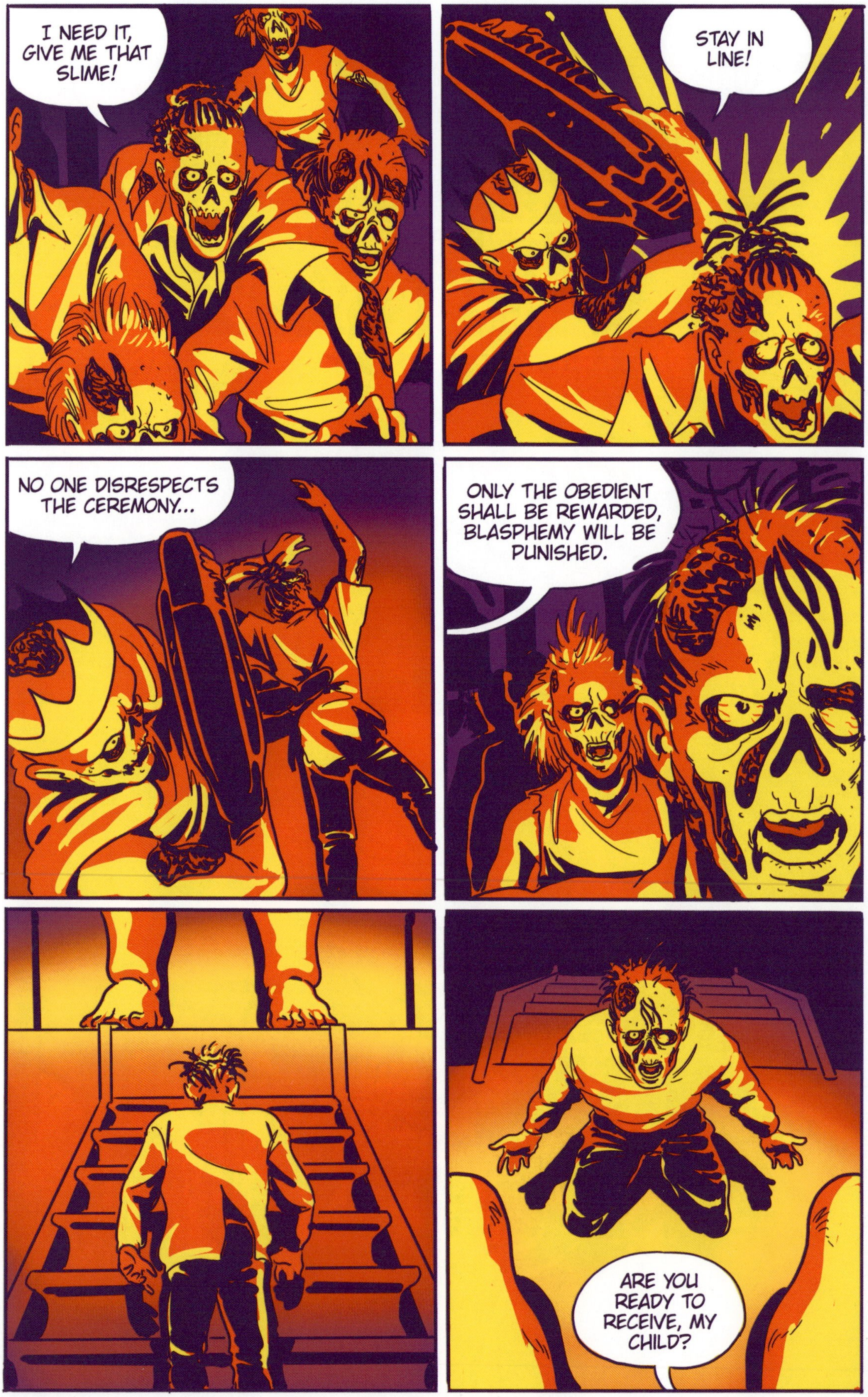
I NEED IT, GIVE ME THAT SLIME!
STAY IN LINE!
NO ONE DISRESPECTS THE CEREMONY...
ONLY THE OBEDIENT SHALL BE REWARDED, BLASPHEMY WILL BE PUNISHED.
ARE YOU READY TO RECEIVE, MY CHILD?

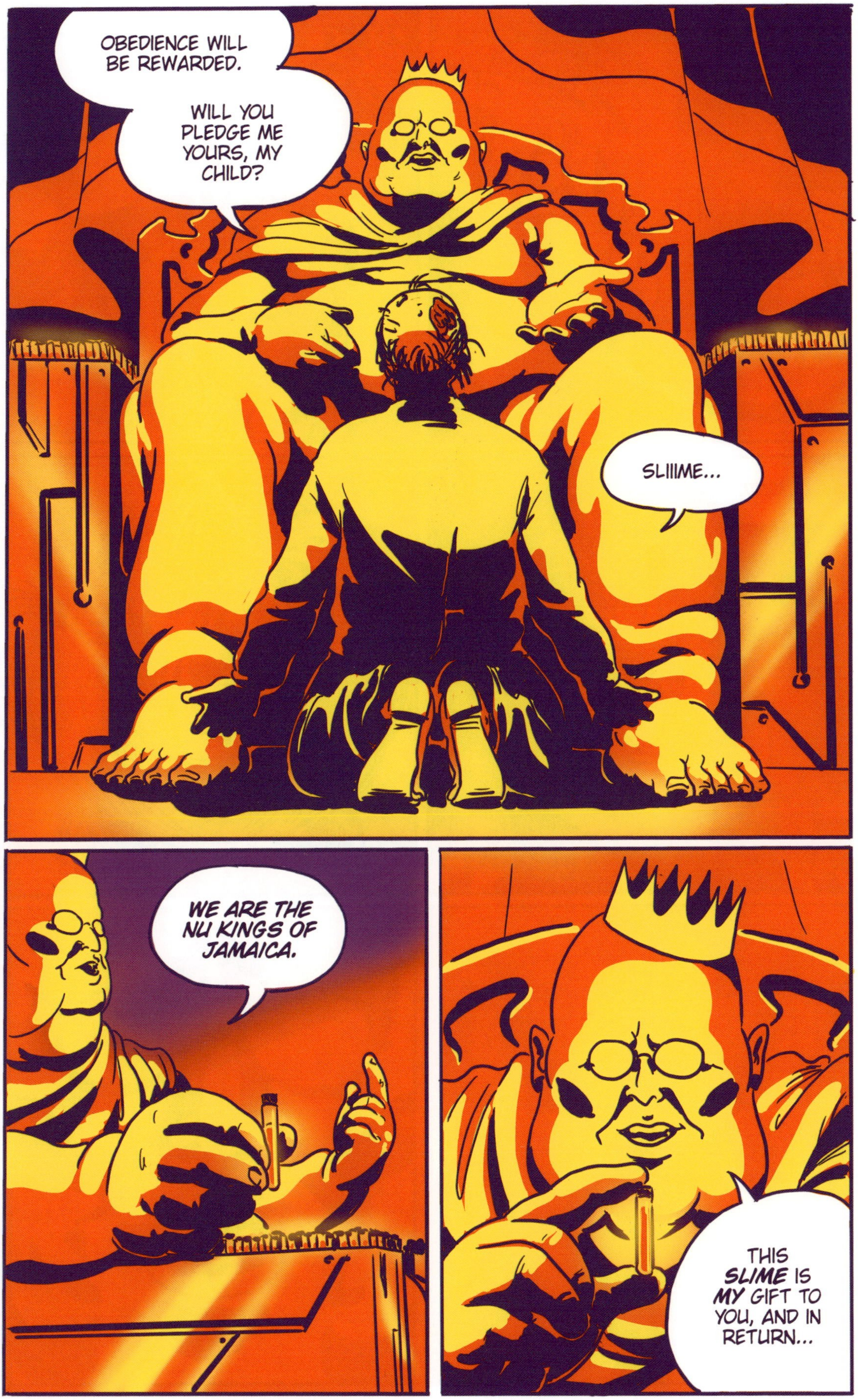
OBEDIENCE WILL BE REWARDED.
WILL YOU PLEDGE ME YOURS, MY CHILD?
SLIIIME...
WE ARE THE NU KINGS OF JAMAICA.
THIS SLIME IS MY GIFT TO YOU, AND IN RETURN...

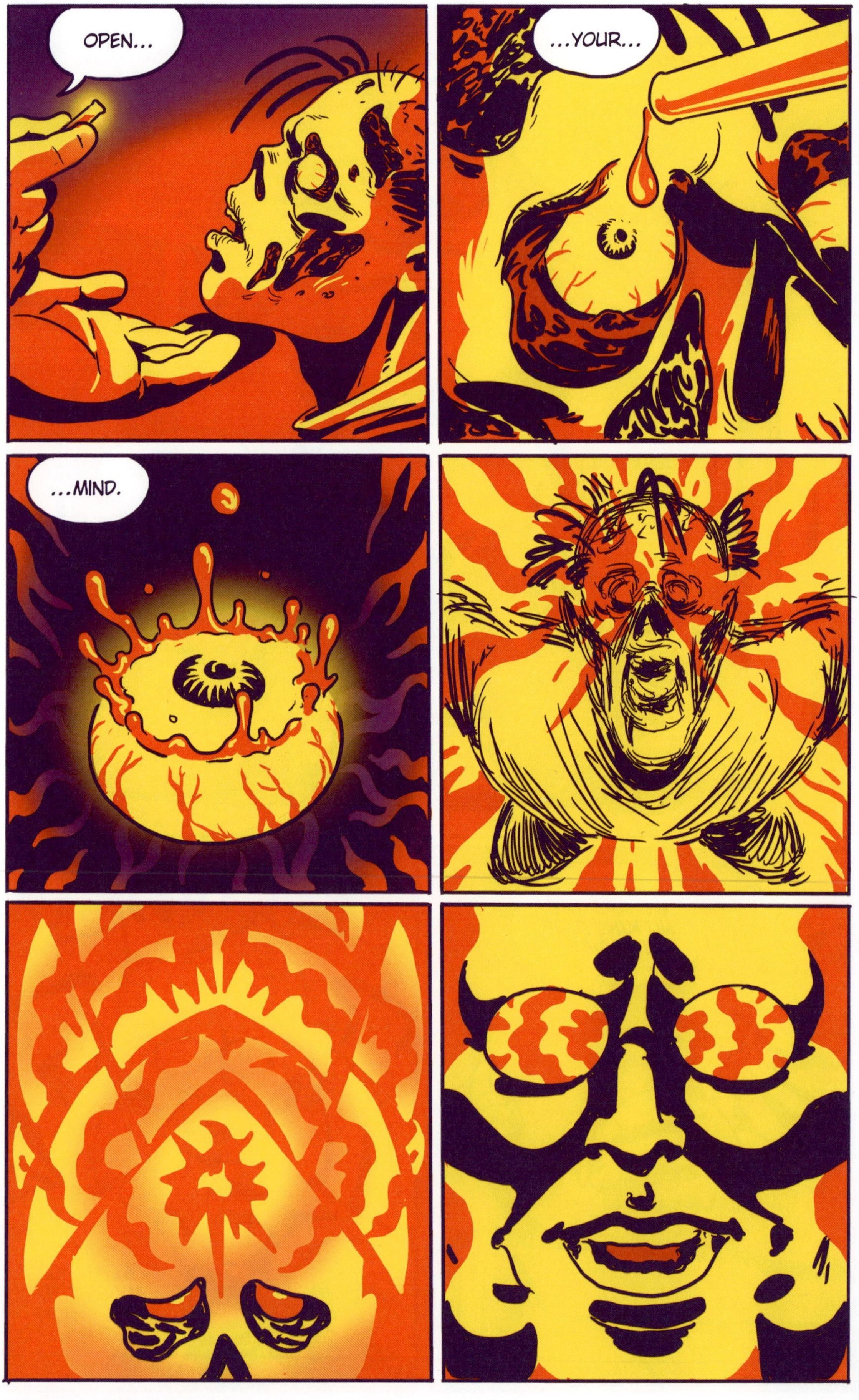
OPEN...
...YOUR...
...MIND.

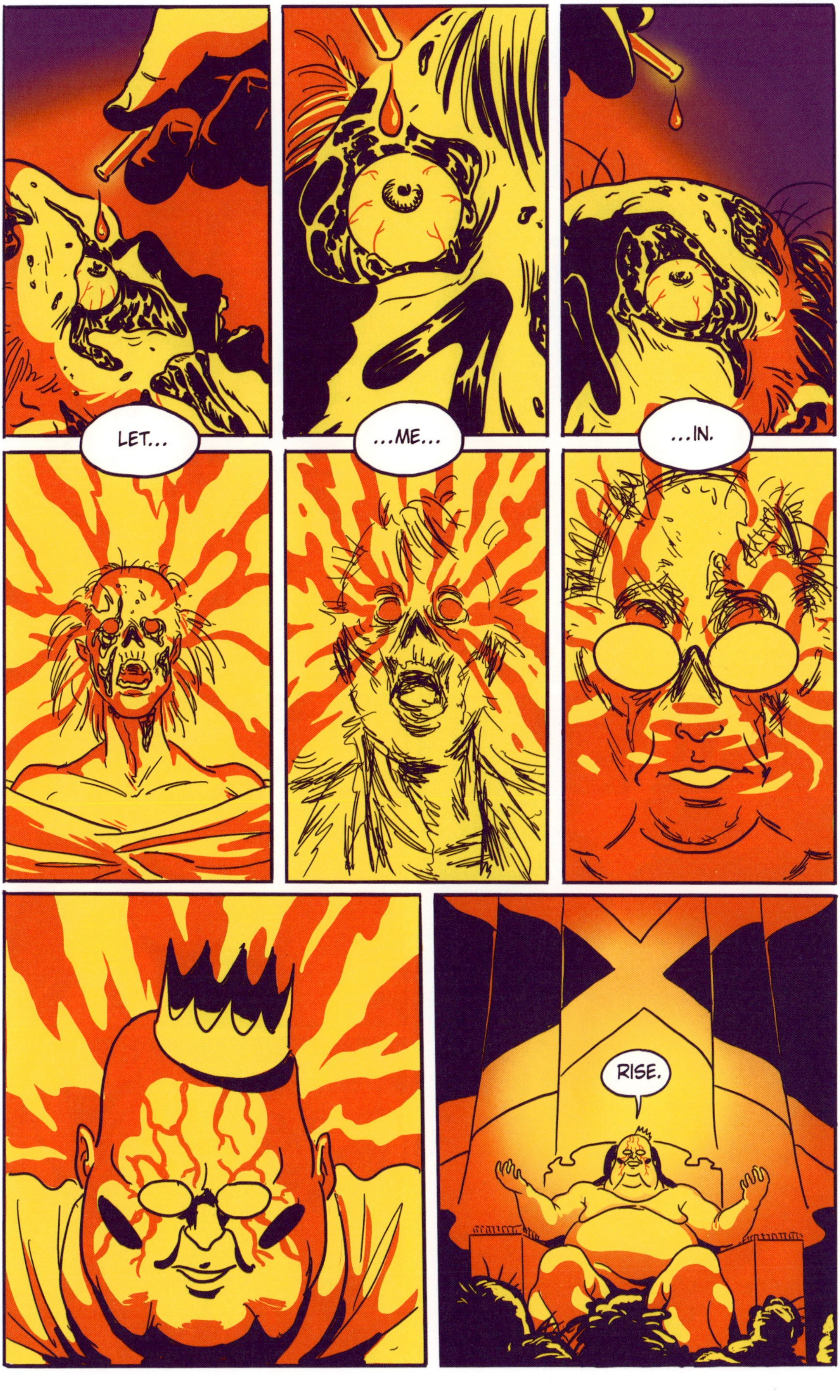
LET...
...ME...
...IN.
RISE.

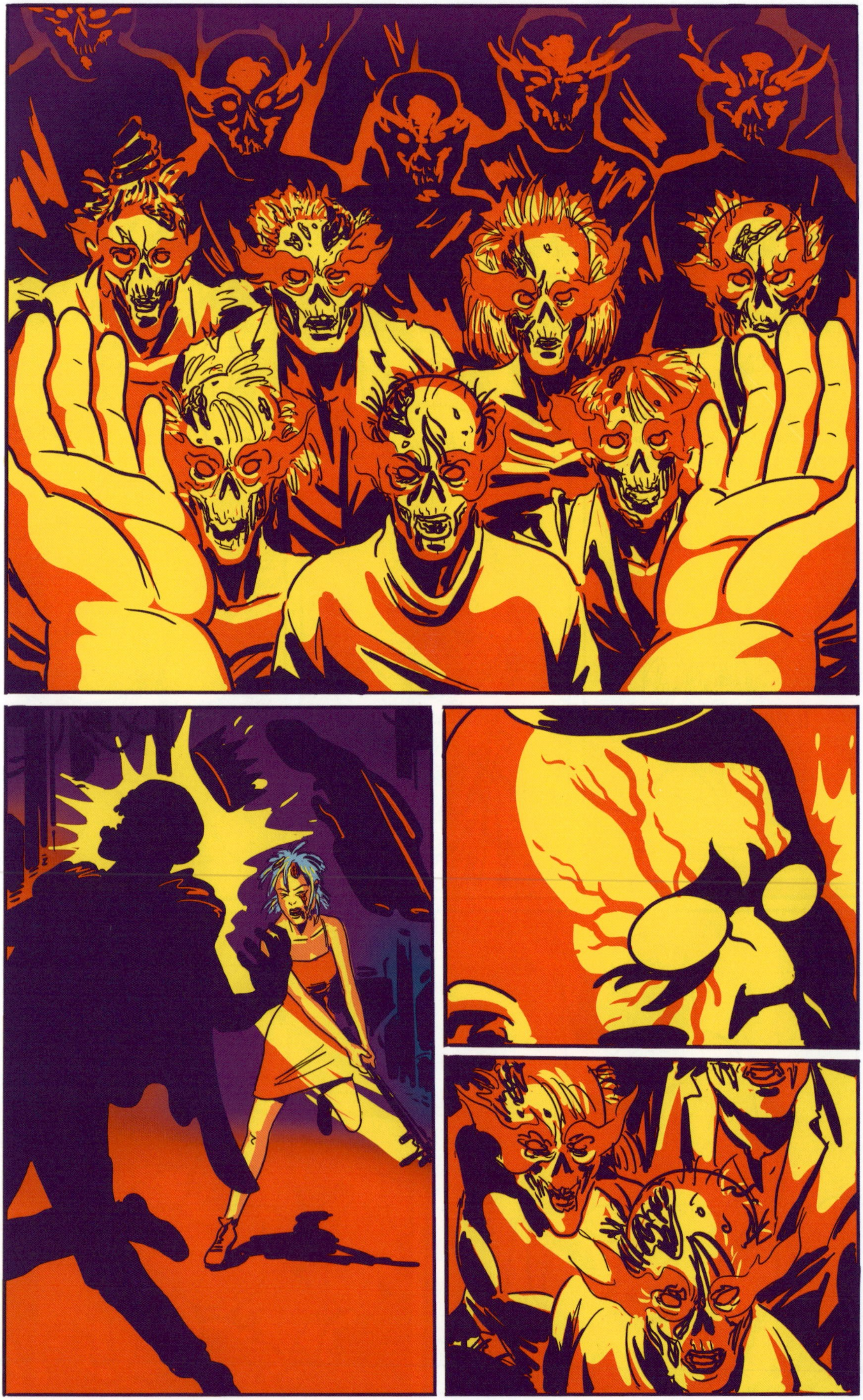

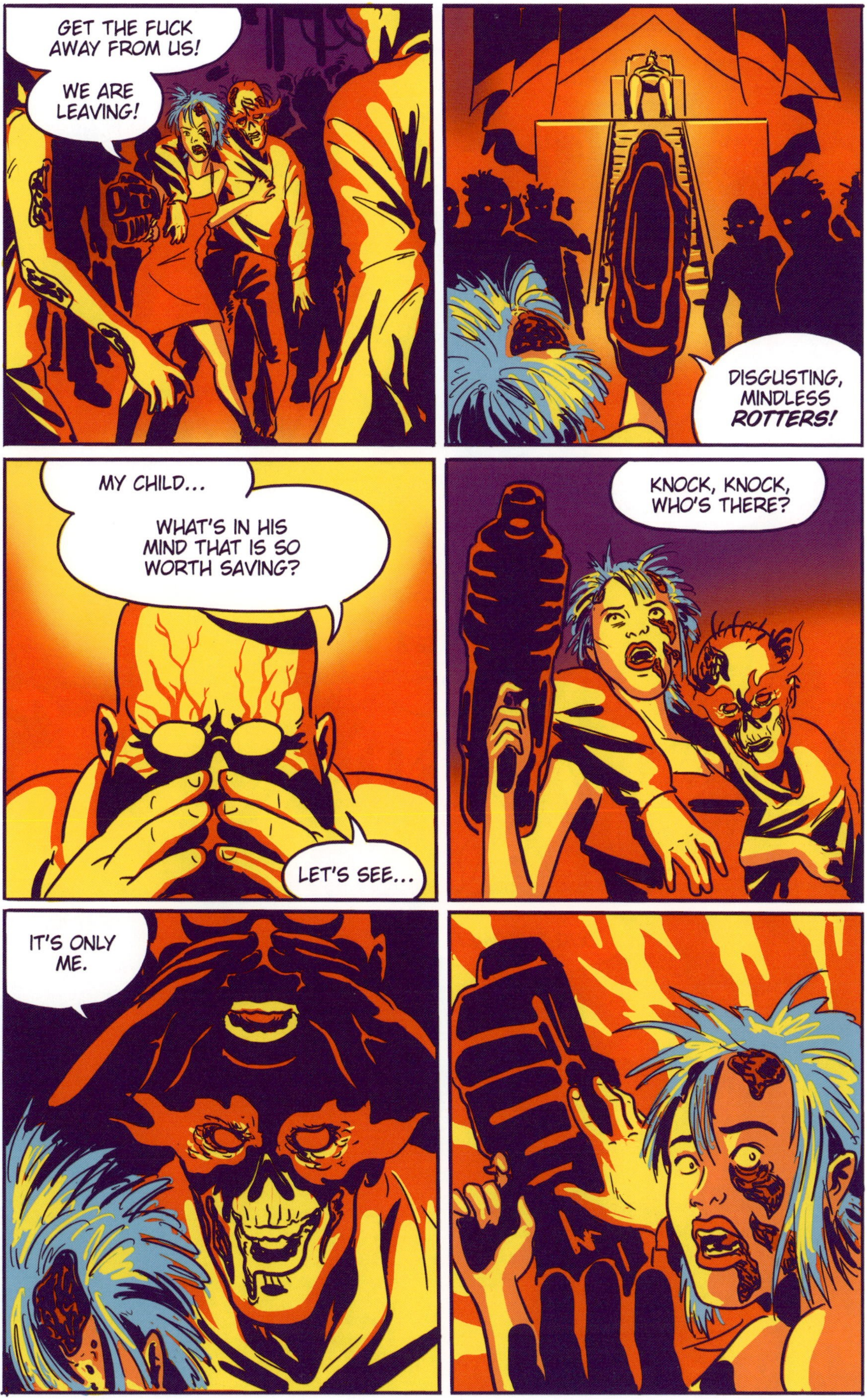
GET THE FUCK AWAY FROM US!
WE ARE LEAVING!
DISGUSTING, MINDLESS ROTTERS!
MY CHILD...
WHAT'S IN HIS MIND THAT IS SO WORTH SAVING?
LET'S SEE...
KNOCK, KNOCK, WHO'S THERE?
IT'S ONLY ME.

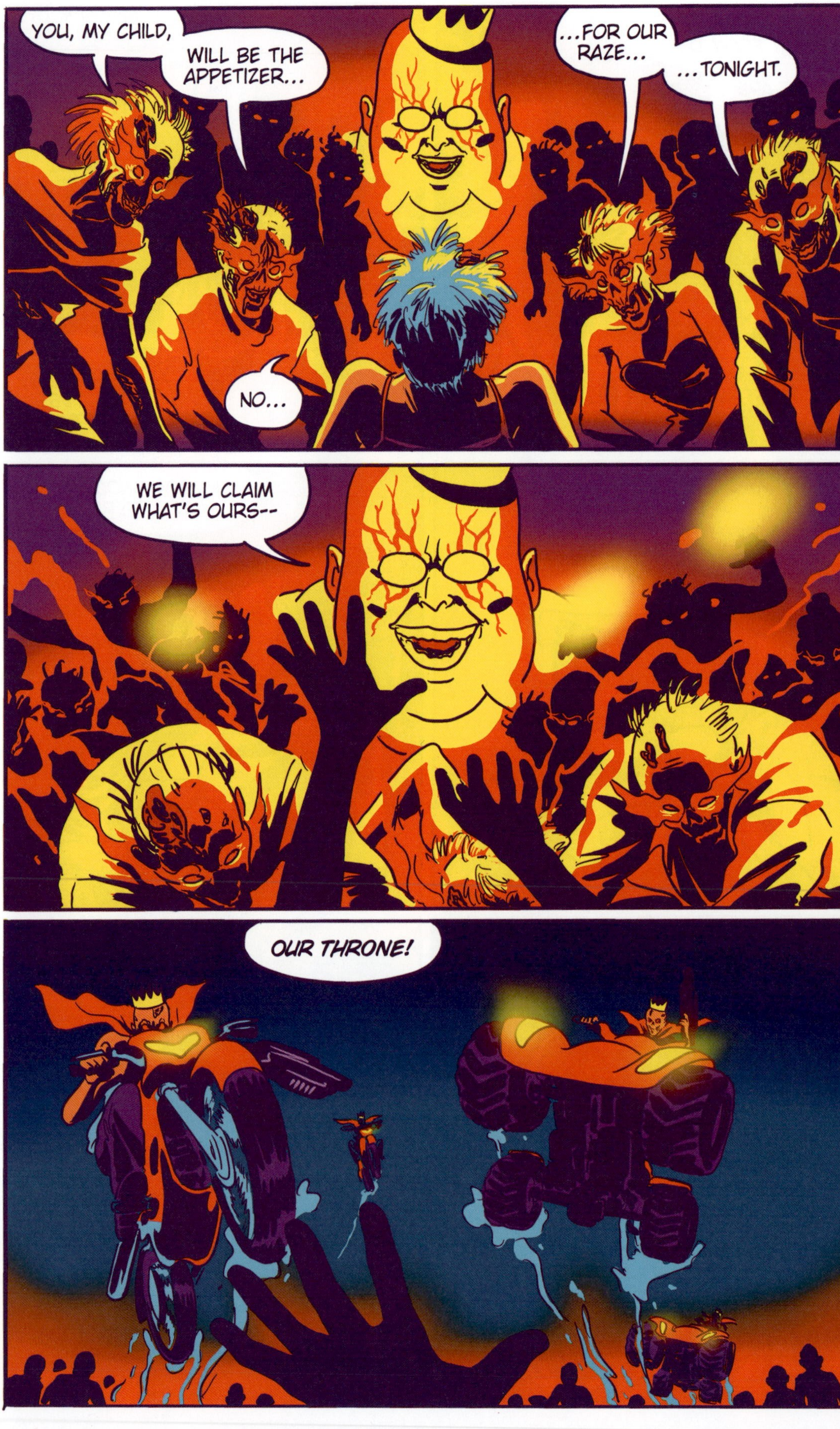
YOU, MY CHILD,
WILL BE THE APPETIZER...
...FOR OUR RAZE...
...TONIGHT.
NO...
WE WILL CLAIM WHAT'S OURS--
OUR THRONE!

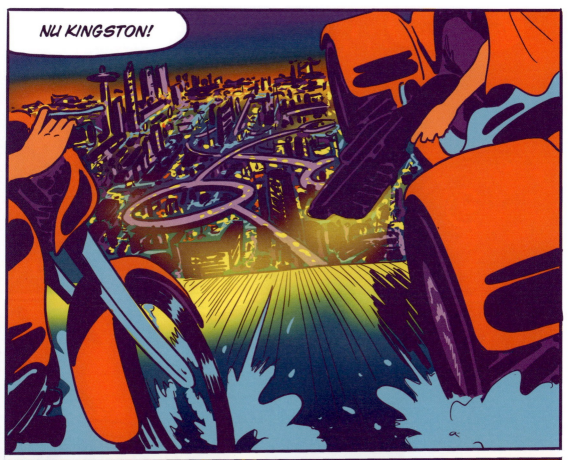

NU KINGSTON!

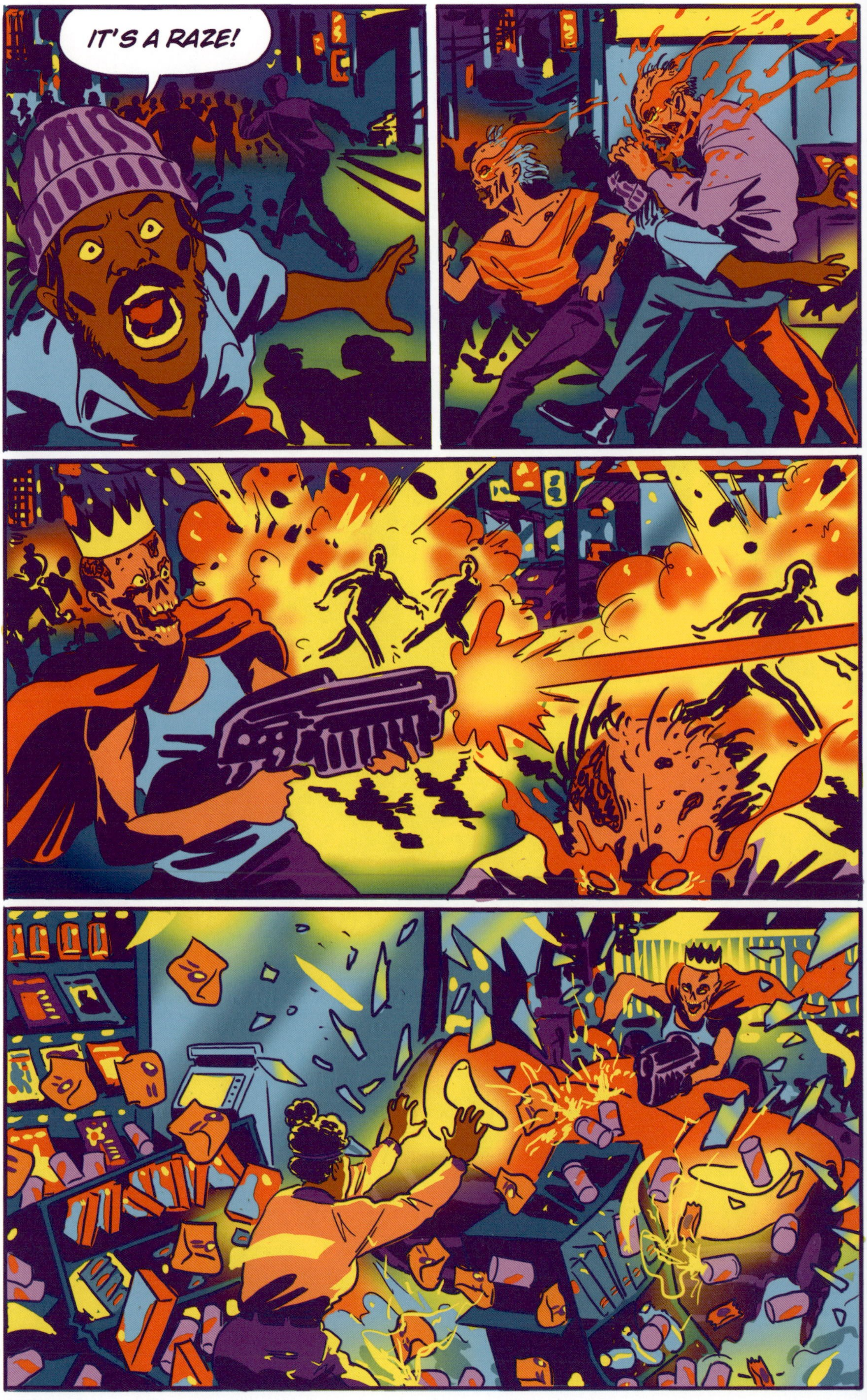
IT'S A RAZE!

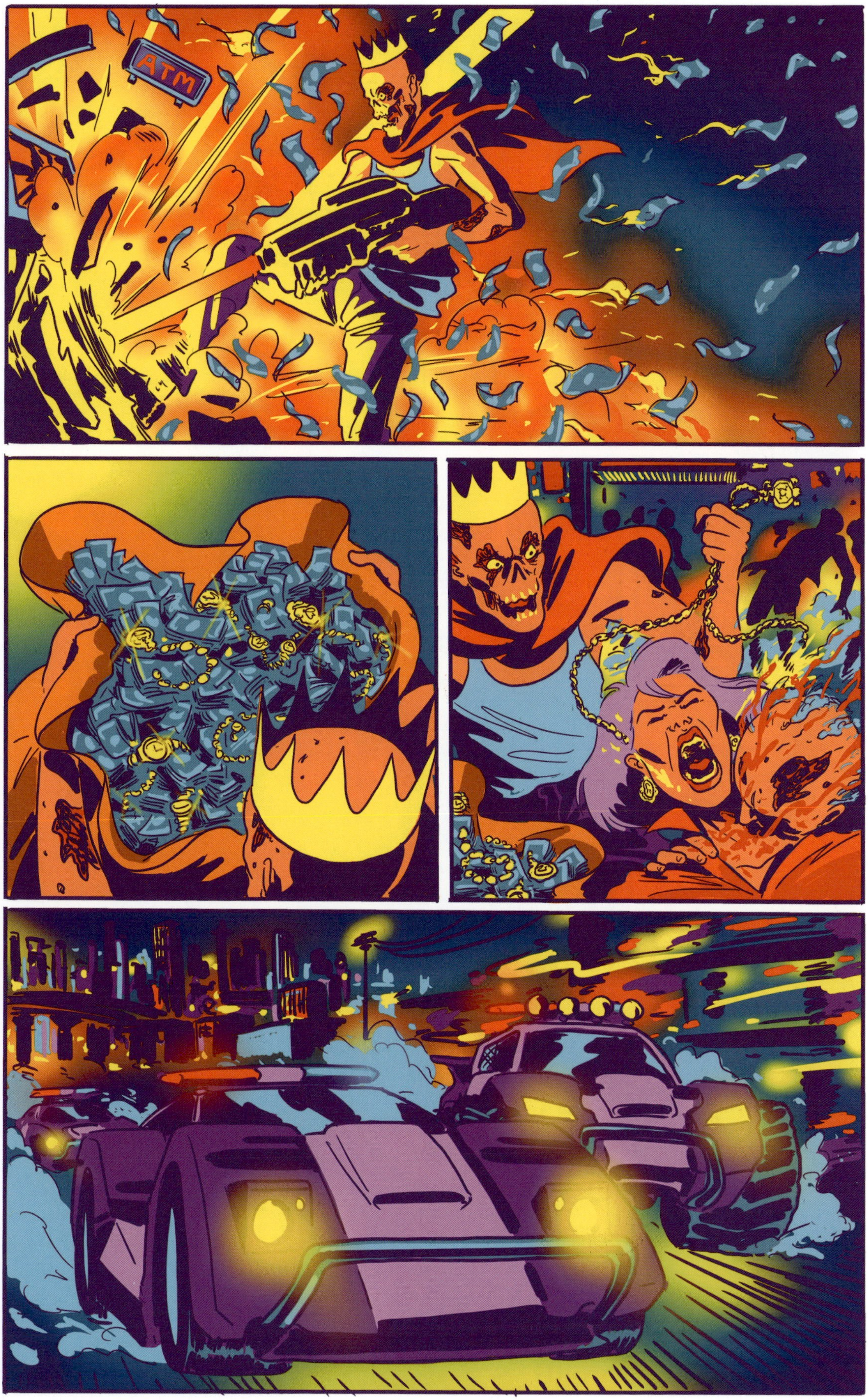
ATM

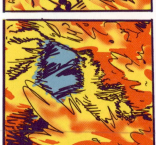

MY BEAUTIFUL CHILDREN...

...NU KINGSTON IS *OURS!*

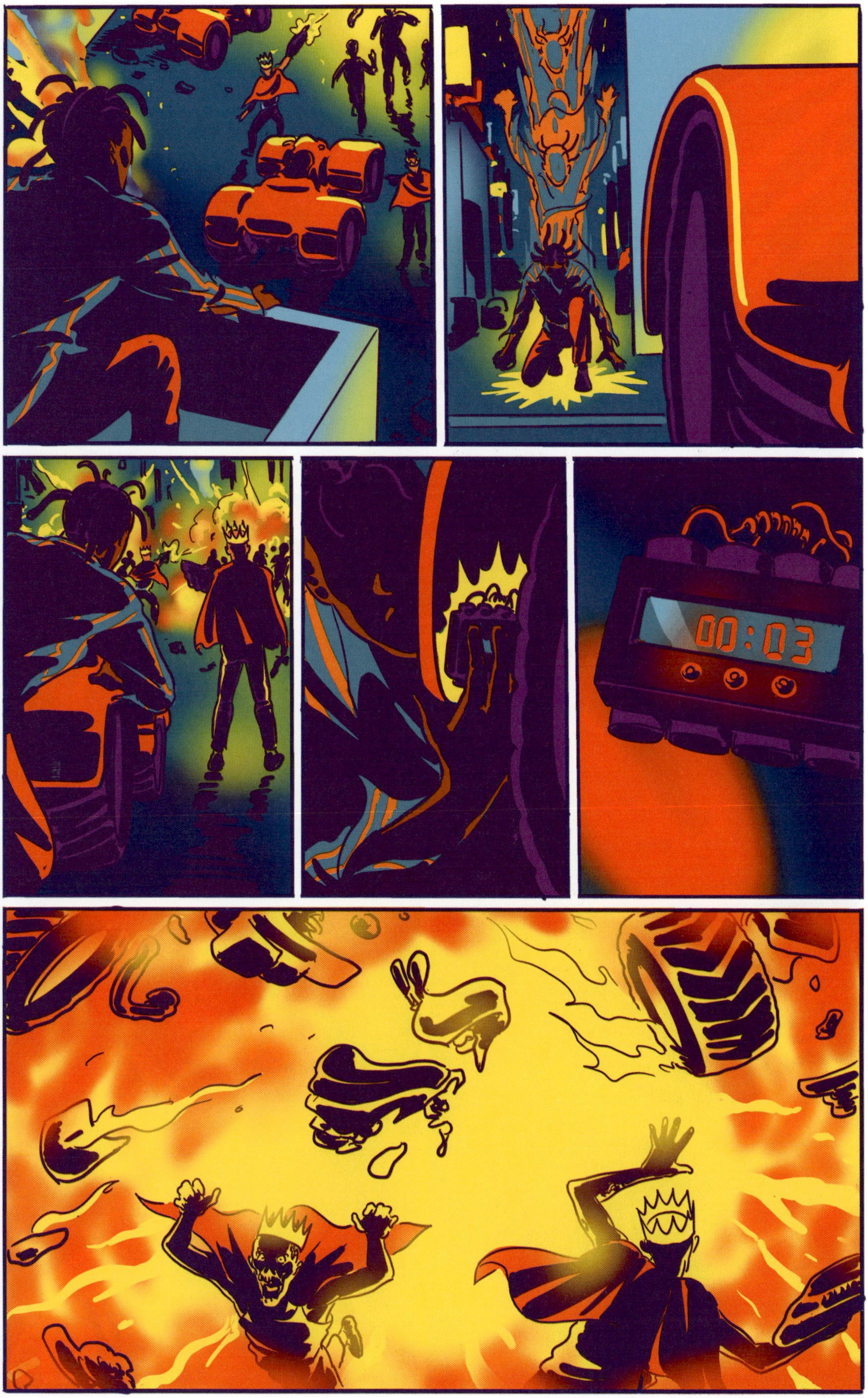

00:03

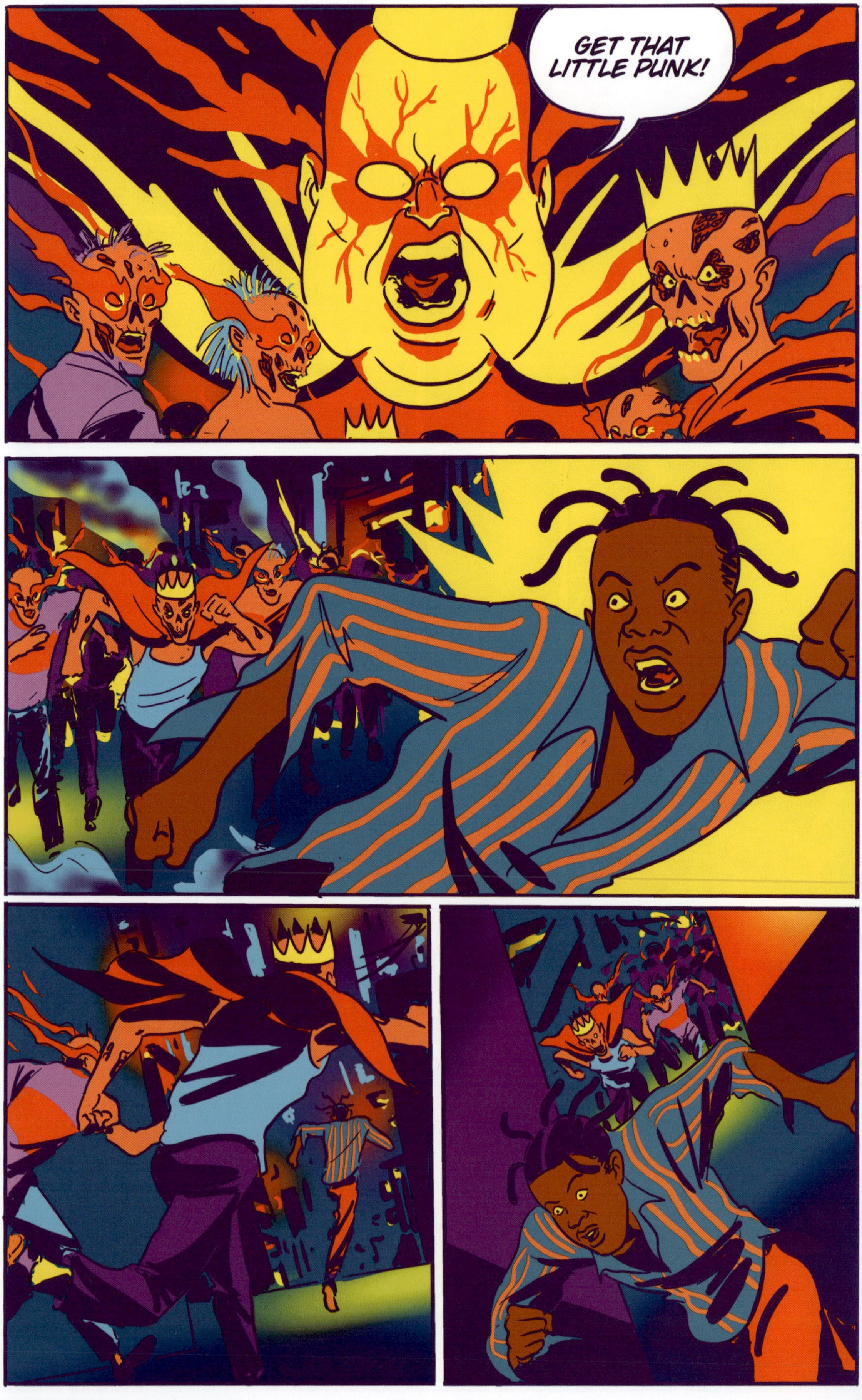
GET THAT LITTLE PUNK!

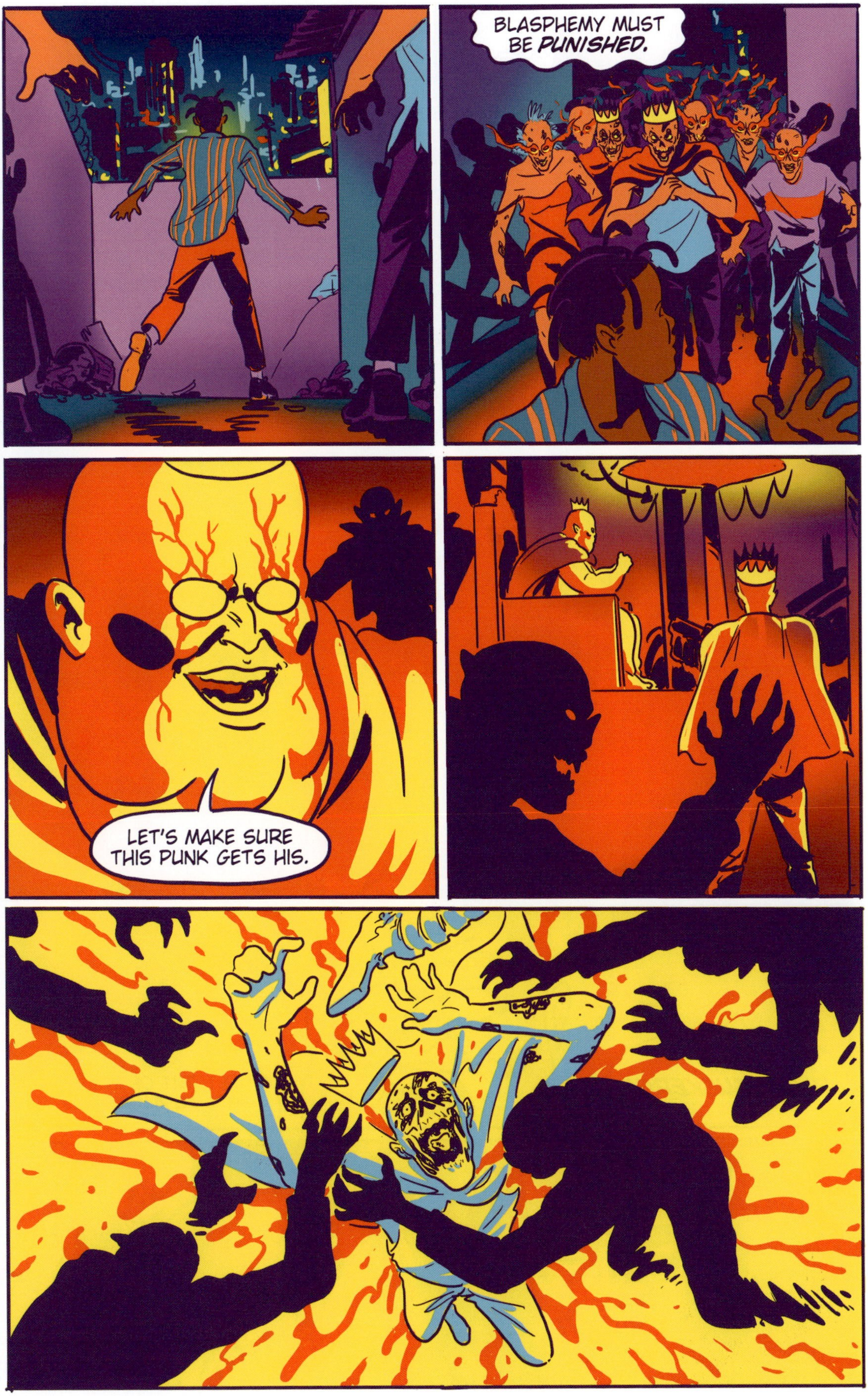
BLASPHEMY MUST BE PUNISHED.
LET'S MAKE SURE THIS PUNK GETS HIS.

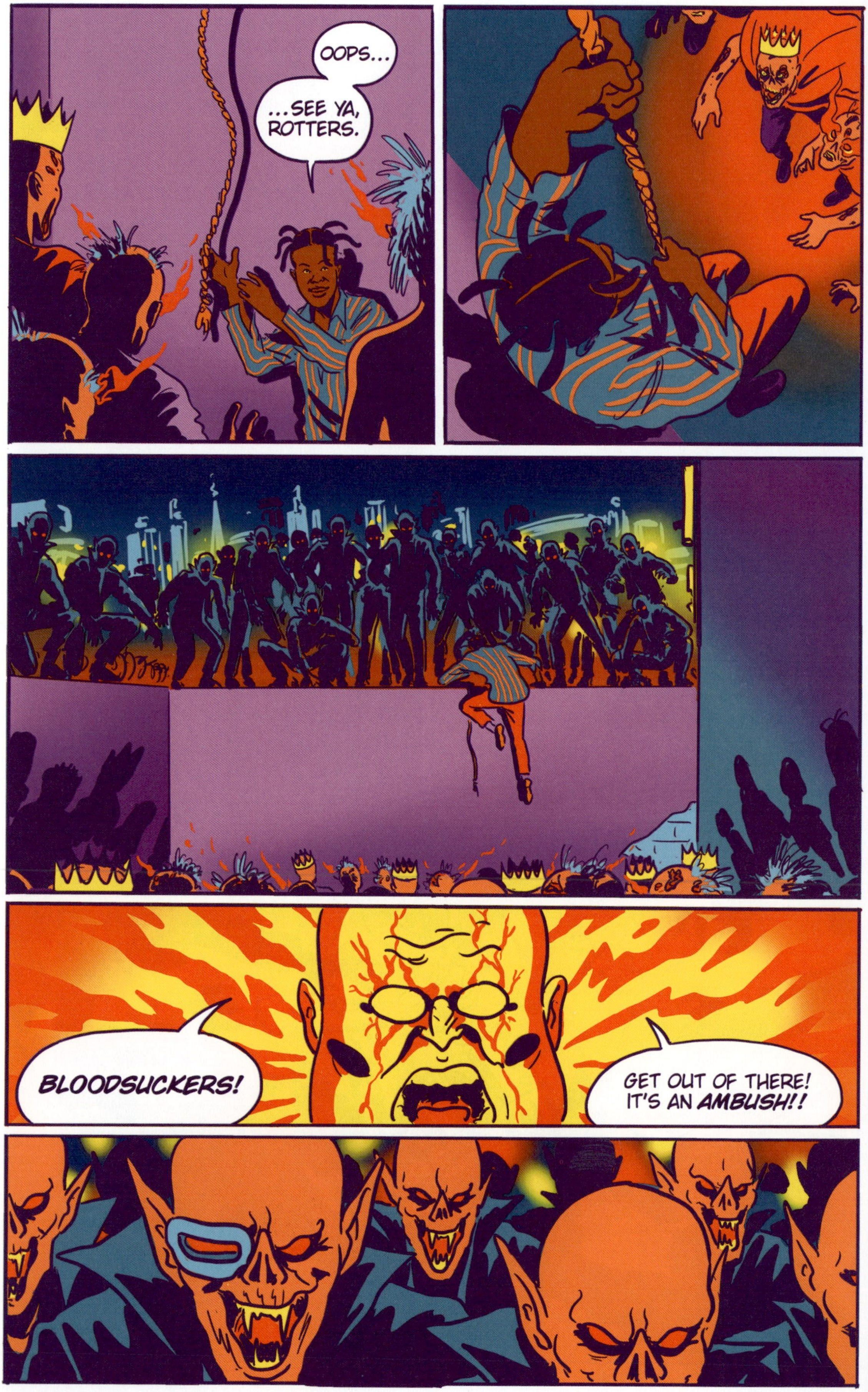
OOPS...
...SEE YA, ROTTERS.
BLOODSUCKERS!
GET OUT OF THERE! IT'S AN AMBUSH!!

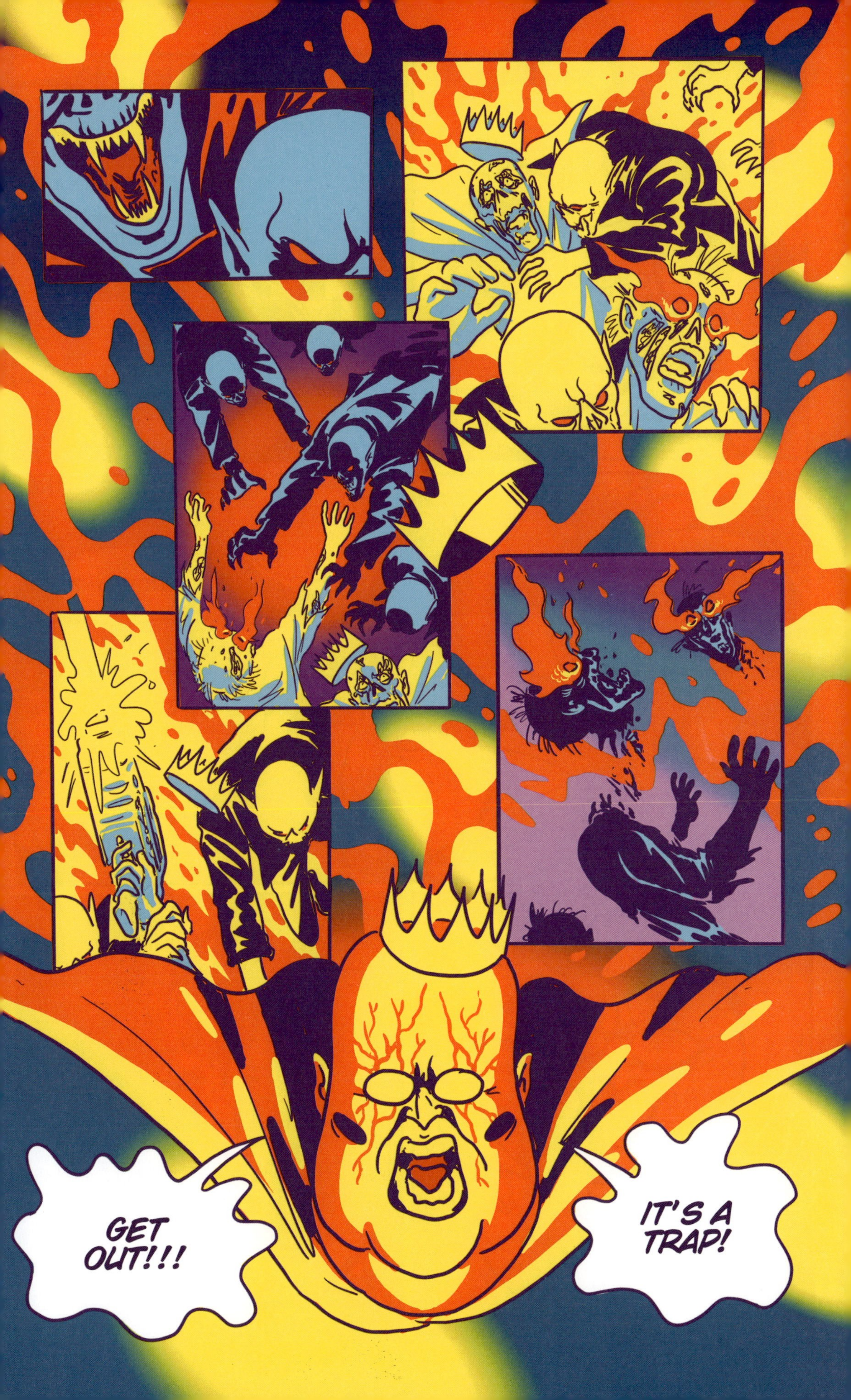
GET OUT!!!
IT'S A TRAP!

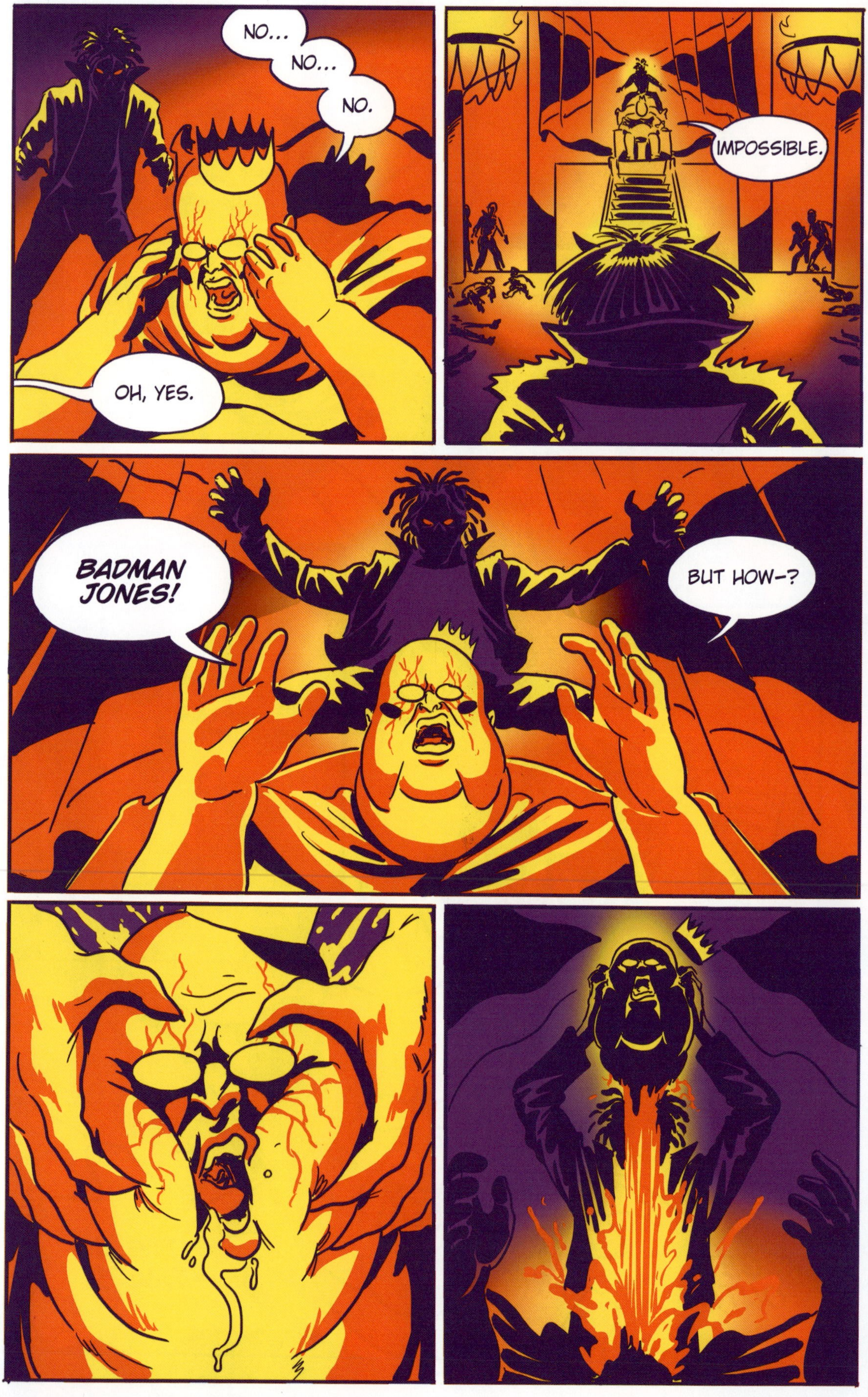
NO...
NO...
NO.
OH, YES.
IMPOSSIBLE.
BADMAN JONES!
BUT HOW-?

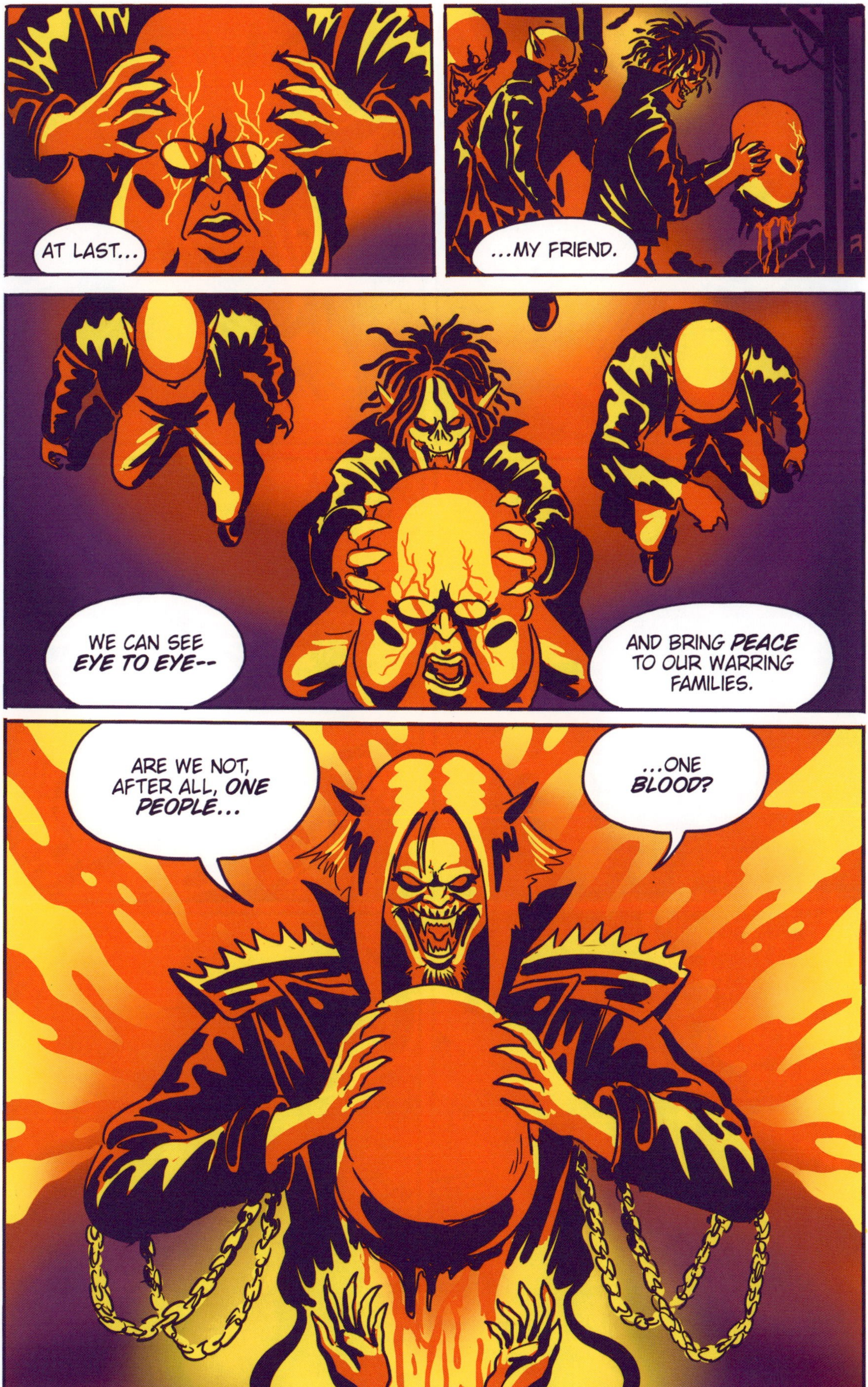
AT LAST...
...MY FRIEND.
WE CAN SEE EYE TO EYE--
AND BRING PEACE TO OUR WARRING FAMILIES.
ARE WE NOT, AFTER ALL, ONE PEOPLE...
...ONE BLOOD?

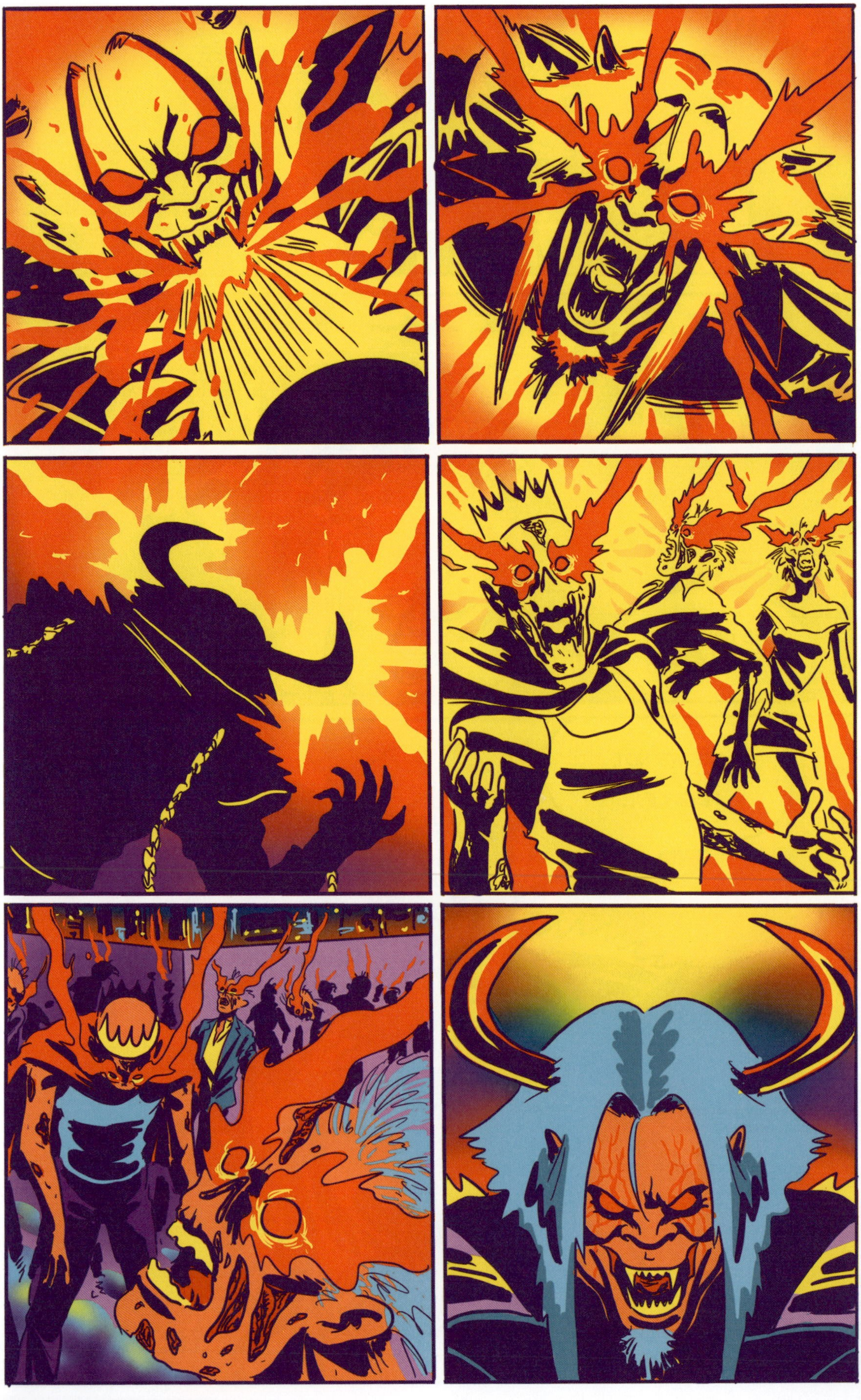

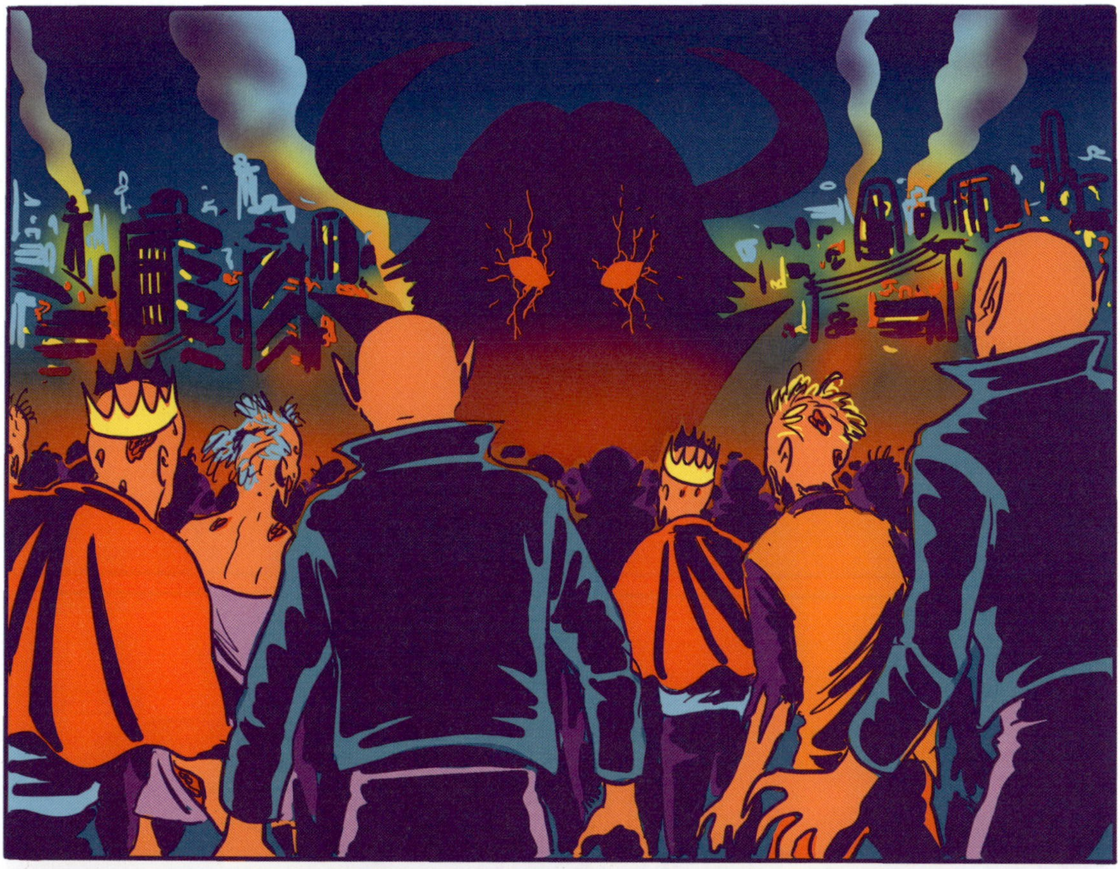
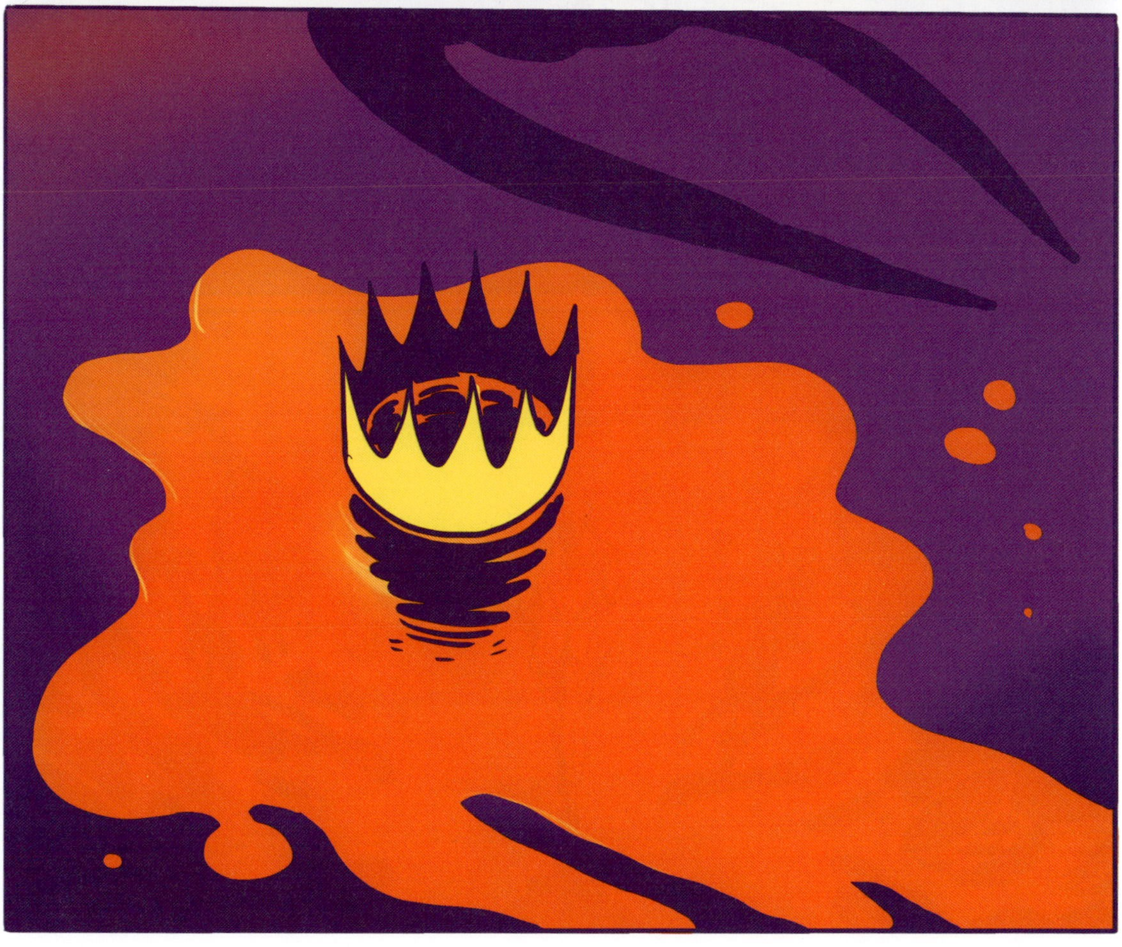

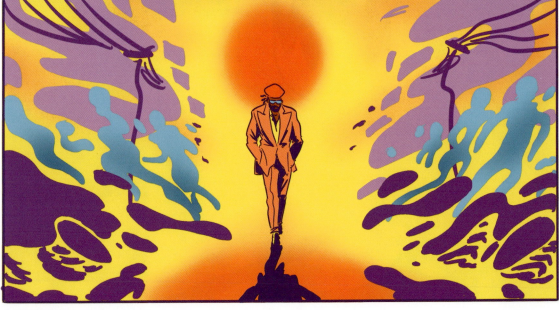

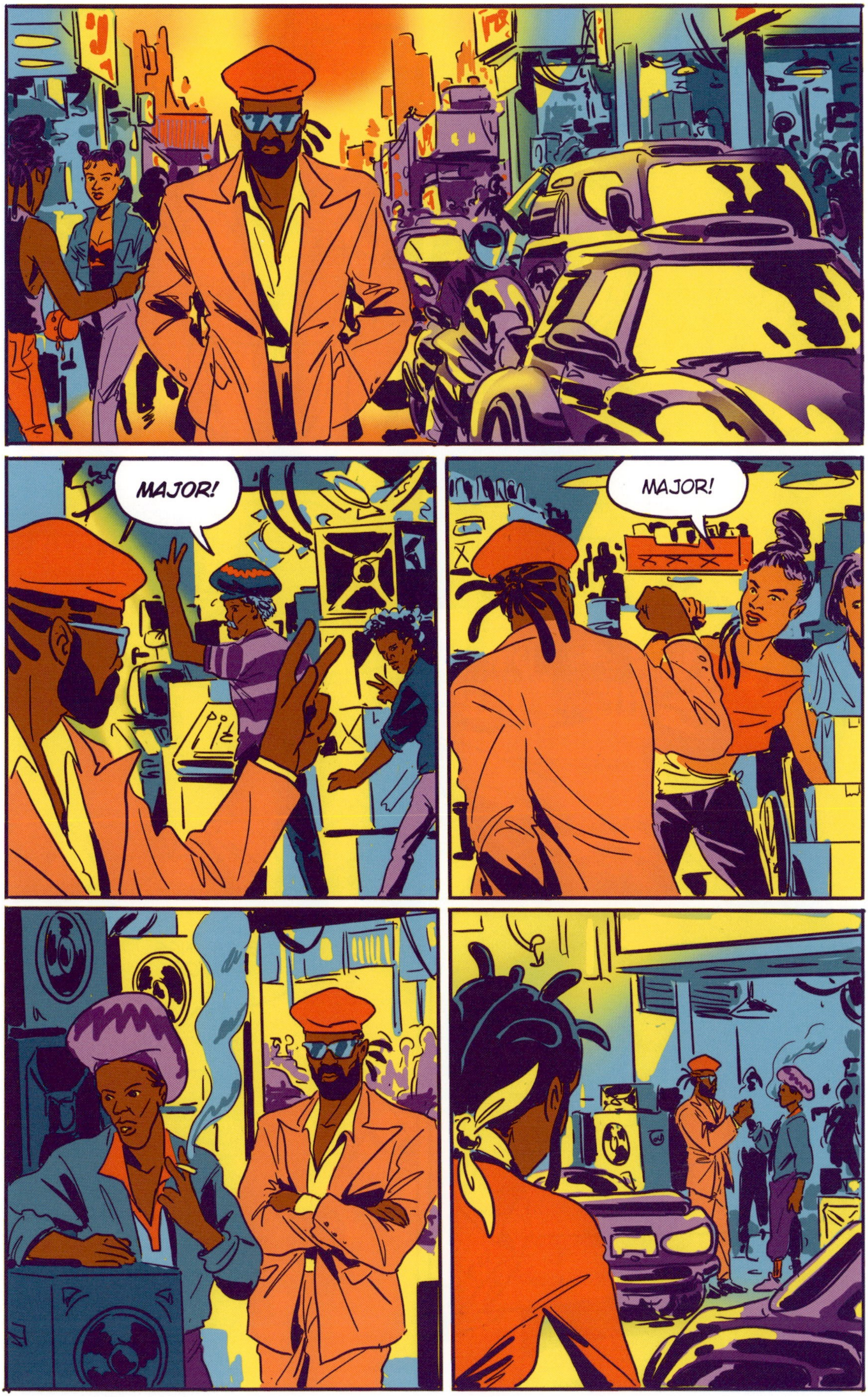
MAJOR!
MAJOR!

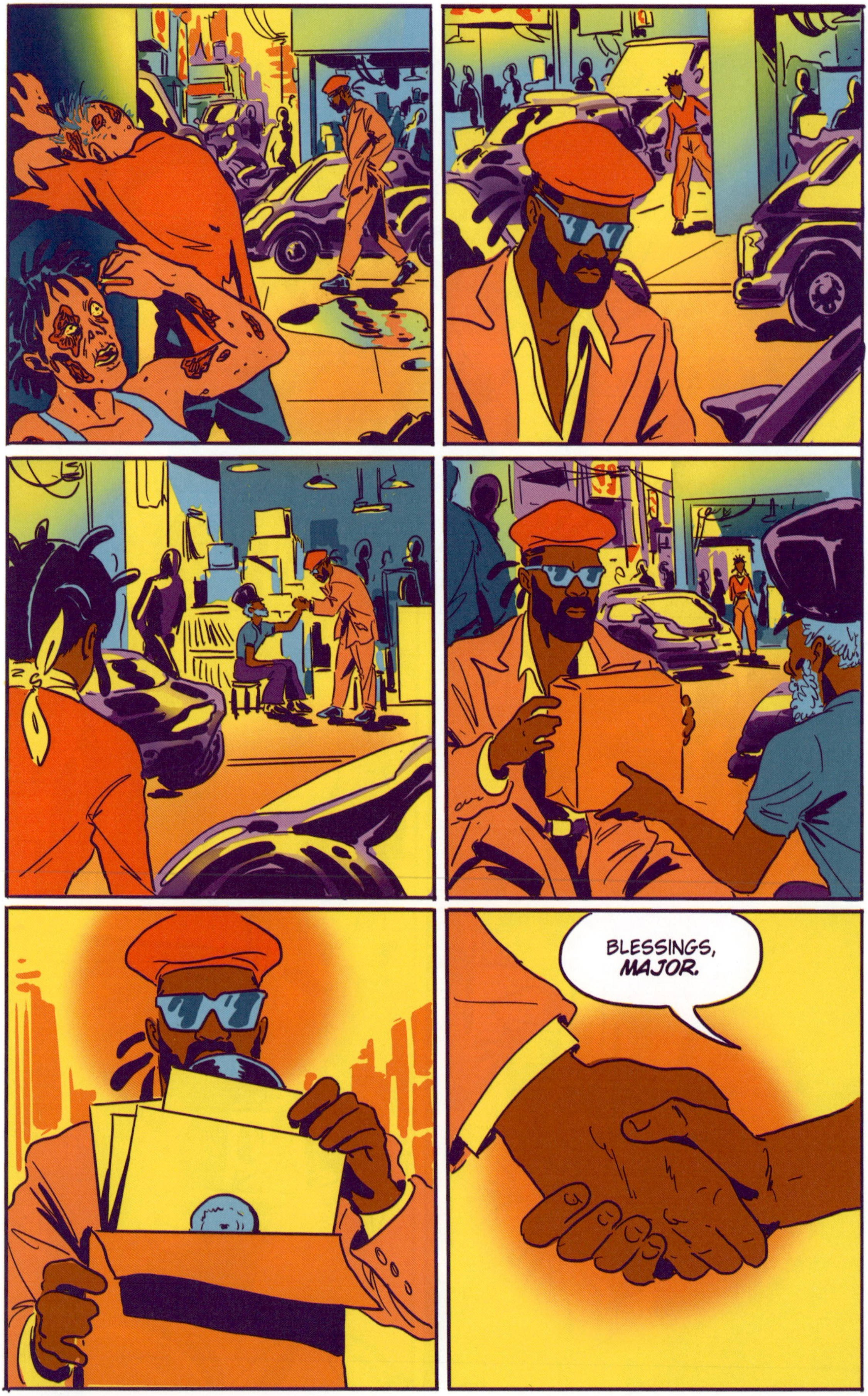
BLESSINGS, **MAJOR.**

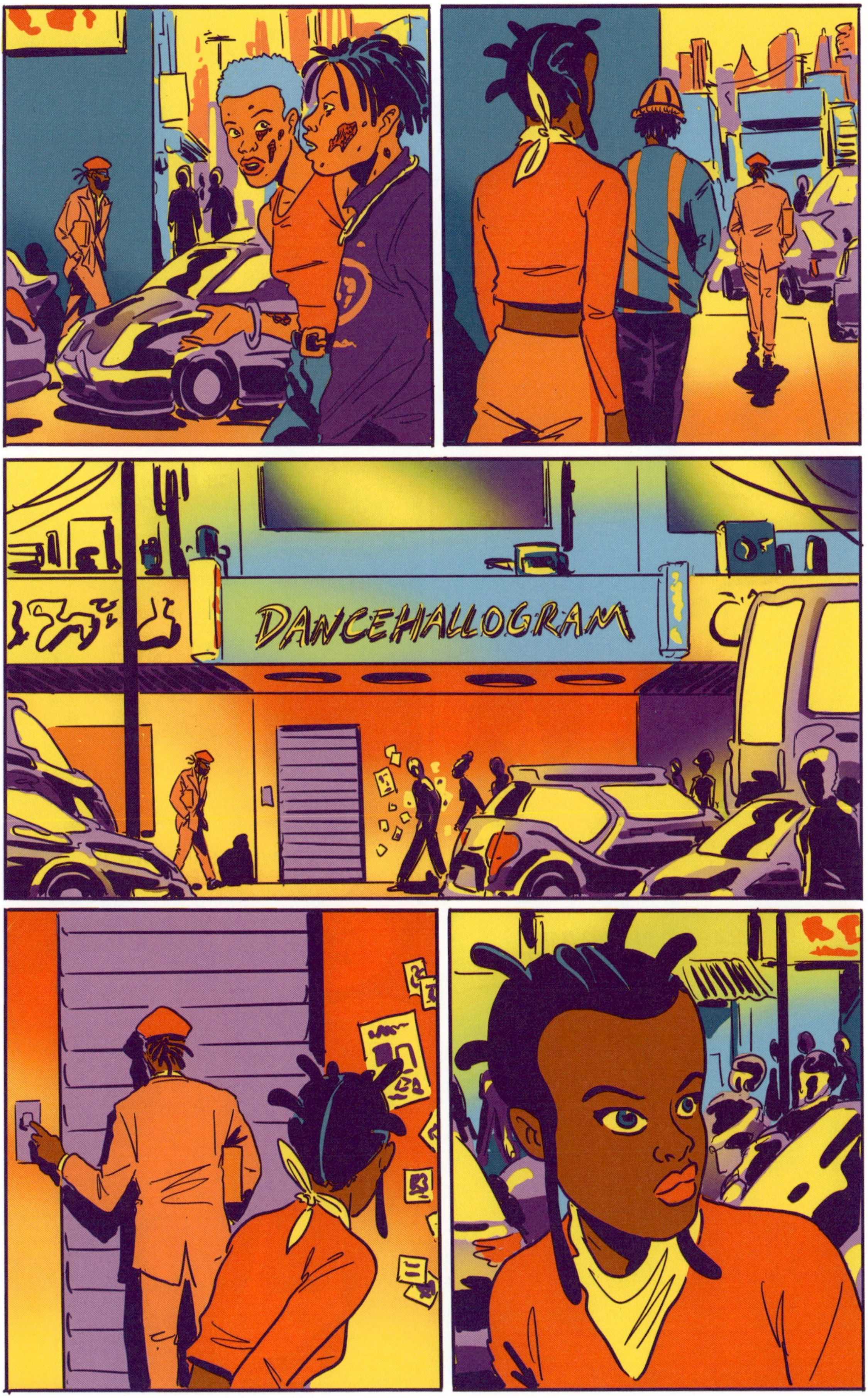
DANCEHALLOGRAM

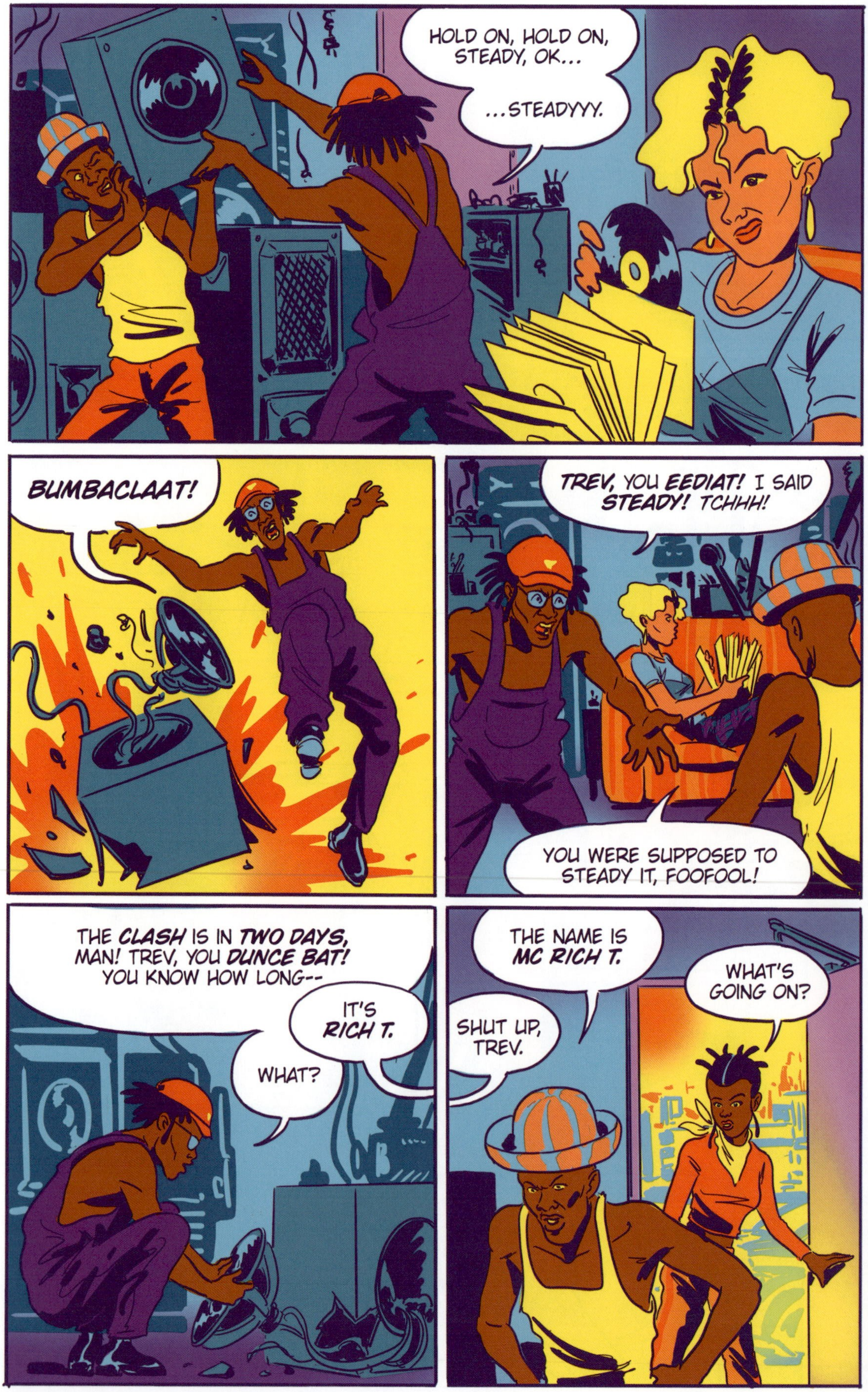
HOLD ON, HOLD ON, STEADY, OK...
...STEADYYY.
BUMBACLAAT!
TREV, YOU EEDIAT! I SAID STEADY! TCHHH!
YOU WERE SUPPOSED TO STEADY IT, FOOFOOL!
THE CLASH IS IN TWO DAYS, MAN! TREV, YOU DUNCE BAT! YOU KNOW HOW LONG--
IT'S RICH T.
WHAT?
THE NAME IS MC RICH T.
SHUT UP, TREV.
WHAT'S GOING ON?

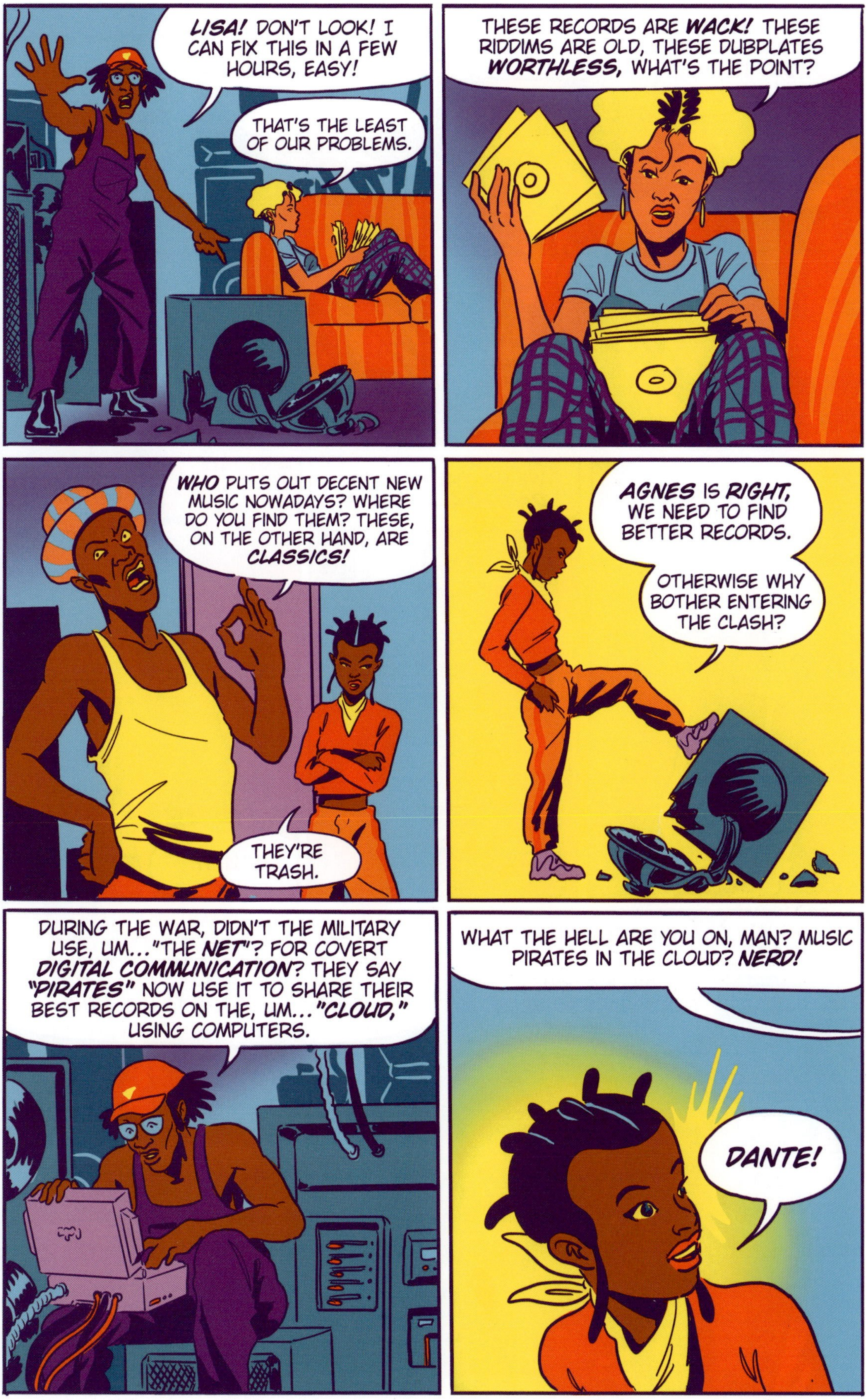
LISA! DON'T LOOK! I CAN FIX THIS IN A FEW HOURS, EASY!
THAT'S THE LEAST OF OUR PROBLEMS.
THESE RECORDS ARE WACK! THESE RIDDIMS ARE OLD, THESE DUBPLATES WORTHLESS, WHAT'S THE POINT?
WHO PUTS OUT DECENT NEW MUSIC NOWADAYS? WHERE DO YOU FIND THEM? THESE, ON THE OTHER HAND, ARE CLASSICS!
THEY'RE TRASH.
AGNES IS RIGHT, WE NEED TO FIND BETTER RECORDS.
OTHERWISE WHY BOTHER ENTERING THE CLASH?
DURING THE WAR, DIDN'T THE MILITARY USE, UM..."THE NET"? FOR COVERT DIGITAL COMMUNICATION? THEY SAY "PIRATES" NOW USE IT TO SHARE THEIR BEST RECORDS ON THE, UM..."CLOUD," USING COMPUTERS.
WHAT THE HELL ARE YOU ON, MAN? MUSIC PIRATES IN THE CLOUD? NERD!
DANTE!

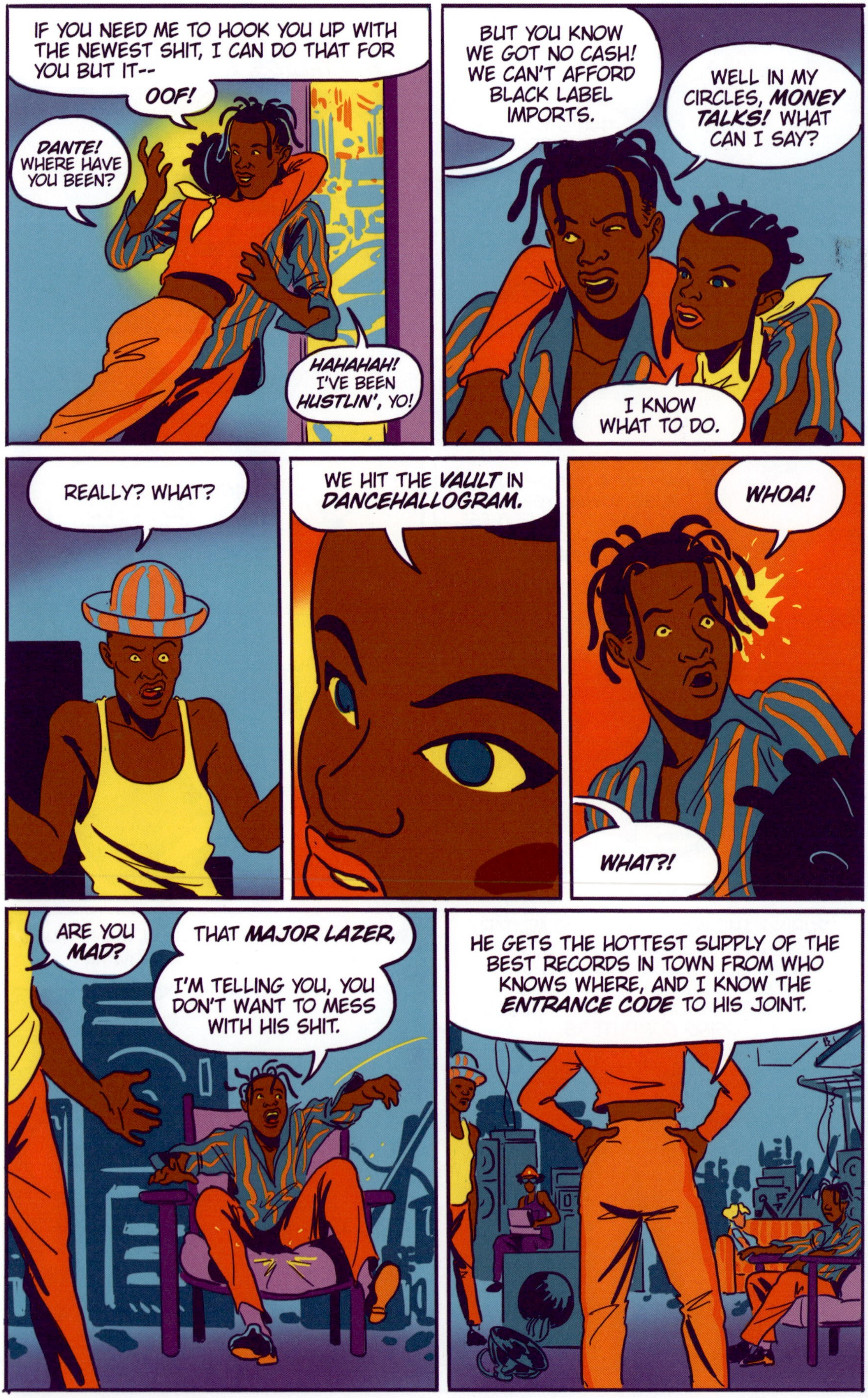
IF YOU NEED ME TO HOOK YOU UP WITH THE NEWEST SHIT, I CAN DO THAT FOR YOU BUT IT--
OOF!
DANTE! WHERE HAVE YOU BEEN?
HAHAHAH! I'VE BEEN HUSTLIN', YO!
BUT YOU KNOW WE GOT NO CASH! WE CAN'T AFFORD BLACK LABEL IMPORTS.
WELL IN MY CIRCLES, MONEY TALKS! WHAT CAN I SAY?
I KNOW WHAT TO DO.
REALLY? WHAT?
WE HIT THE VAULT IN DANCEHALLOGRAM.
WHOA!
WHAT?!
ARE YOU MAD?
THAT MAJOR LAZER,
I'M TELLING YOU, YOU DON'T WANT TO MESS WITH HIS SHIT.
HE GETS THE HOTTEST SUPPLY OF THE BEST RECORDS IN TOWN FROM WHO KNOWS WHERE, AND I KNOW THE ENTRANCE CODE TO HIS JOINT.

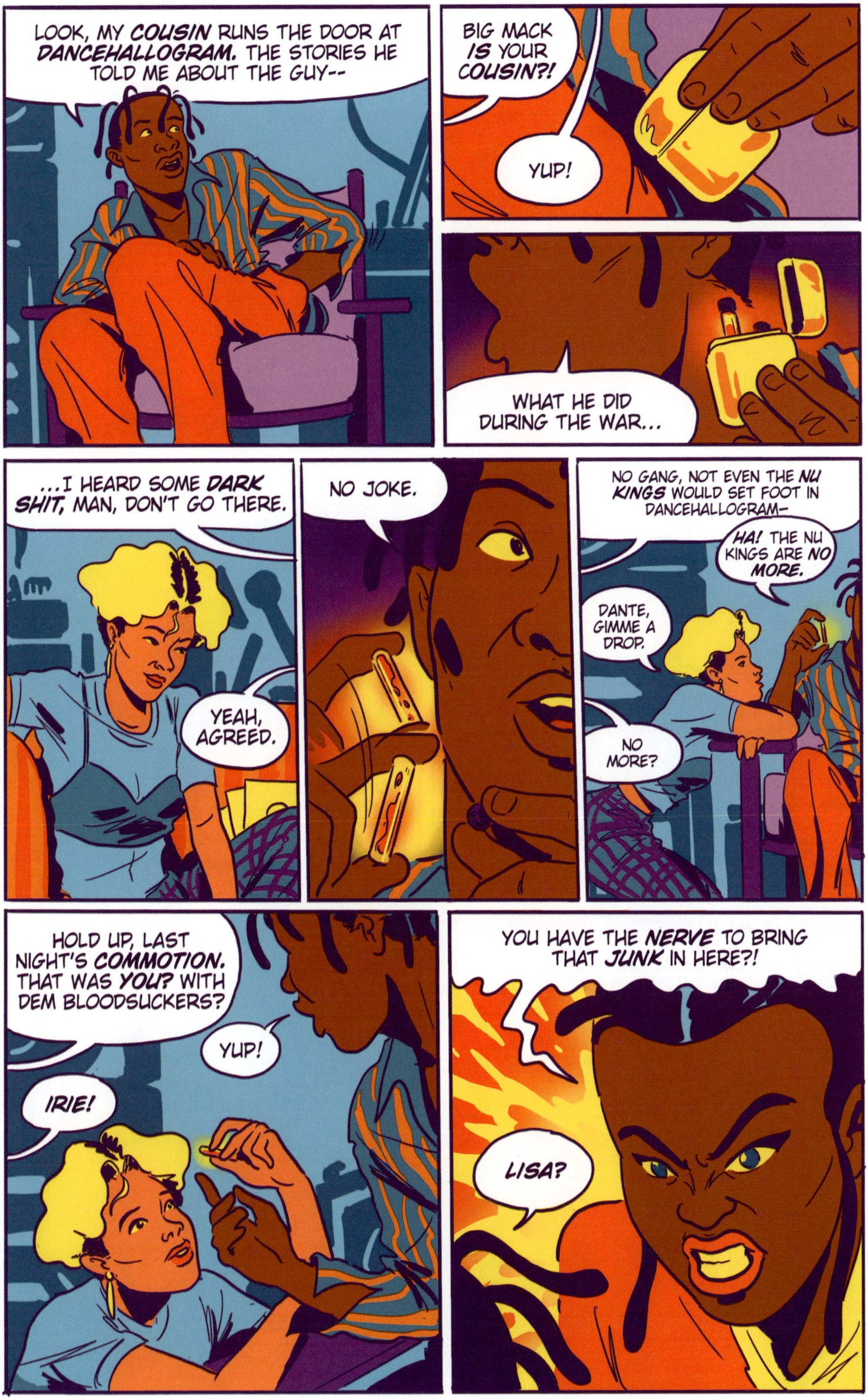
LOOK, MY COUSIN RUNS THE DOOR AT DANCEHALLOGRAM. THE STORIES HE TOLD ME ABOUT THE GUY--
BIG MACK IS YOUR COUSIN?!
YUP!
WHAT HE DID DURING THE WAR...
...I HEARD SOME DARK SHIT, MAN, DON'T GO THERE.
YEAH, AGREED.
NO JOKE.
NO GANG, NOT EVEN THE NU KINGS WOULD SET FOOT IN DANCEHALLOGRAM—
HA! THE NU KINGS ARE NO MORE.
DANTE, GIMME A DROP.
NO MORE?
HOLD UP, LAST NIGHT'S COMMOTION. THAT WAS YOU? WITH DEM BLOODSUCKERS?
YUP!
IRIE!
YOU HAVE THE NERVE TO BRING THAT JUNK IN HERE?!
LISA?

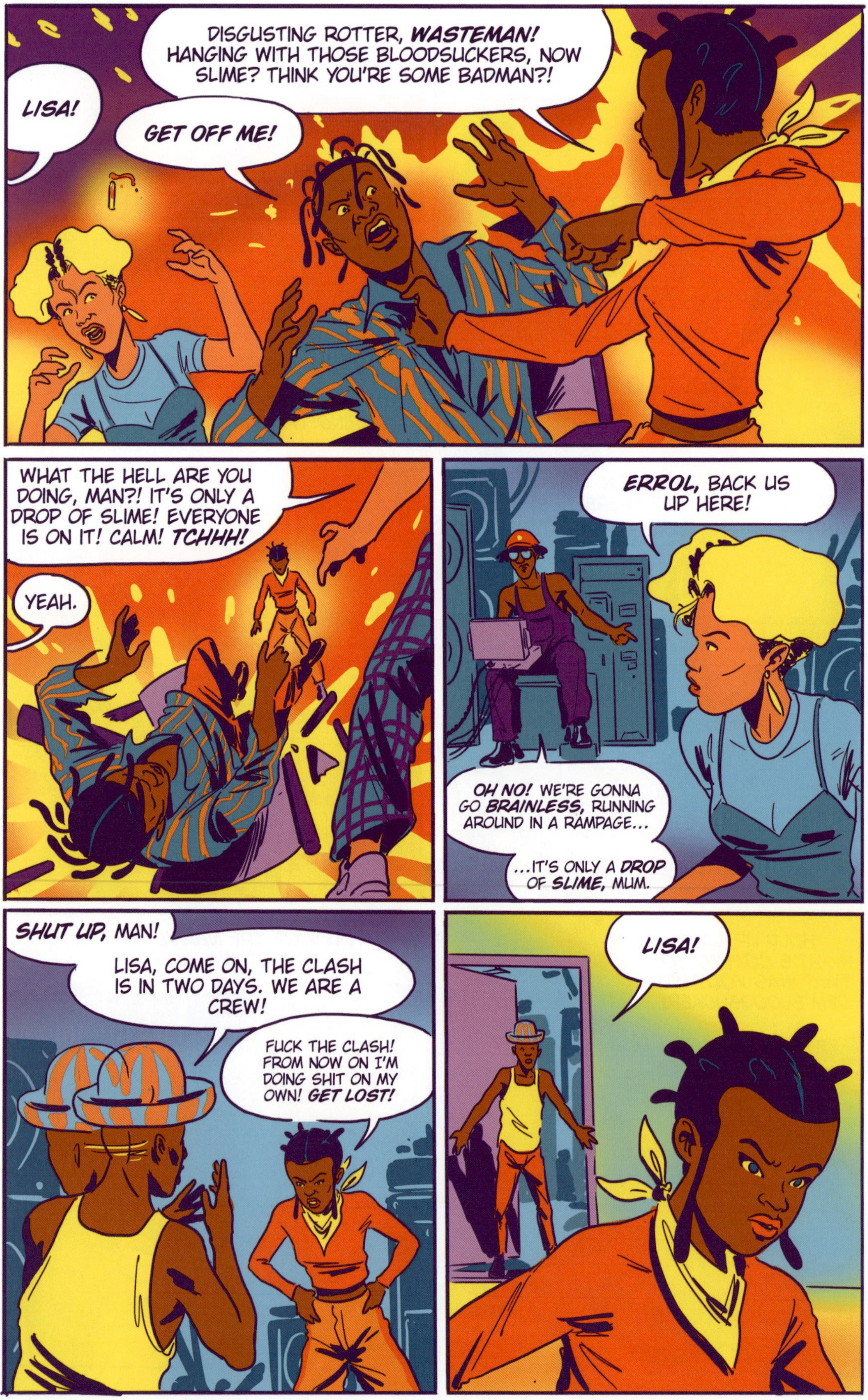

LISA!
DISGUSTING ROTTER, **WASTEMAN!** HANGING WITH THOSE BLOODSUCKERS, NOW SLIME? THINK YOU'RE SOME BADMAN?!
GET OFF ME!
WHAT THE HELL ARE YOU DOING, MAN?! IT'S ONLY A DROP OF SLIME! EVERYONE IS ON IT! CALM! **TCHHH!**
YEAH.
ERROL, BACK US UP HERE!
OH NO! WE'RE GONNA GO **BRAINLESS,** RUNNING AROUND IN A RAMPAGE...
...IT'S ONLY A **DROP** OF **SLIME,** MUM.
SHUT UP, MAN!
LISA, COME ON, THE CLASH IS IN TWO DAYS. WE ARE A CREW!
FUCK THE CLASH! FROM NOW ON I'M DOING SHIT ON MY OWN! **GET LOST!**
LISA!

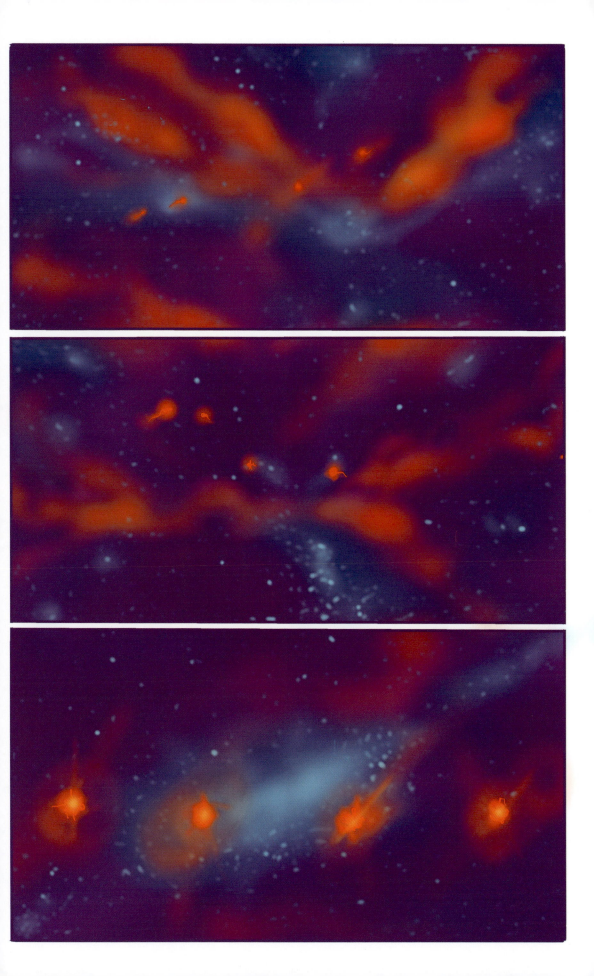

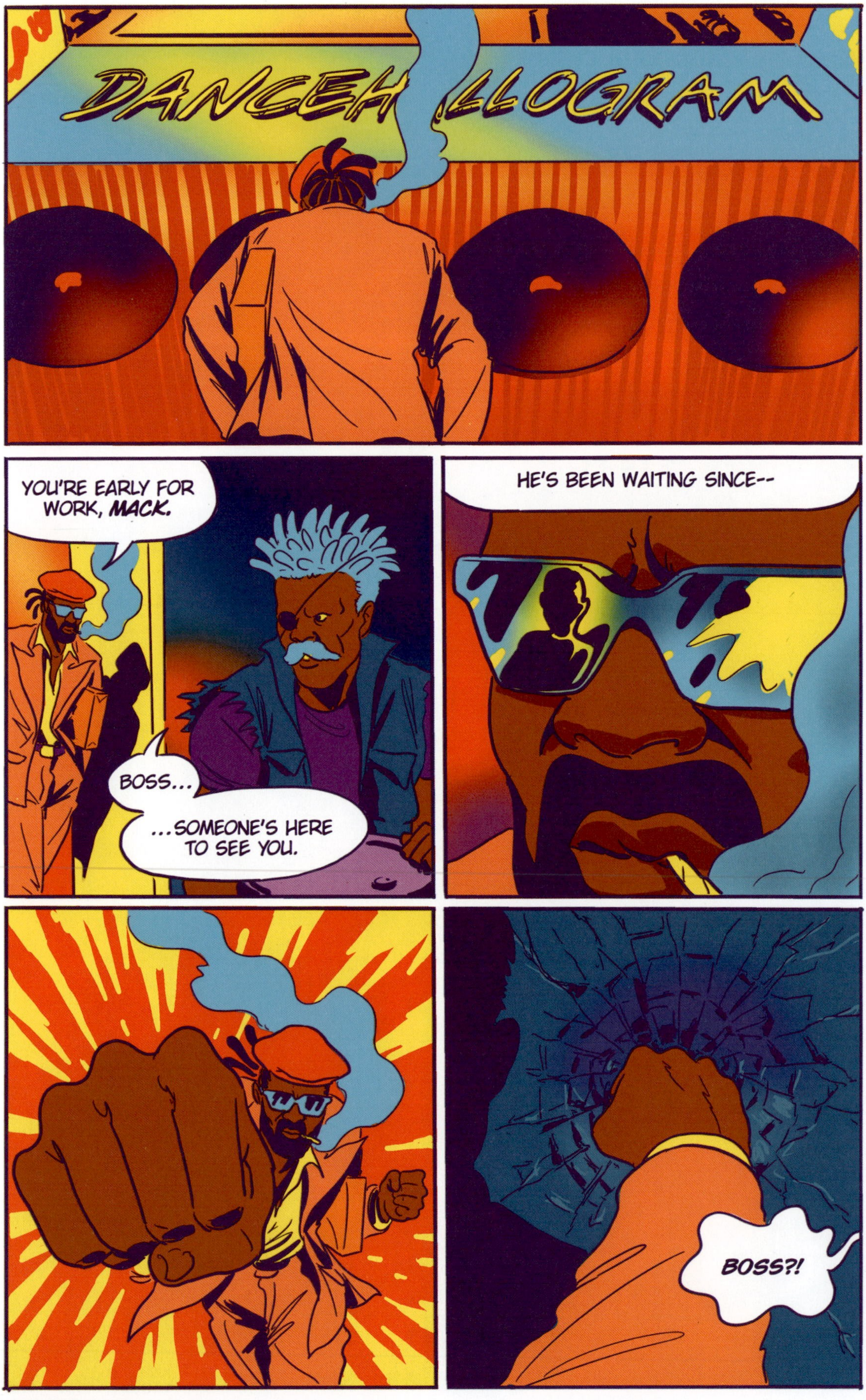
DANCEH LLOGRAM
YOU'RE EARLY FOR WORK, MACK.
BOSS...
...SOMEONE'S HERE TO SEE YOU.
HE'S BEEN WAITING SINCE--
BOSS?!

IS THAT HOW YOU GREET AN *OLD FRIEND?*

WHAT DO YOU WANT, *WALLACE?*

BOSS?

IT'S FINE, MACK.

I'M ONLY HERE FOR A FRIENDLY CATCH UP, LAZER.

I GUESS YOU'VE HEARD THE WORD ON THE STREETS?

NU KINGS ARE NO MORE.

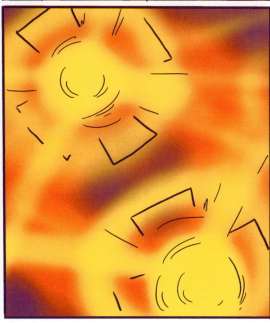

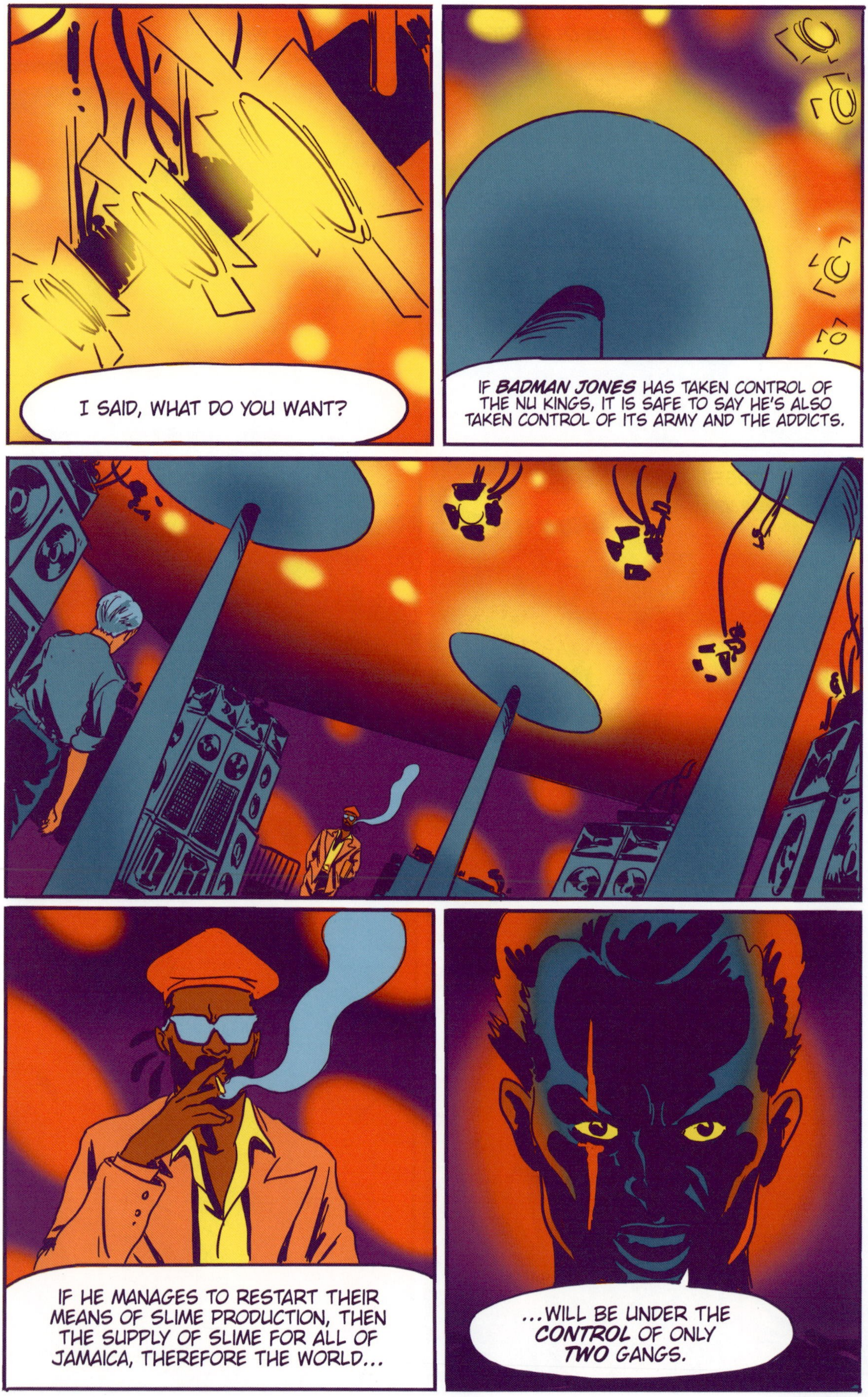
I SAID, WHAT DO YOU WANT?
IF BADMAN JONES HAS TAKEN CONTROL OF THE NU KINGS, IT IS SAFE TO SAY HE'S ALSO TAKEN CONTROL OF ITS ARMY AND THE ADDICTS.
IF HE MANAGES TO RESTART THEIR MEANS OF SLIME PRODUCTION, THEN THE SUPPLY OF SLIME FOR ALL OF JAMAICA, THEREFORE THE WORLD...
...WILL BE UNDER THE CONTROL OF ONLY TWO GANGS.

THE BLOODSUCKERS...

MASTER...

...WE HAVE FOUND THE SOURCE.

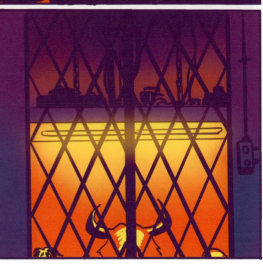

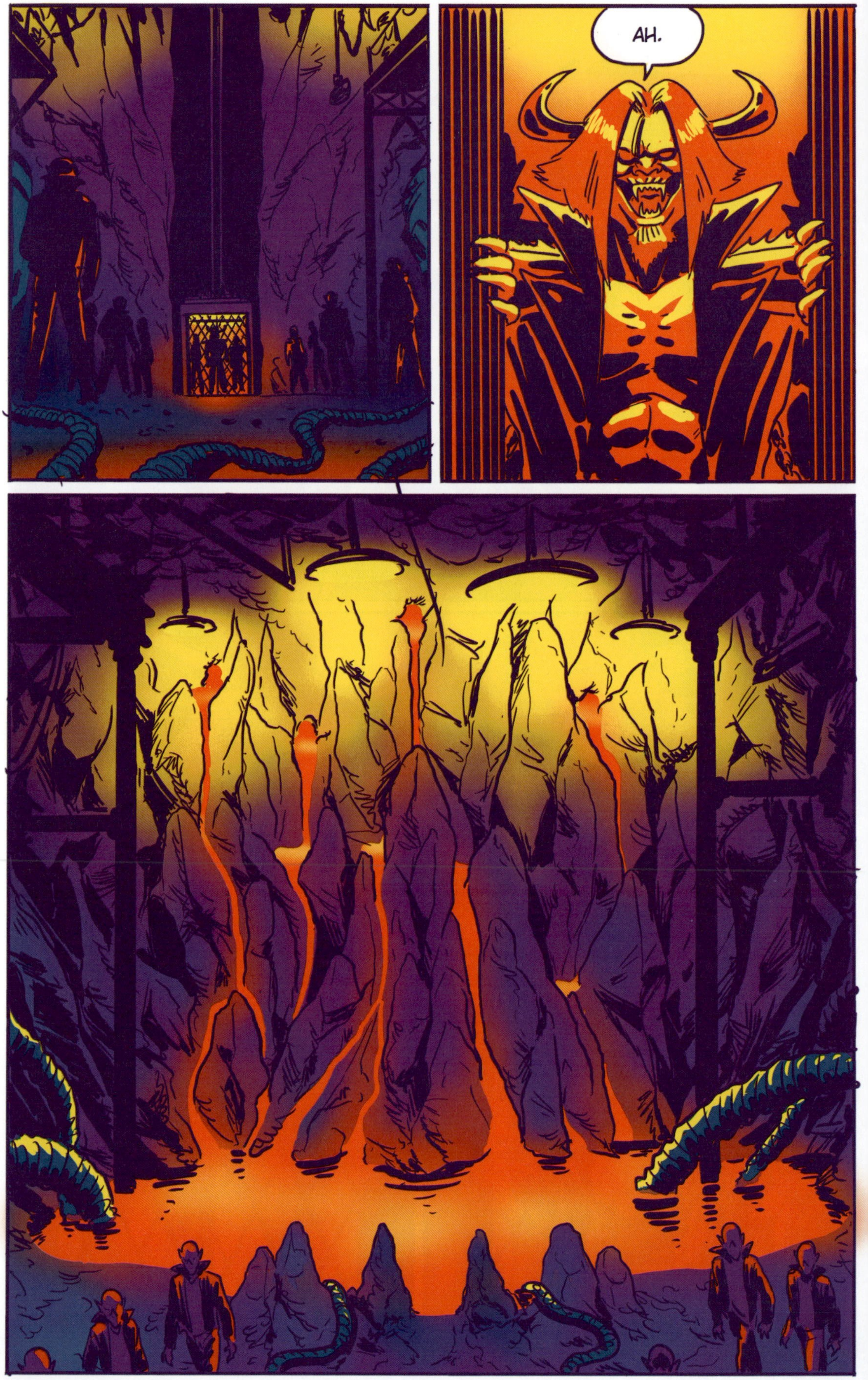
AH.

...AND THE *LOWEST* OF 'EM ALL, THE *JUNKIES.*

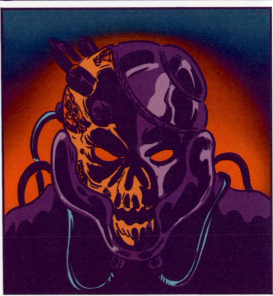

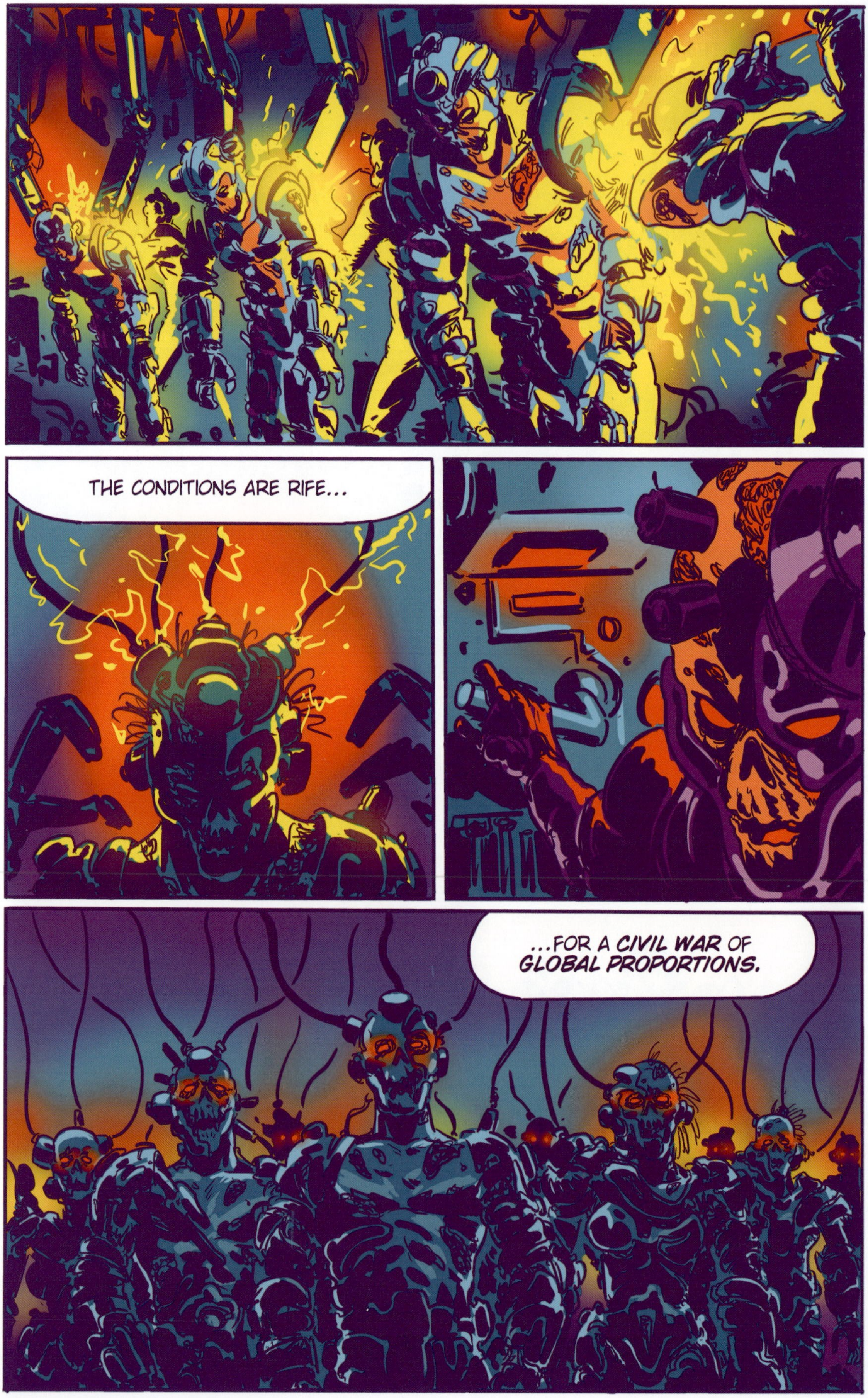
THE CONDITIONS ARE RIFE...
...FOR A CIVIL WAR OF GLOBAL PROPORTIONS.

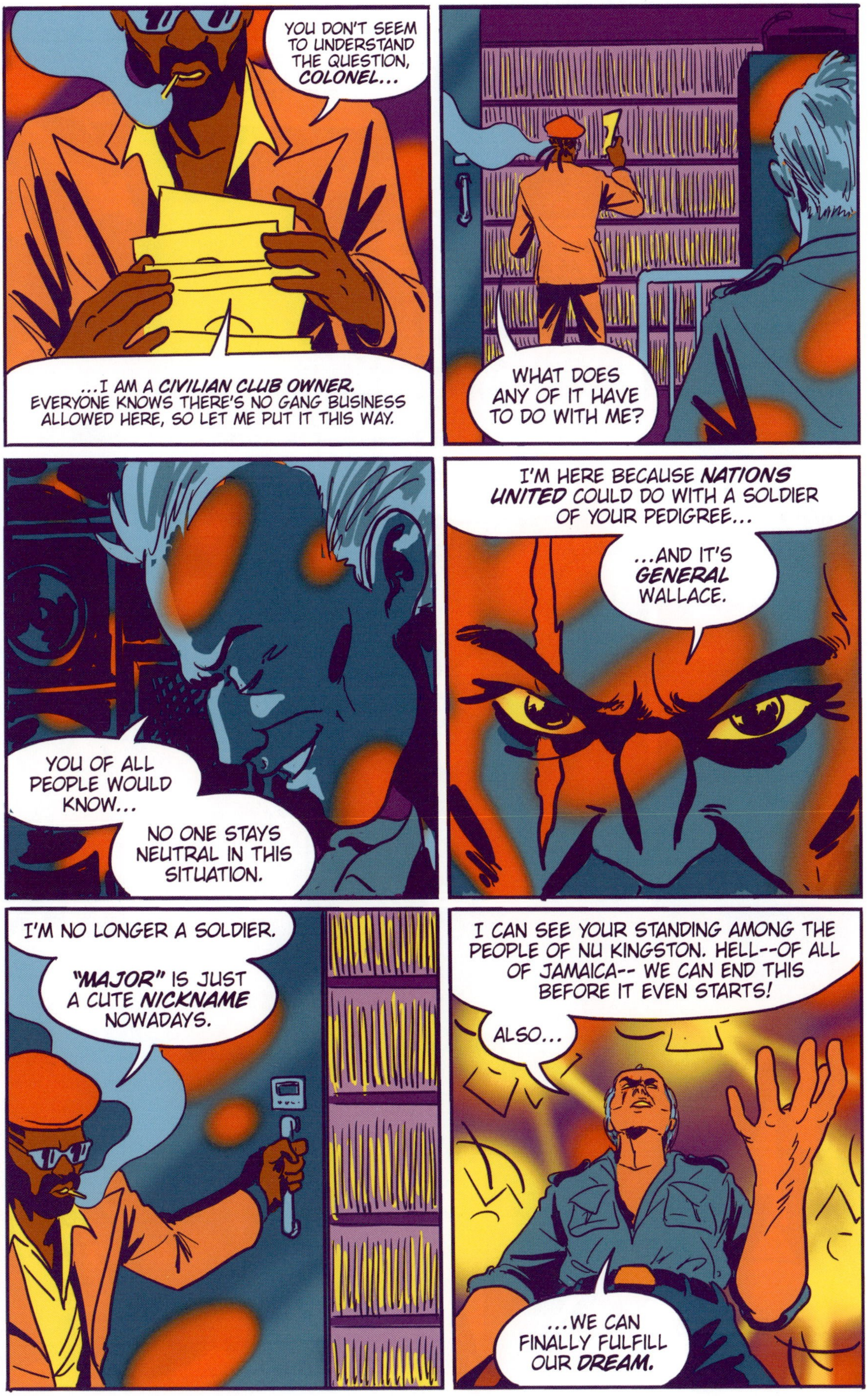
YOU DON'T SEEM TO UNDERSTAND THE QUESTION, COLONEL...
...I AM A CIVILIAN CLUB OWNER. EVERYONE KNOWS THERE'S NO GANG BUSINESS ALLOWED HERE, SO LET ME PUT IT THIS WAY.
WHAT DOES ANY OF IT HAVE TO DO WITH ME?
YOU OF ALL PEOPLE WOULD KNOW...
NO ONE STAYS NEUTRAL IN THIS SITUATION.
I'M HERE BECAUSE NATIONS UNITED COULD DO WITH A SOLDIER OF YOUR PEDIGREE...
...AND IT'S GENERAL WALLACE.
I'M NO LONGER A SOLDIER.
"MAJOR" IS JUST A CUTE NICKNAME NOWADAYS.
I CAN SEE YOUR STANDING AMONG THE PEOPLE OF NU KINGSTON. HELL--OF ALL OF JAMAICA-- WE CAN END THIS BEFORE IT EVEN STARTS!
ALSO...
...WE CAN FINALLY FULFILL OUR DREAM.

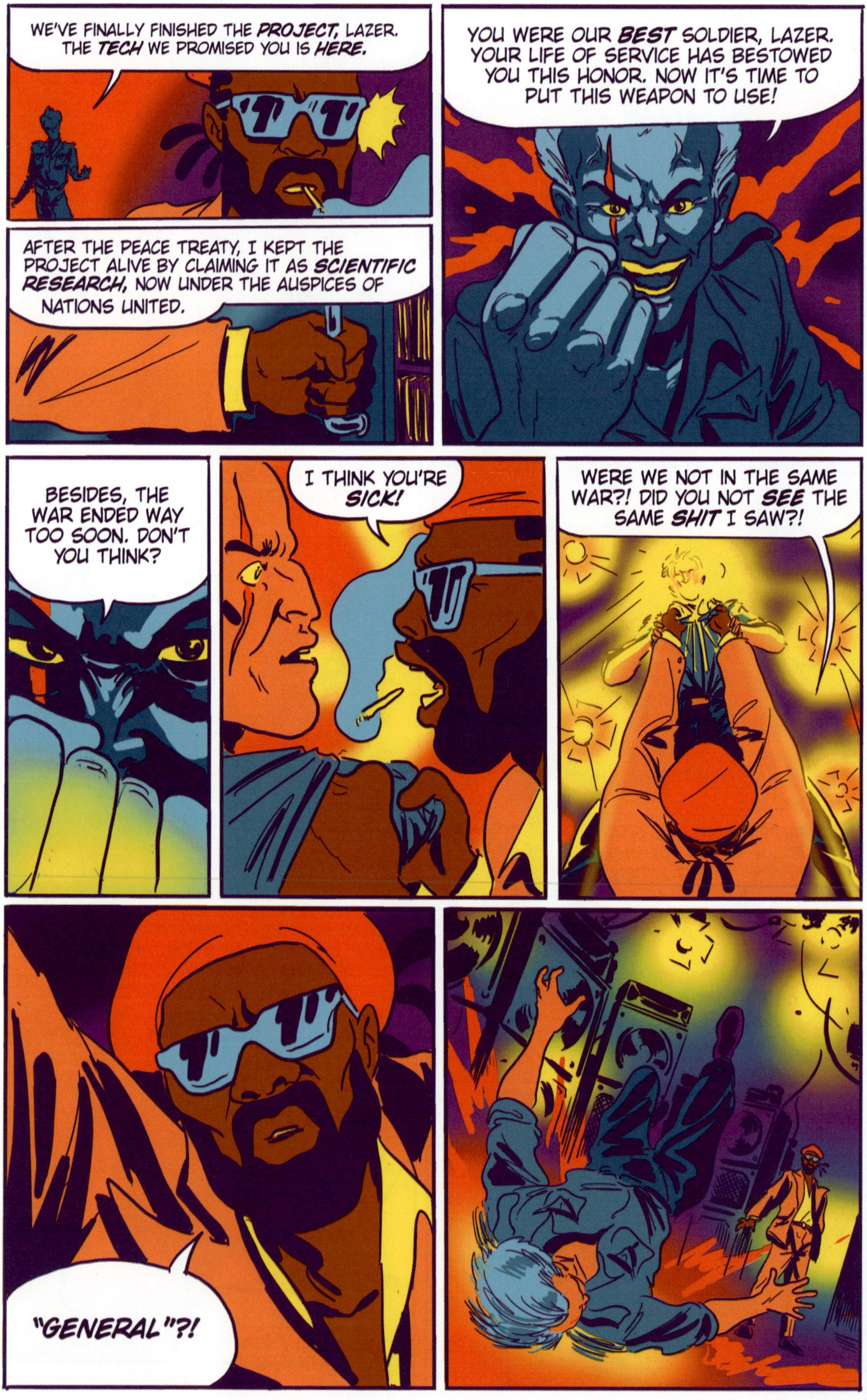
WE'VE FINALLY FINISHED THE PROJECT, LAZER. THE TECH WE PROMISED YOU IS HERE.
AFTER THE PEACE TREATY, I KEPT THE PROJECT ALIVE BY CLAIMING IT AS SCIENTIFIC RESEARCH, NOW UNDER THE AUSPICES OF NATIONS UNITED.
YOU WERE OUR BEST SOLDIER, LAZER. YOUR LIFE OF SERVICE HAS BESTOWED YOU THIS HONOR. NOW IT'S TIME TO PUT THIS WEAPON TO USE!
BESIDES, THE WAR ENDED WAY TOO SOON. DON'T YOU THINK?
I THINK YOU'RE SICK!
WERE WE NOT IN THE SAME WAR?! DID YOU NOT SEE THE SAME SHIT I SAW?!
"GENERAL"?!

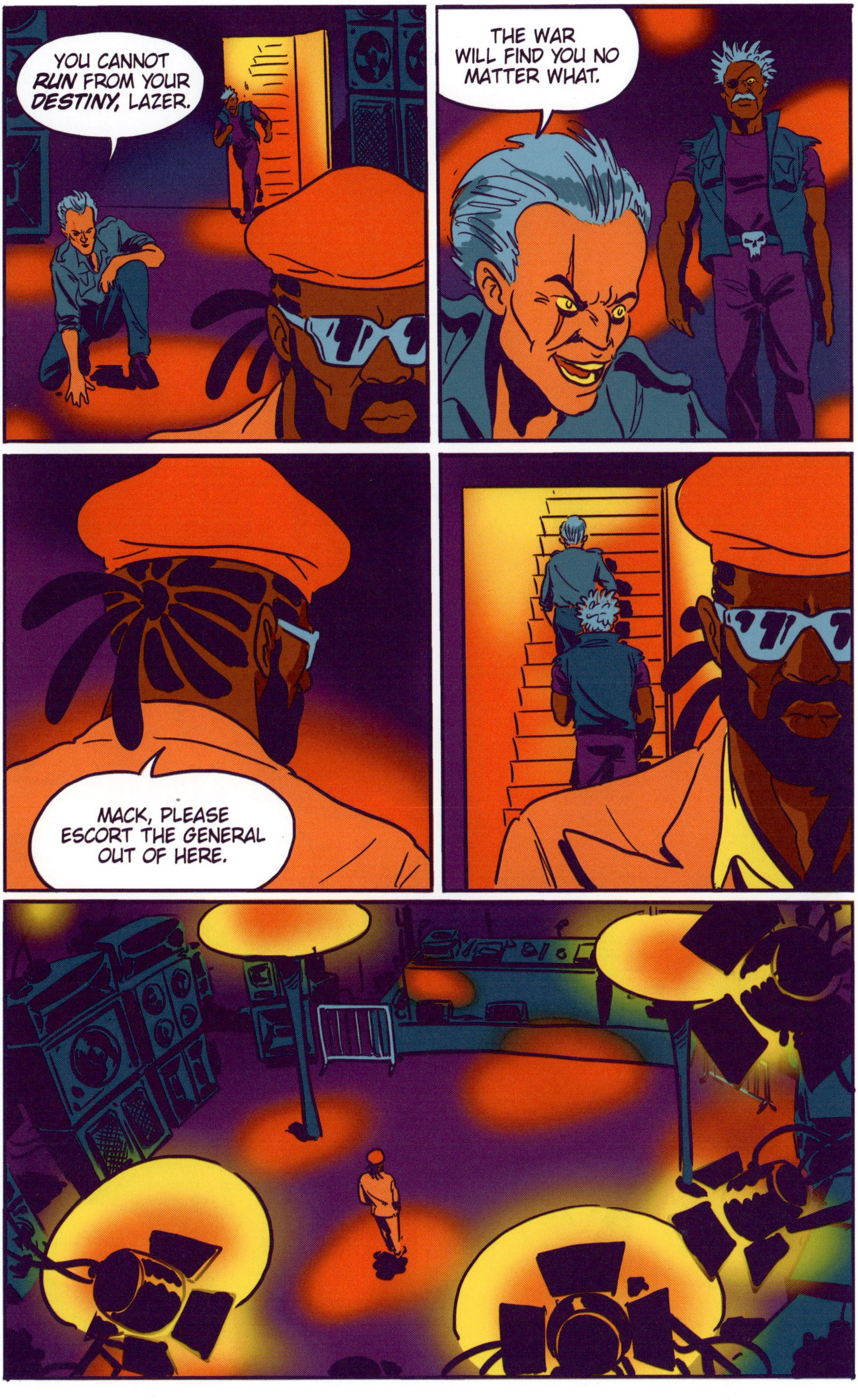
YOU CANNOT RUN FROM YOUR DESTINY, LAZER.
THE WAR WILL FIND YOU NO MATTER WHAT.
MACK, PLEASE ESCORT THE GENERAL OUT OF HERE.

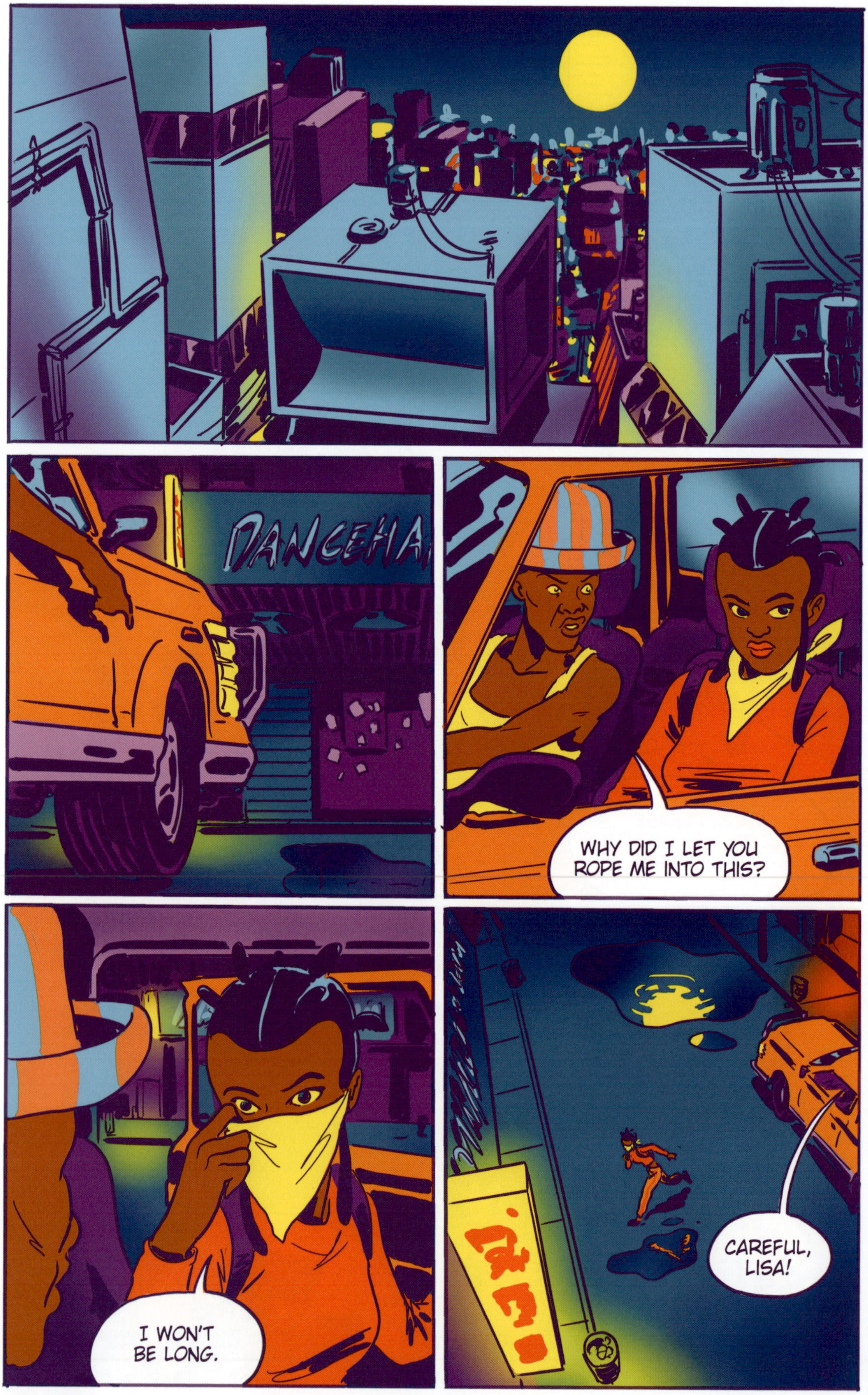
WHY DID I LET YOU ROPE ME INTO THIS?
I WON'T BE LONG.
CAREFUL, LISA!

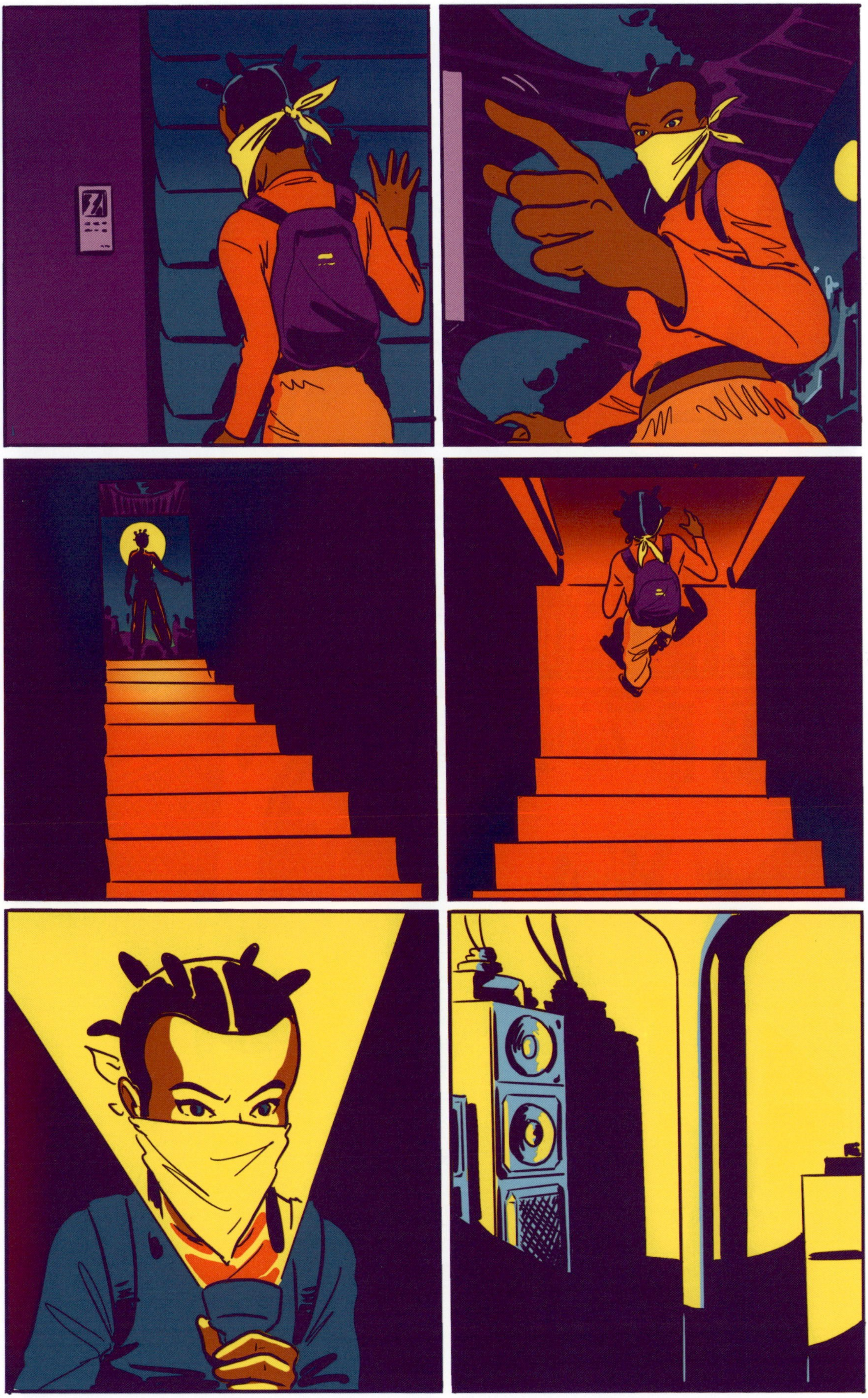

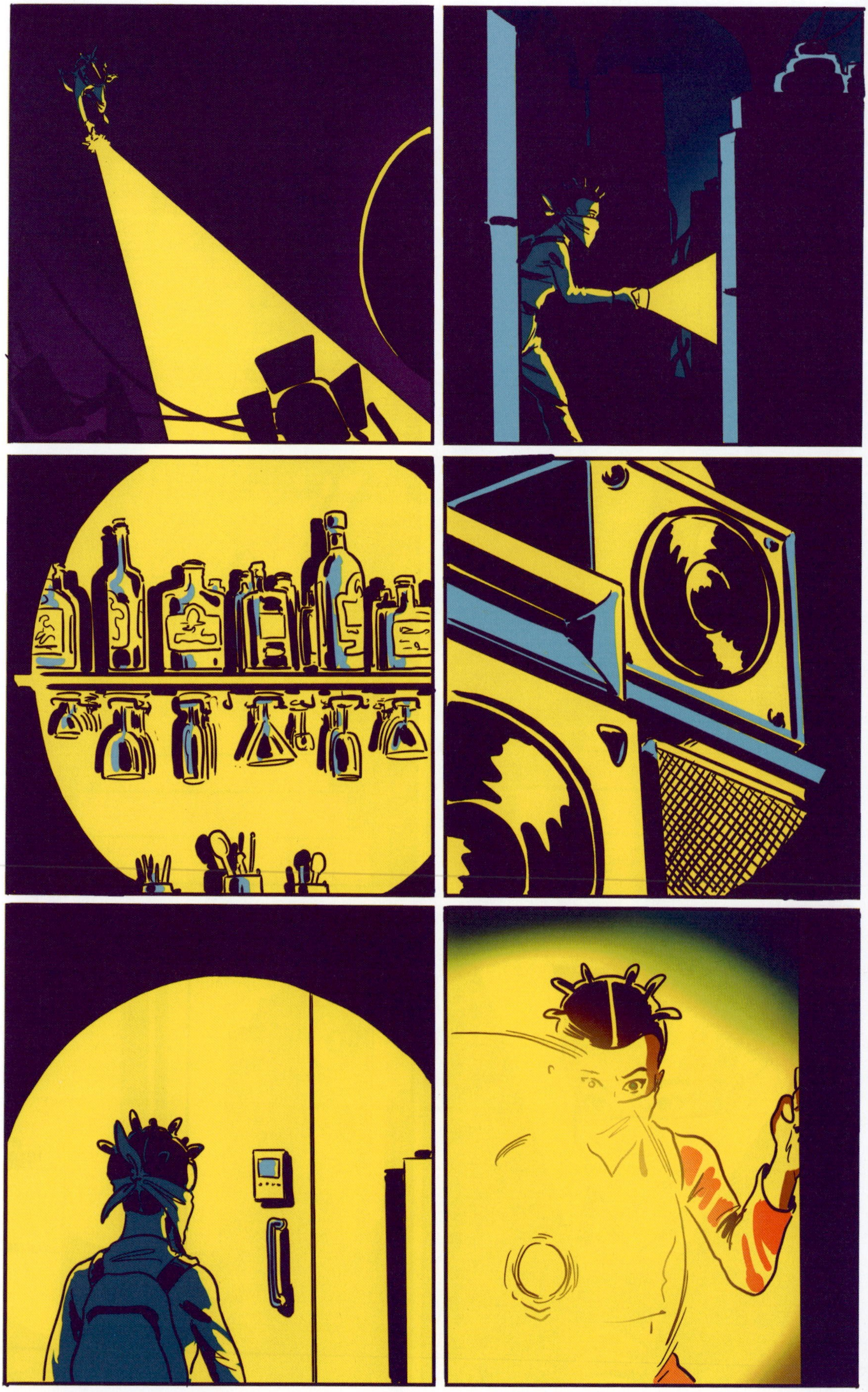

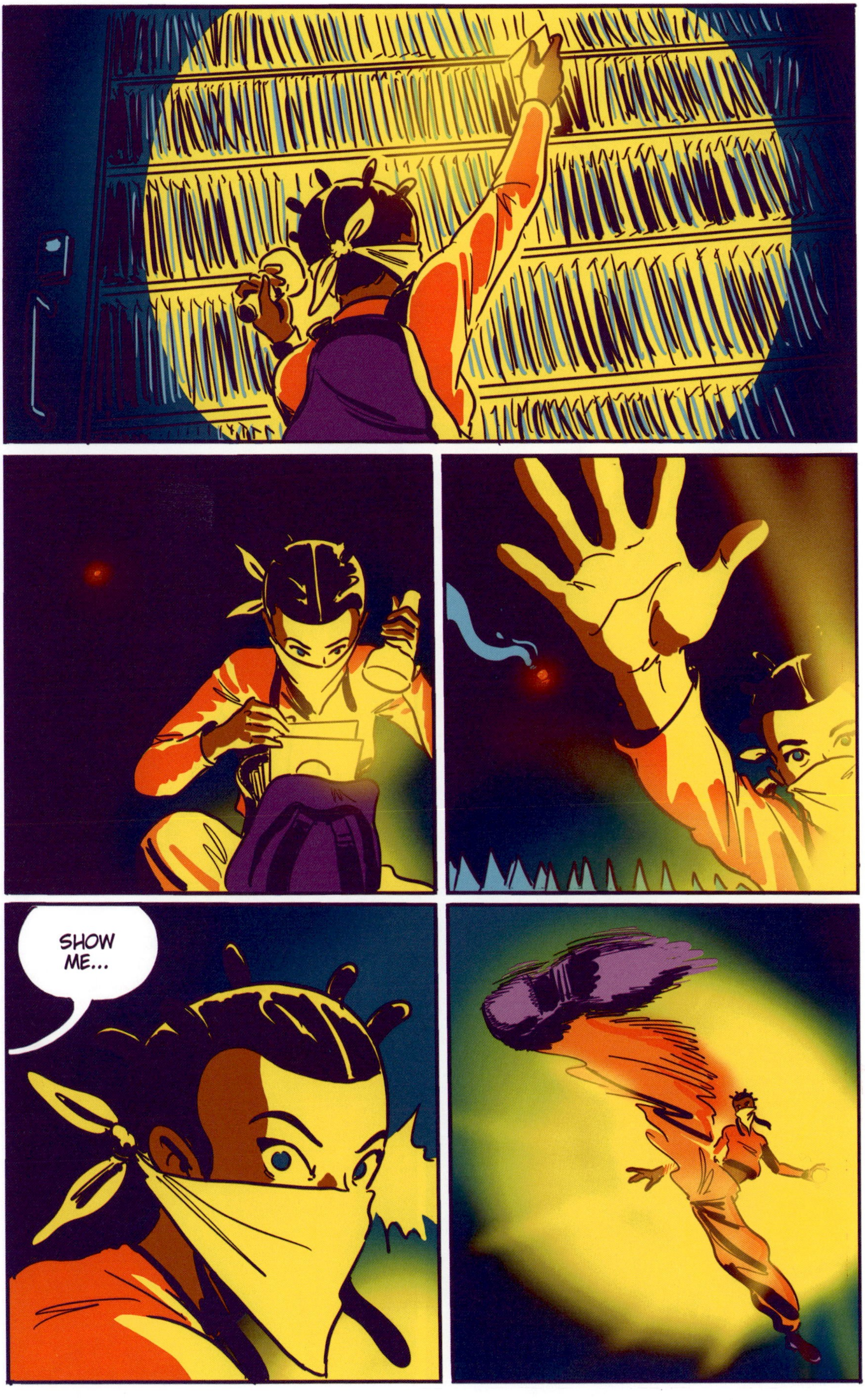
SHOW ME...

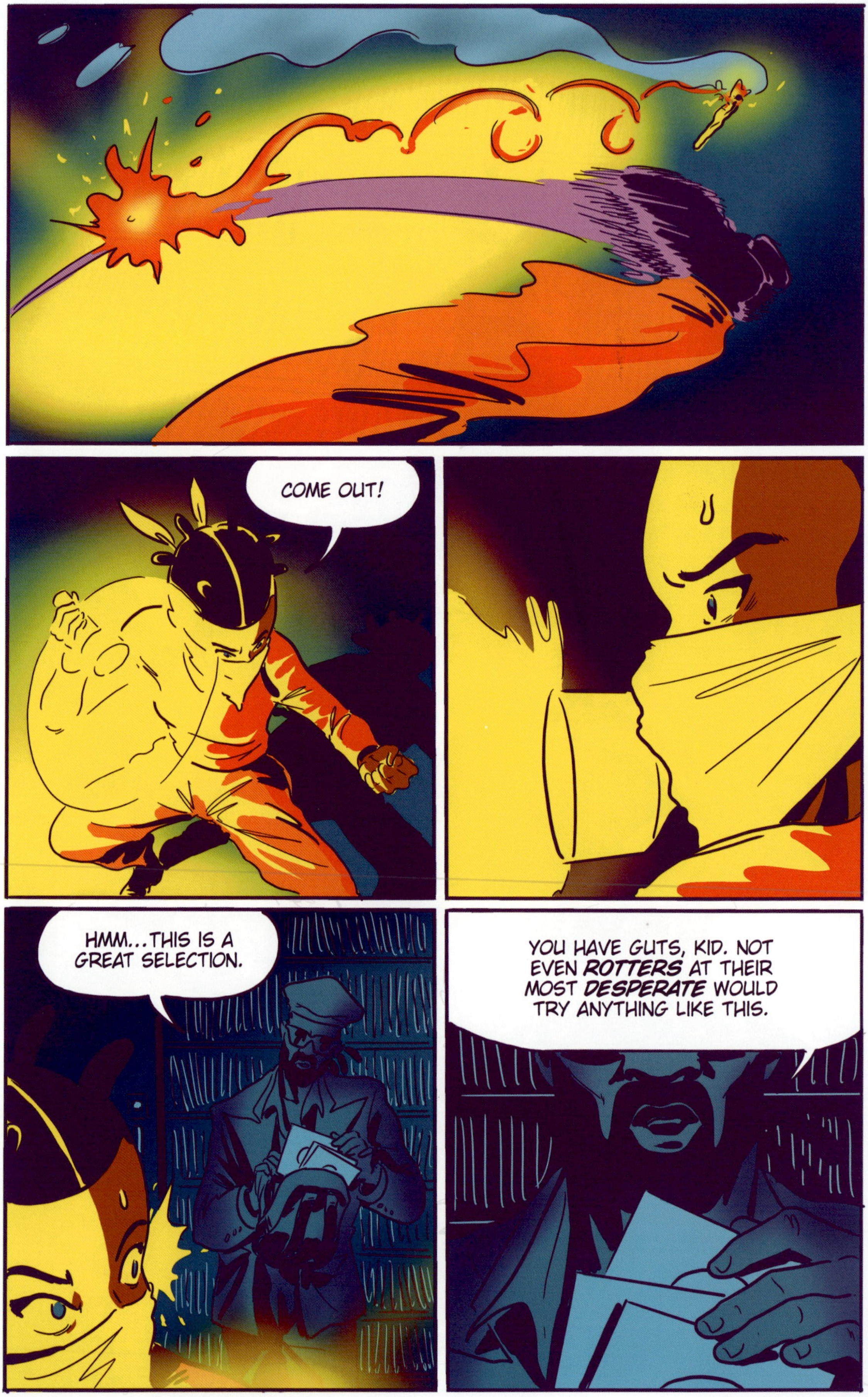
COME OUT!
HMM...THIS IS A GREAT SELECTION.
YOU HAVE GUTS, KID. NOT EVEN ROTTERS AT THEIR MOST DESPERATE WOULD TRY ANYTHING LIKE THIS.

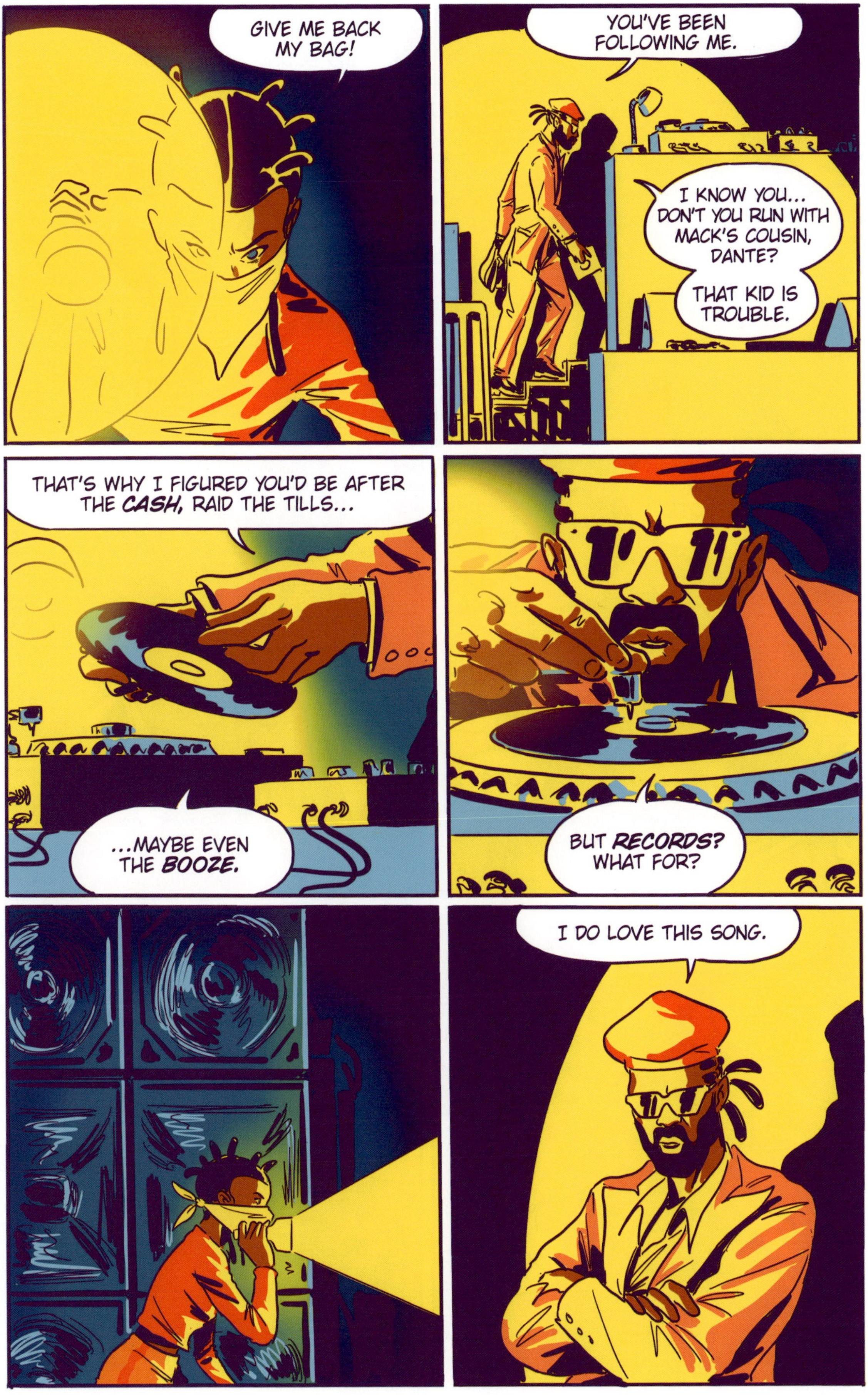
GIVE ME BACK MY BAG!
YOU'VE BEEN FOLLOWING ME.
I KNOW YOU... DON'T YOU RUN WITH MACK'S COUSIN, DANTE?
THAT KID IS TROUBLE.
THAT'S WHY I FIGURED YOU'D BE AFTER THE CASH, RAID THE TILLS...
...MAYBE EVEN THE BOOZE.
BUT RECORDS? WHAT FOR?
I DO LOVE THIS SONG.

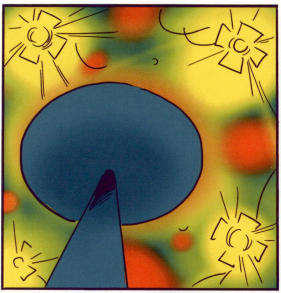

THE RECORDS ARE FOR THE BIG SOUNDCLASH ACCORDING TO THIS GUY.

GET OFF ME, BLOODCLOT!

BOSS?

SHIT.

DANTE'S CREW, RIGHT?

'FRAID SO, BOSS.

SHIT.

HE CAME OUT OF NOWHERE, LISA!

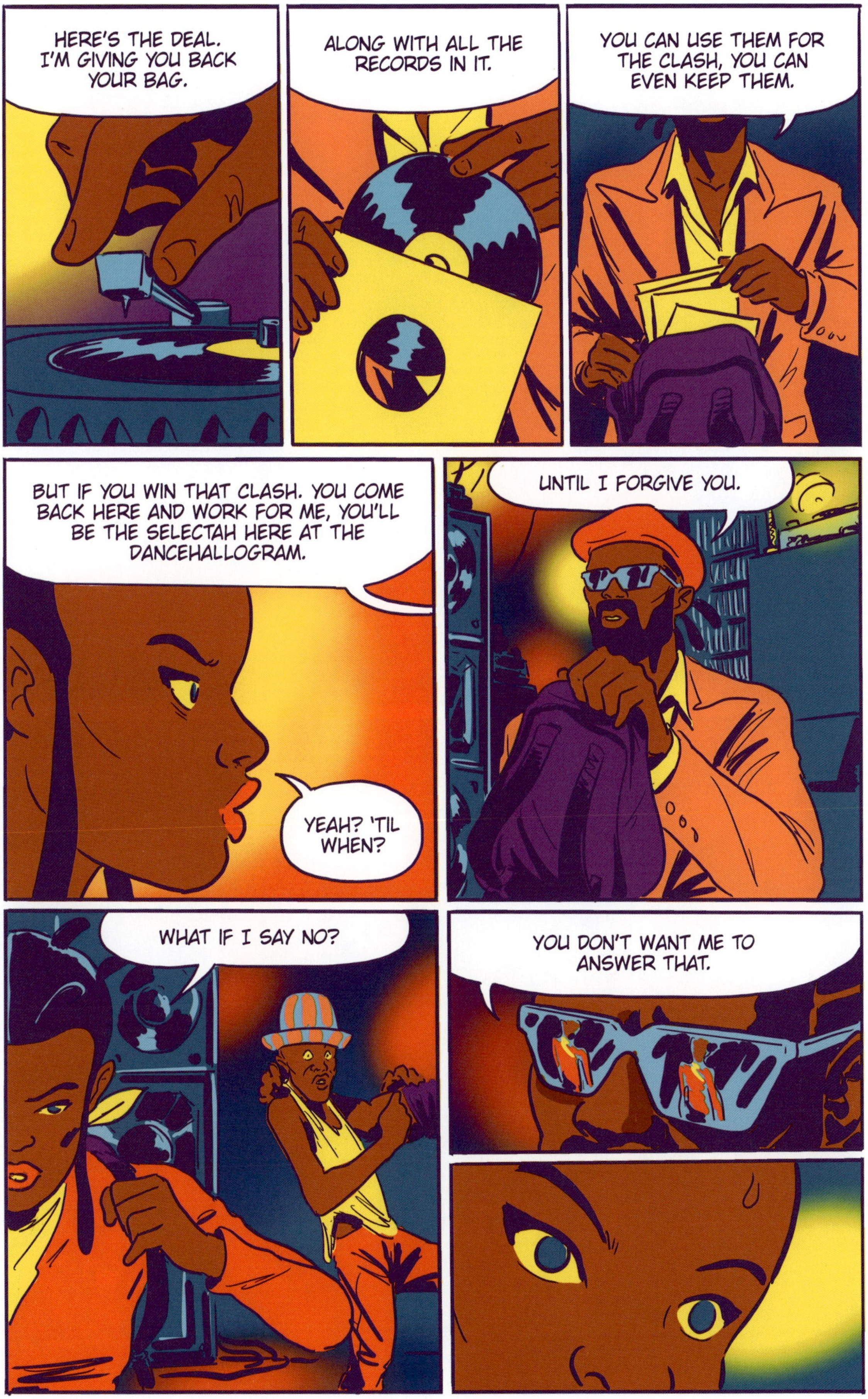
HERE'S THE DEAL. I'M GIVING YOU BACK YOUR BAG.
ALONG WITH ALL THE RECORDS IN IT.
YOU CAN USE THEM FOR THE CLASH, YOU CAN EVEN KEEP THEM.
BUT IF YOU WIN THAT CLASH. YOU COME BACK HERE AND WORK FOR ME, YOU'LL BE THE SELECTAH HERE AT THE DANCEHALLOGRAM.
YEAH? 'TIL WHEN?
UNTIL I FORGIVE YOU.
WHAT IF I SAY NO?
YOU DON'T WANT ME TO ANSWER THAT.

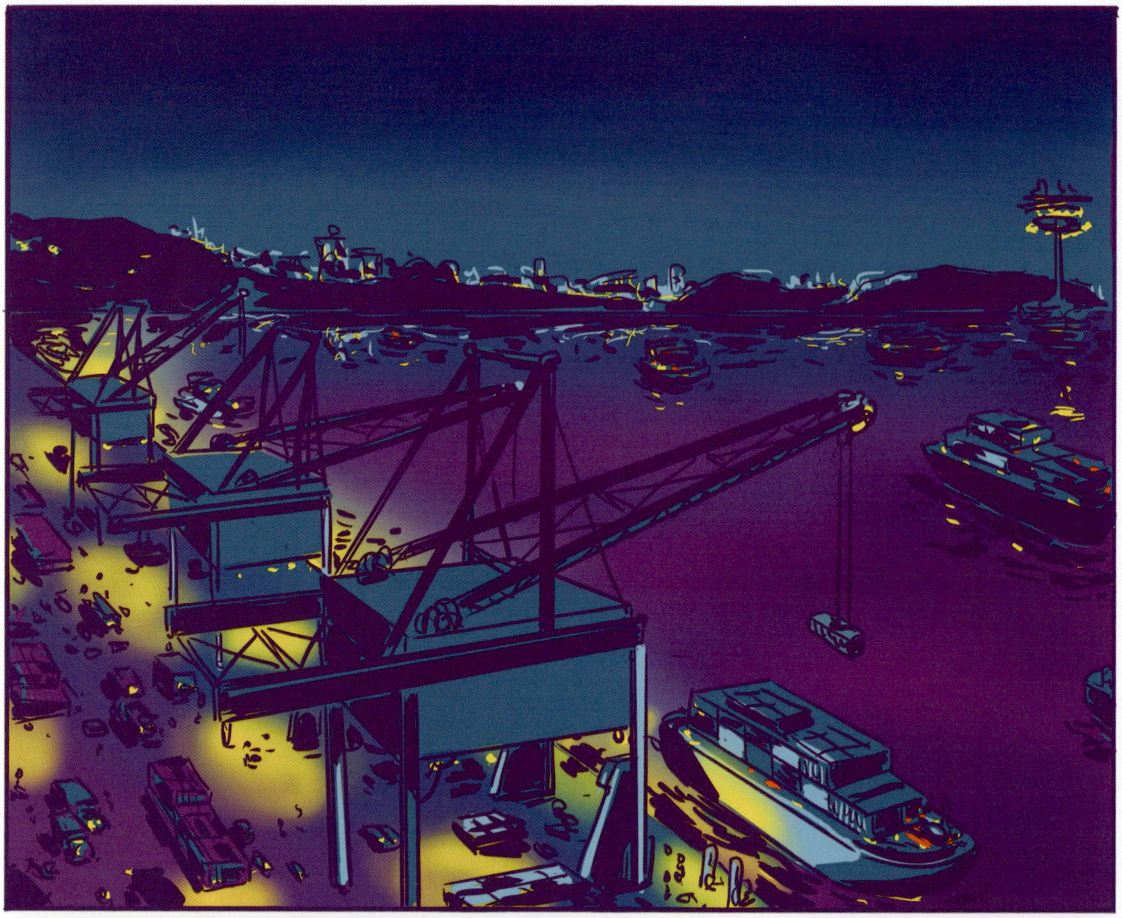

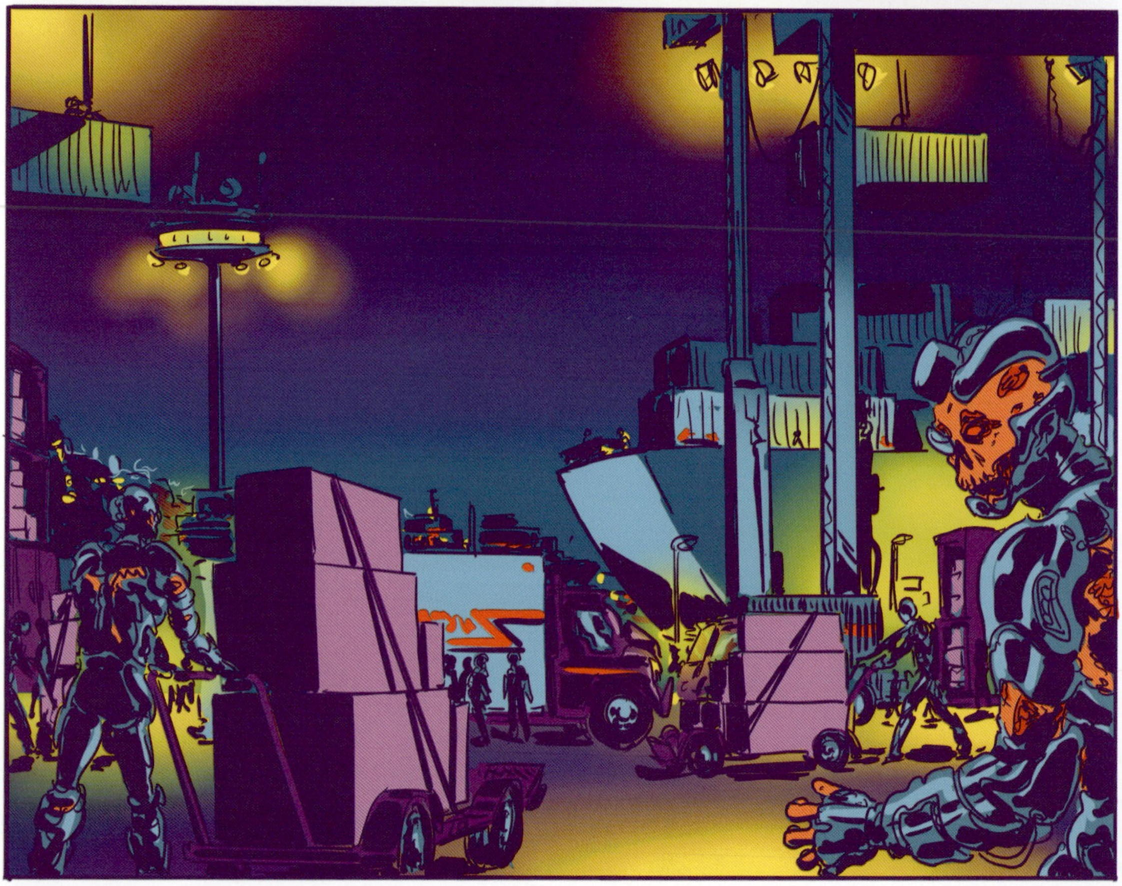

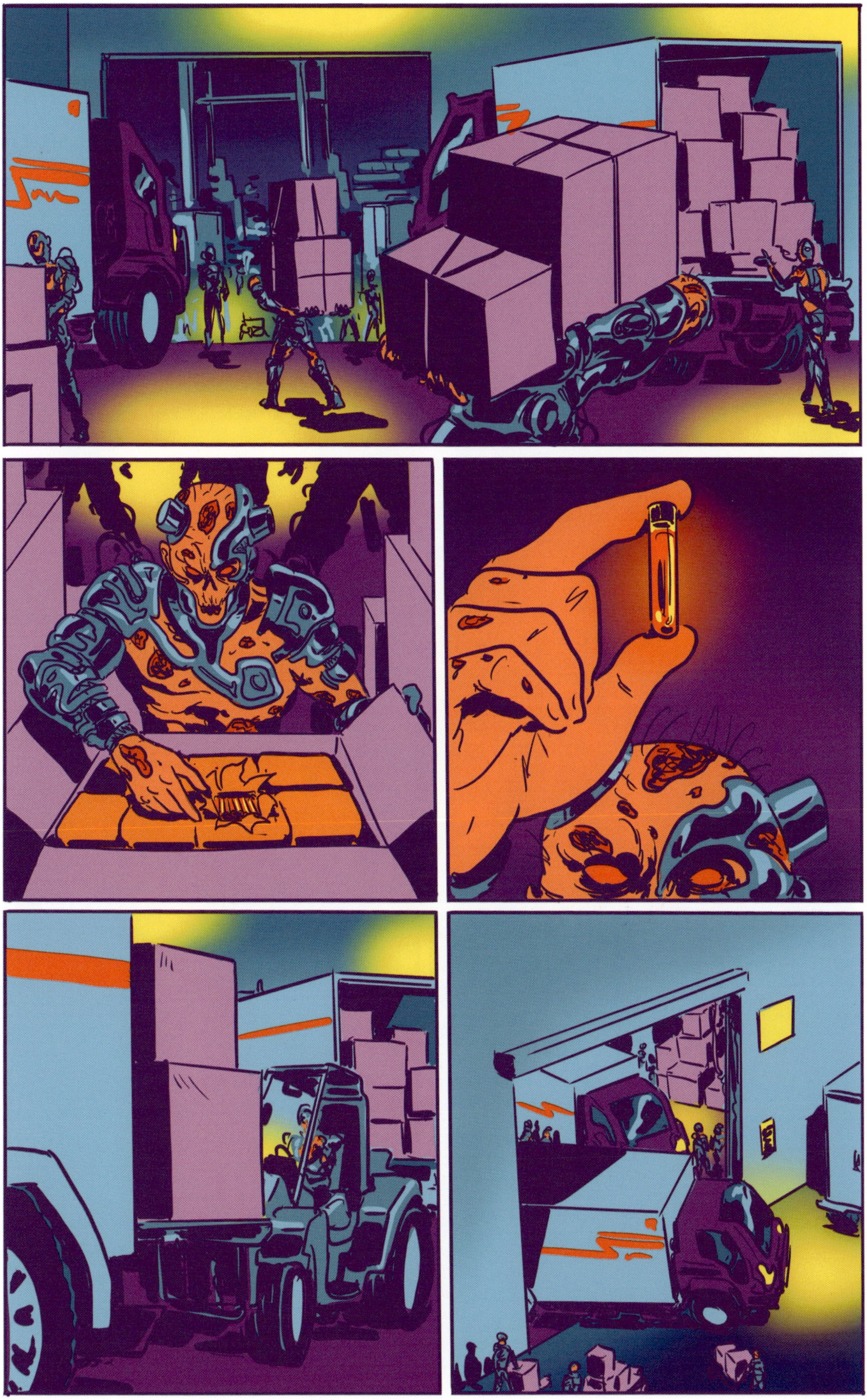

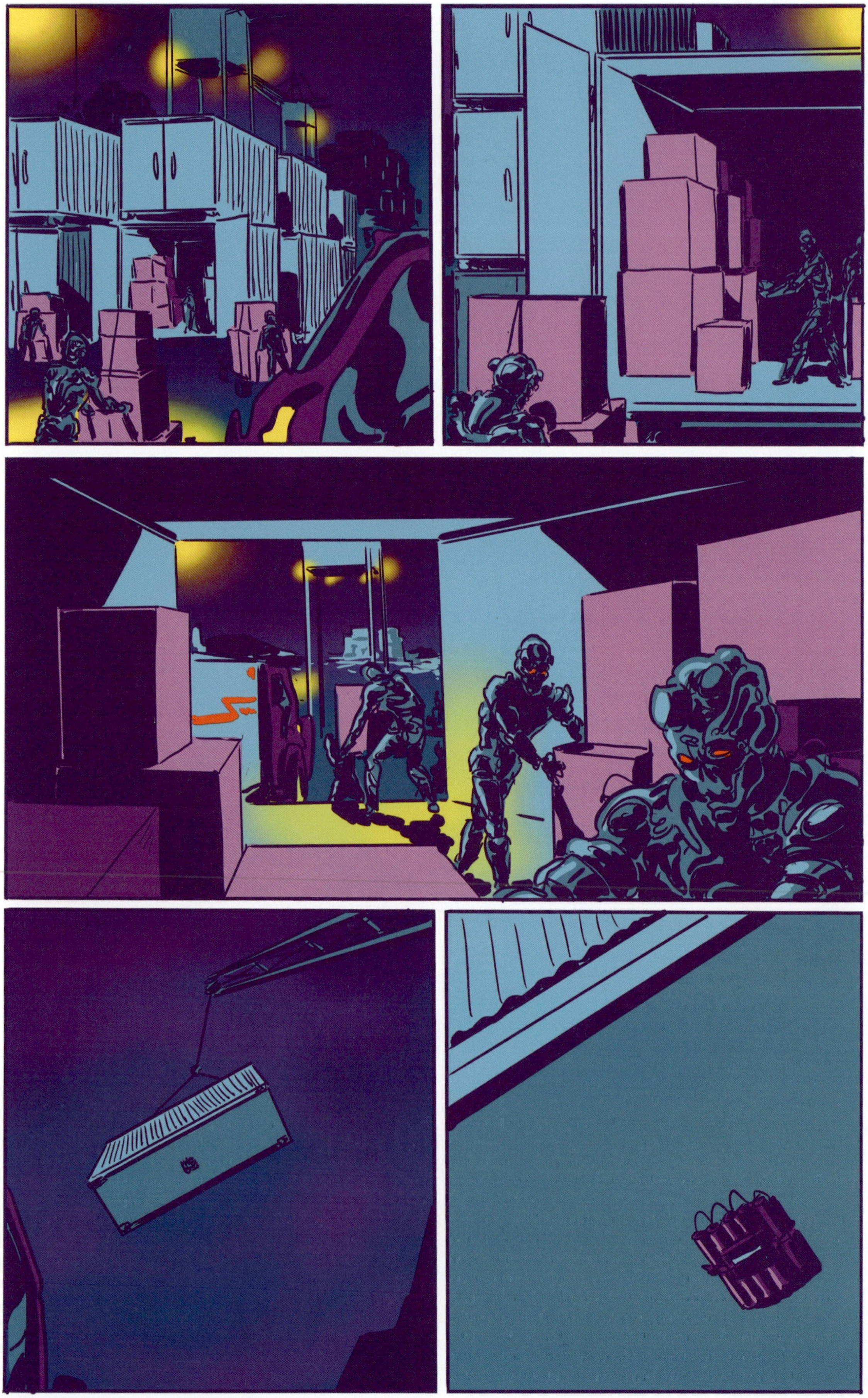

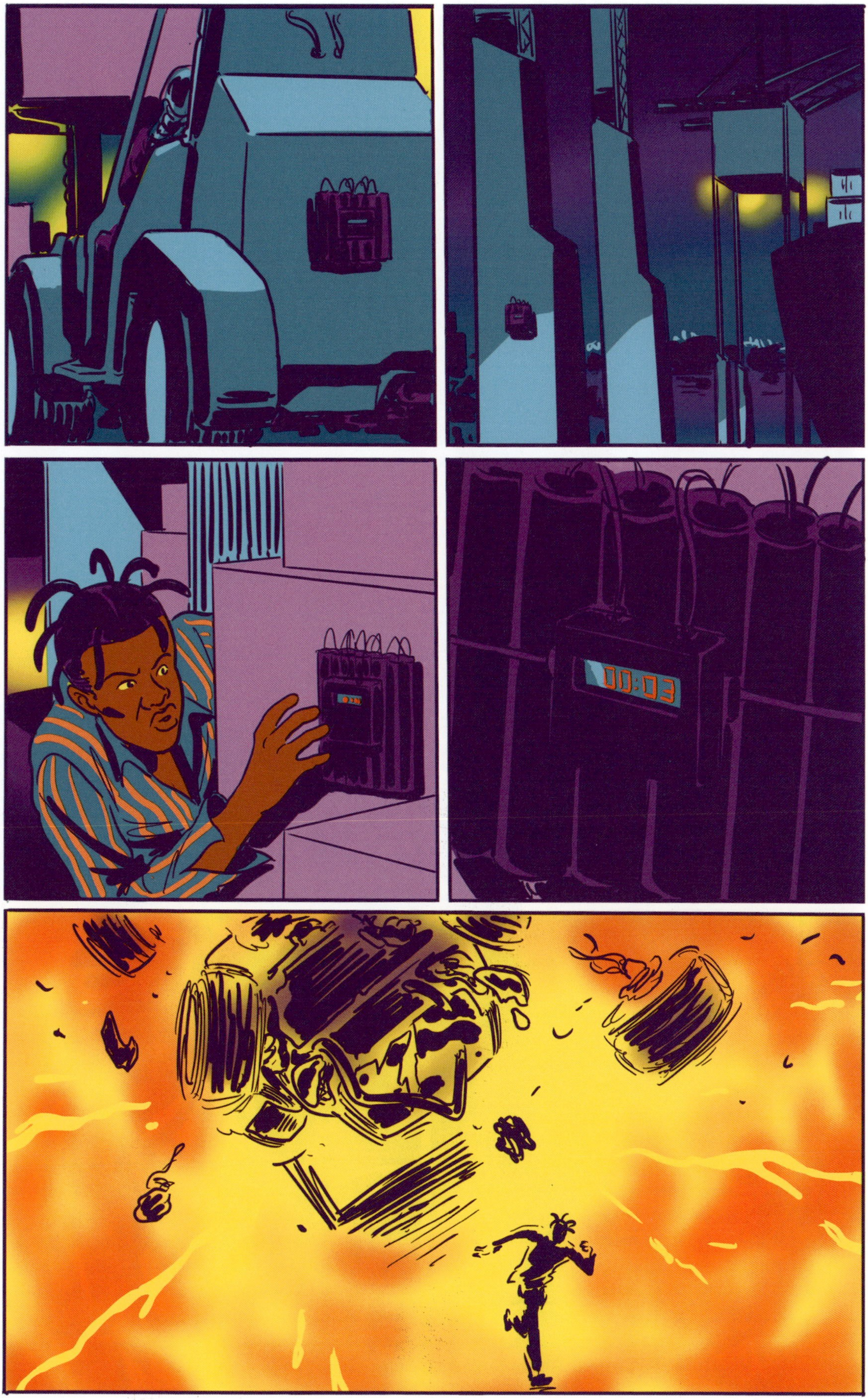
00:03

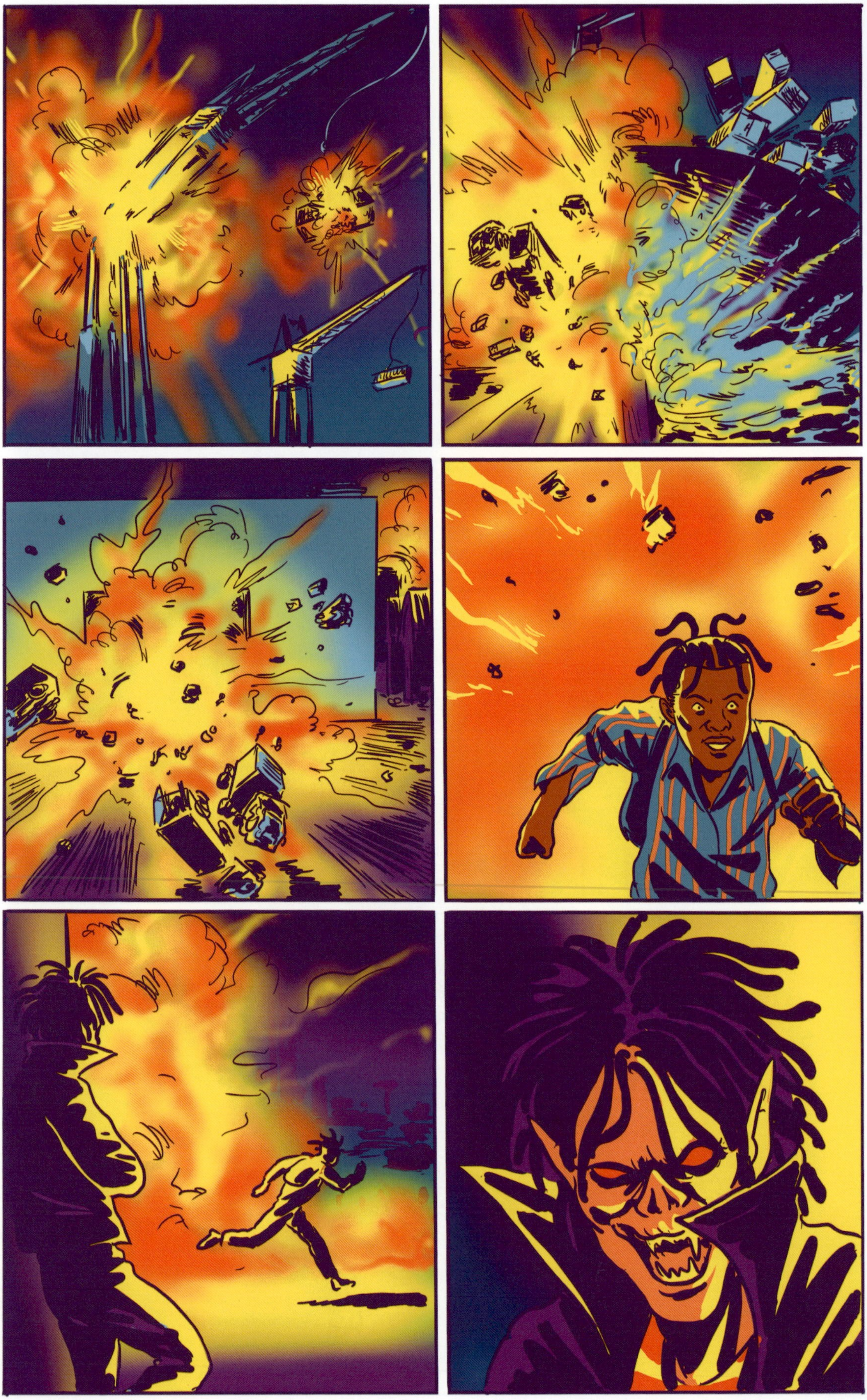

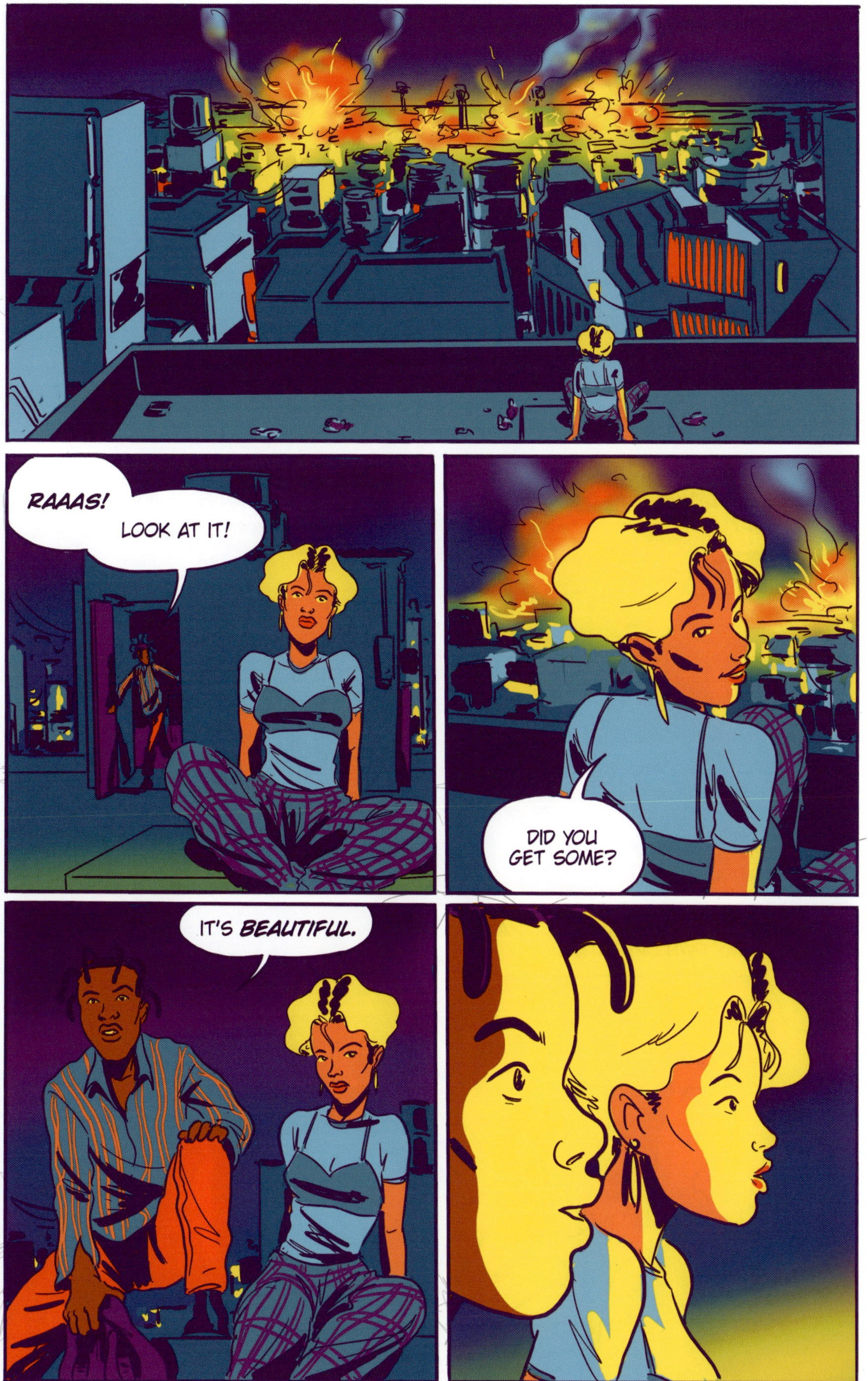
RAAAS!
LOOK AT IT!
DID YOU GET SOME?
IT'S BEAUTIFUL.

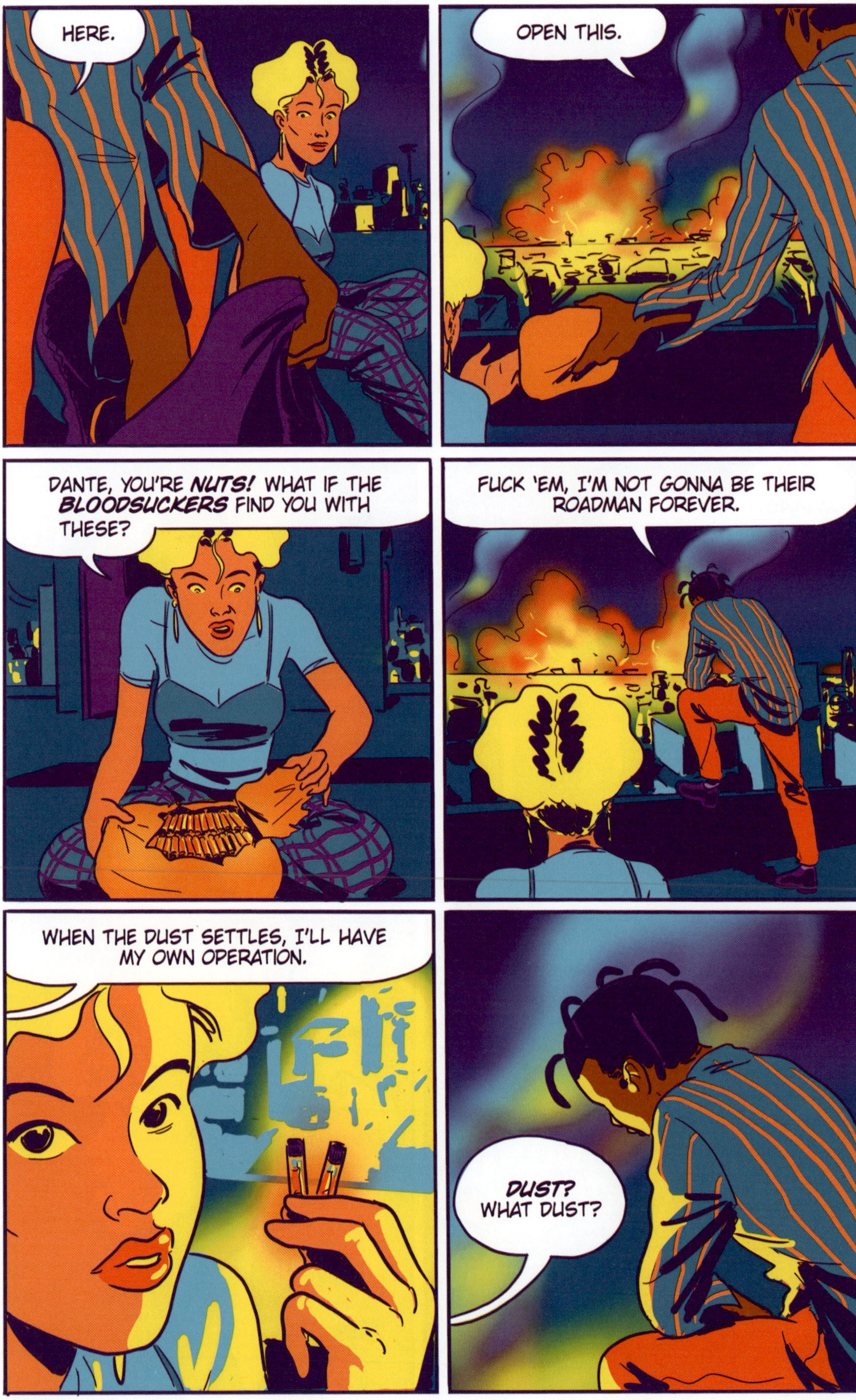
HERE.
OPEN THIS.
DANTE, YOU'RE NUTS! WHAT IF THE BLOODSUCKERS FIND YOU WITH THESE?
FUCK 'EM, I'M NOT GONNA BE THEIR ROADMAN FOREVER.
WHEN THE DUST SETTLES, I'LL HAVE MY OWN OPERATION.
DUST? WHAT DUST?

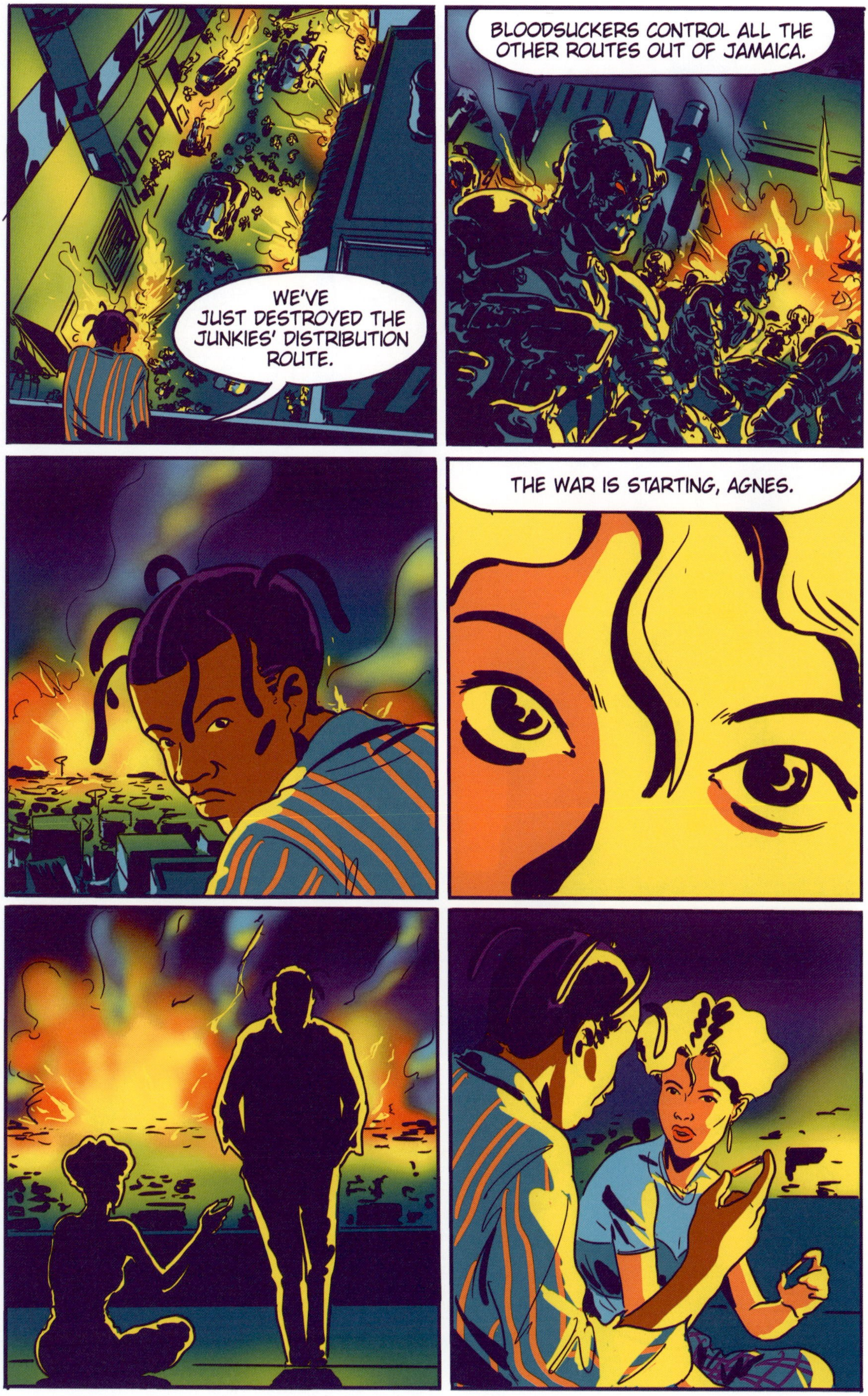
WE'VE JUST DESTROYED THE JUNKIES' DISTRIBUTION ROUTE.
BLOODSUCKERS CONTROL ALL THE OTHER ROUTES OUT OF JAMAICA.
THE WAR IS STARTING, AGNES.

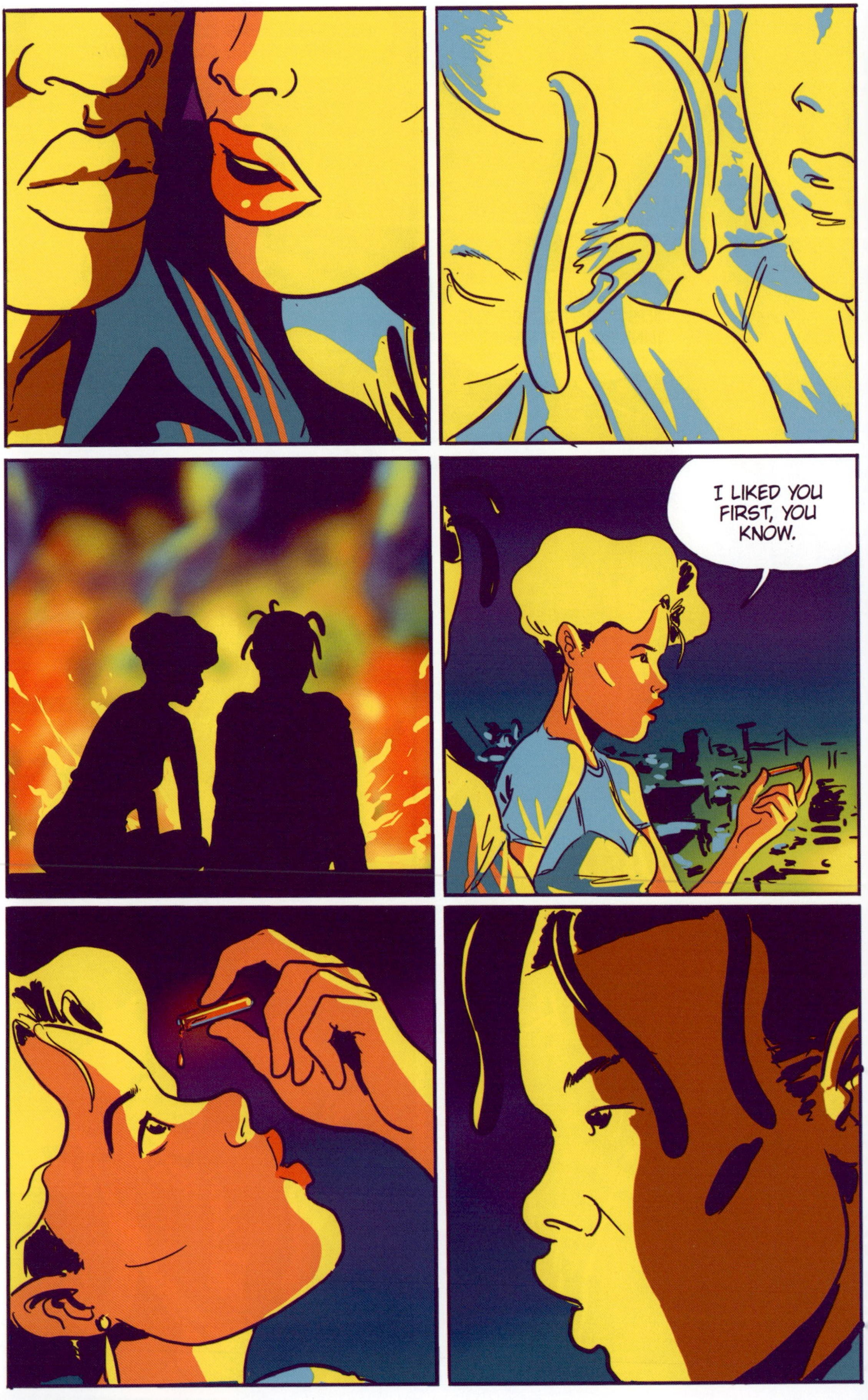
I LIKED YOU FIRST, YOU KNOW.

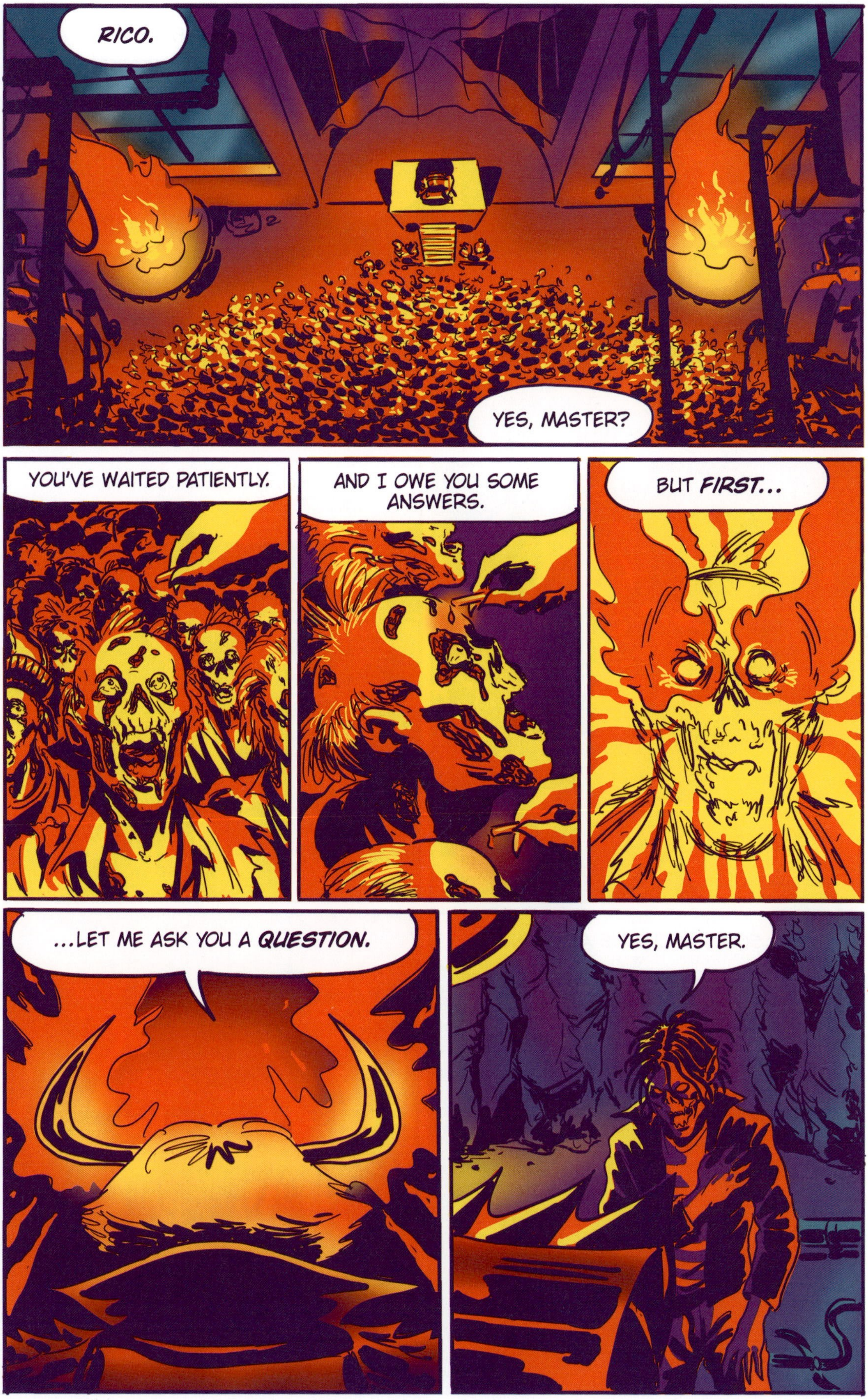
RICO.
YES, MASTER?
YOU'VE WAITED PATIENTLY.
AND I OWE YOU SOME ANSWERS.
BUT FIRST...
...LET ME ASK YOU A QUESTION.
YES, MASTER.

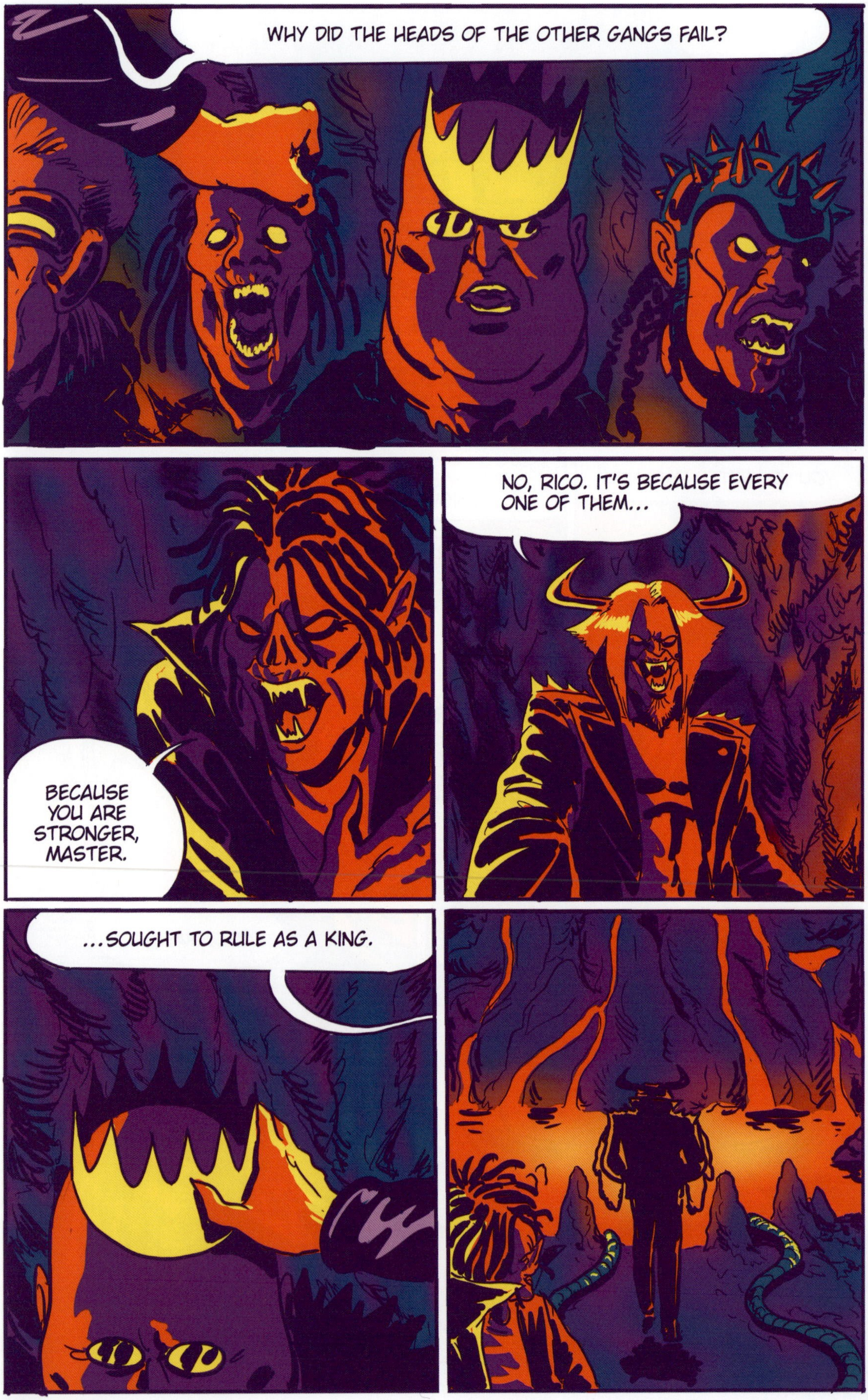
WHY DID THE HEADS OF THE OTHER GANGS FAIL?
BECAUSE YOU ARE STRONGER, MASTER.
NO, RICO. IT'S BECAUSE EVERY ONE OF THEM...
...SOUGHT TO RULE AS A KING.

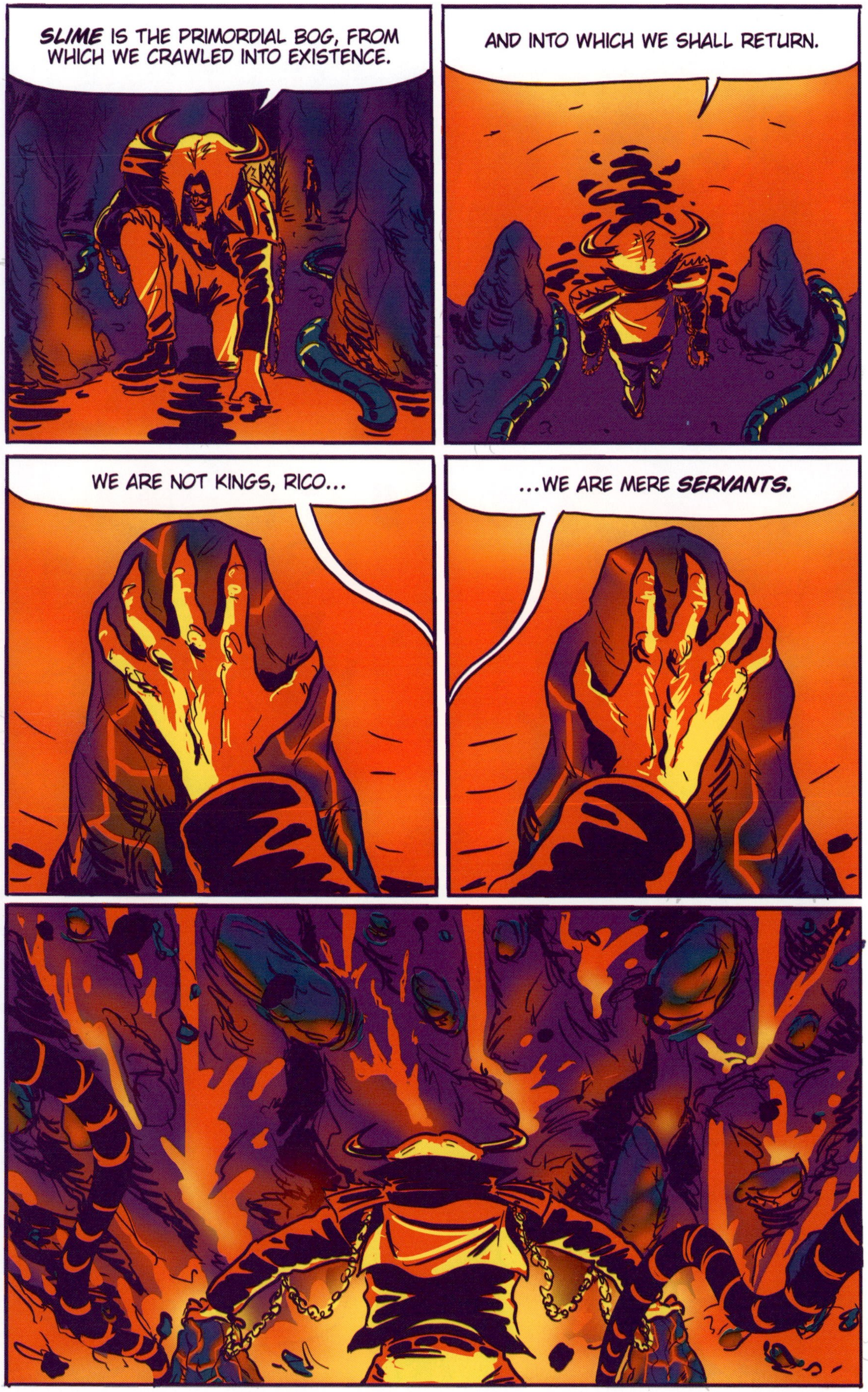
SLIME IS THE PRIMORDIAL BOG, FROM WHICH WE CRAWLED INTO EXISTENCE.
AND INTO WHICH WE SHALL RETURN.
WE ARE NOT KINGS, RICO...
...WE ARE MERE SERVANTS.

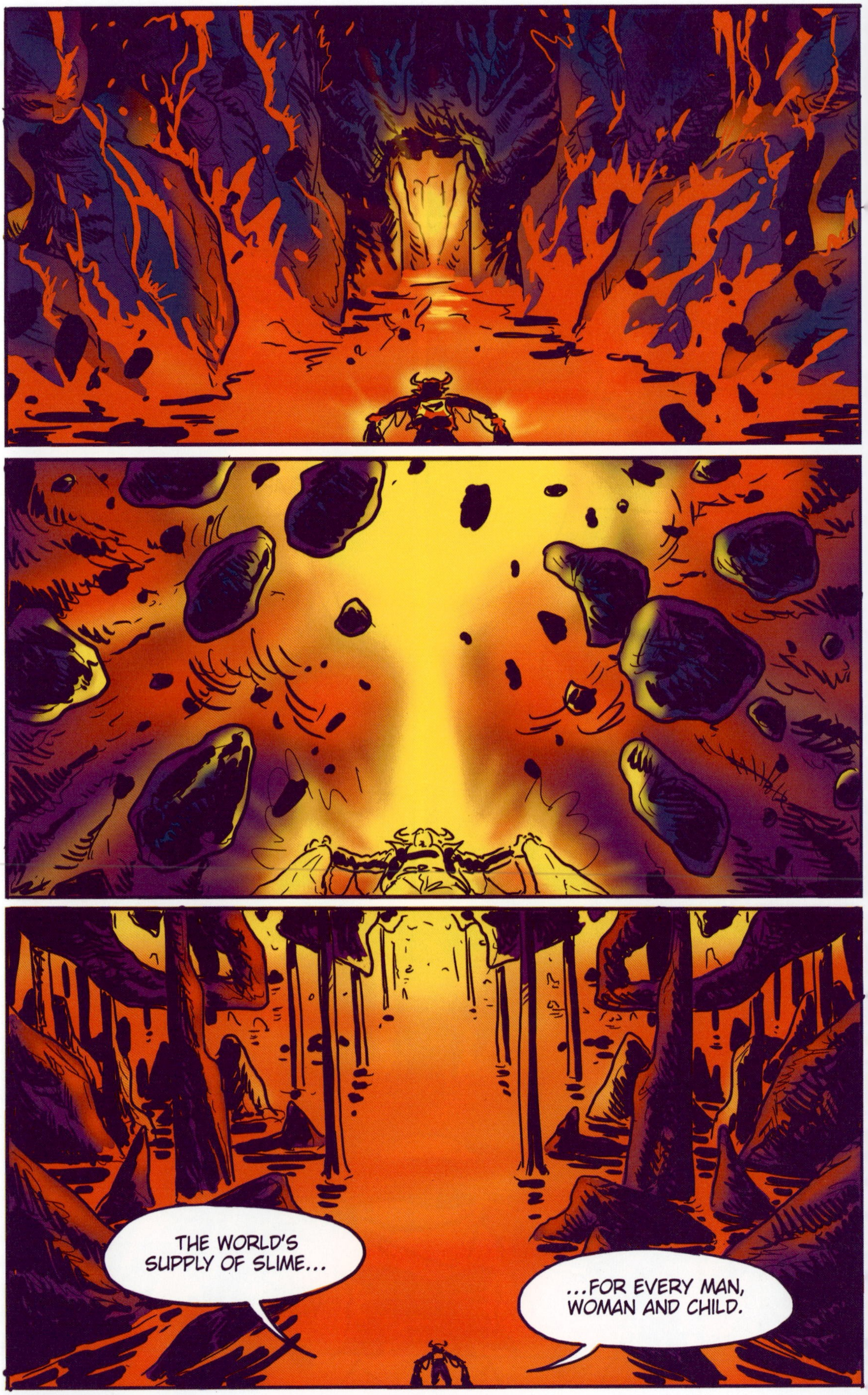
THE WORLD'S SUPPLY OF SLIME...
...FOR EVERY MAN, WOMAN AND CHILD.

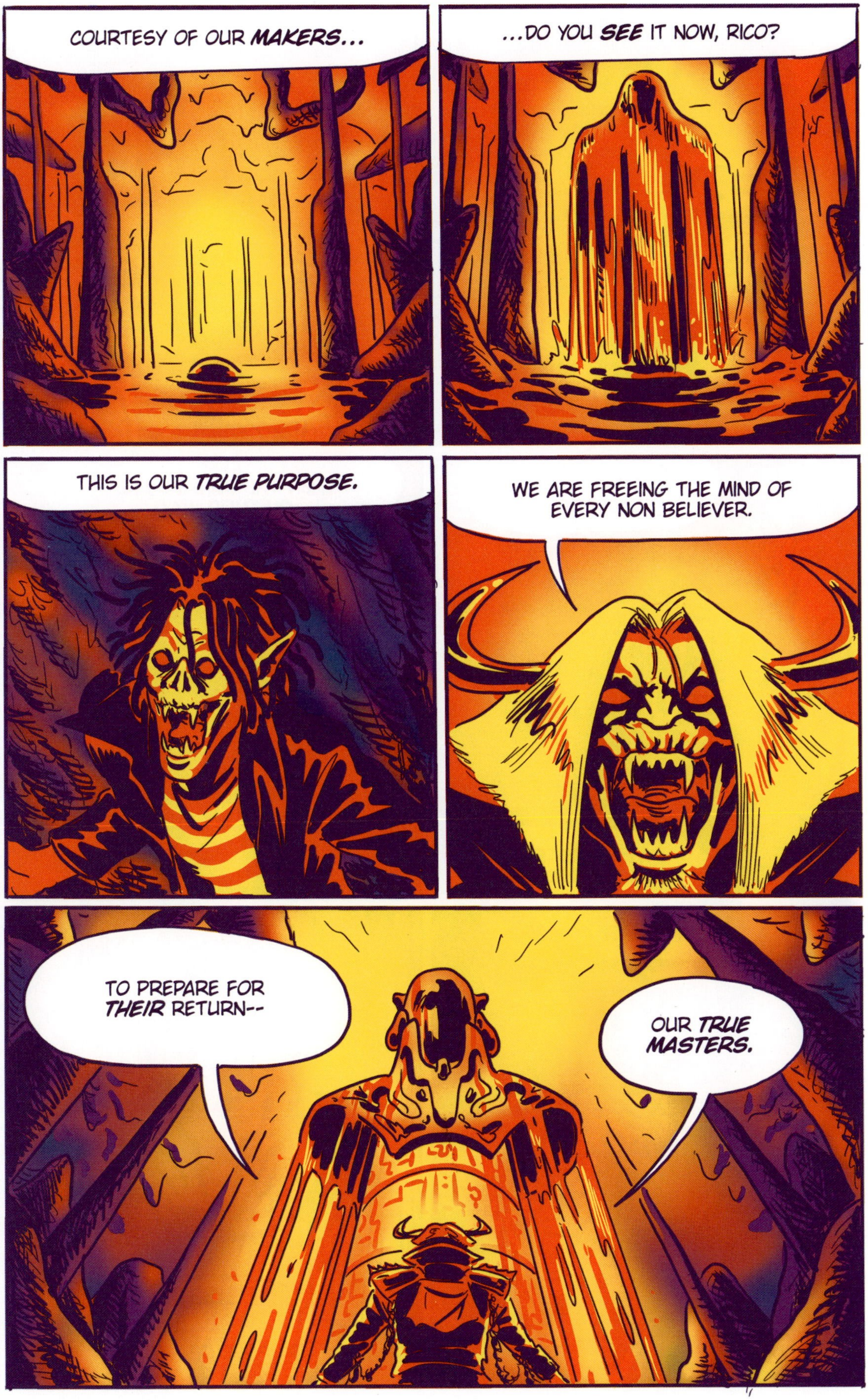
COURTESY OF OUR MAKERS...
...DO YOU SEE IT NOW, RICO?
THIS IS OUR TRUE PURPOSE.
WE ARE FREEING THE MIND OF EVERY NON BELIEVER.
TO PREPARE FOR THEIR RETURN--
OUR TRUE MASTERS.

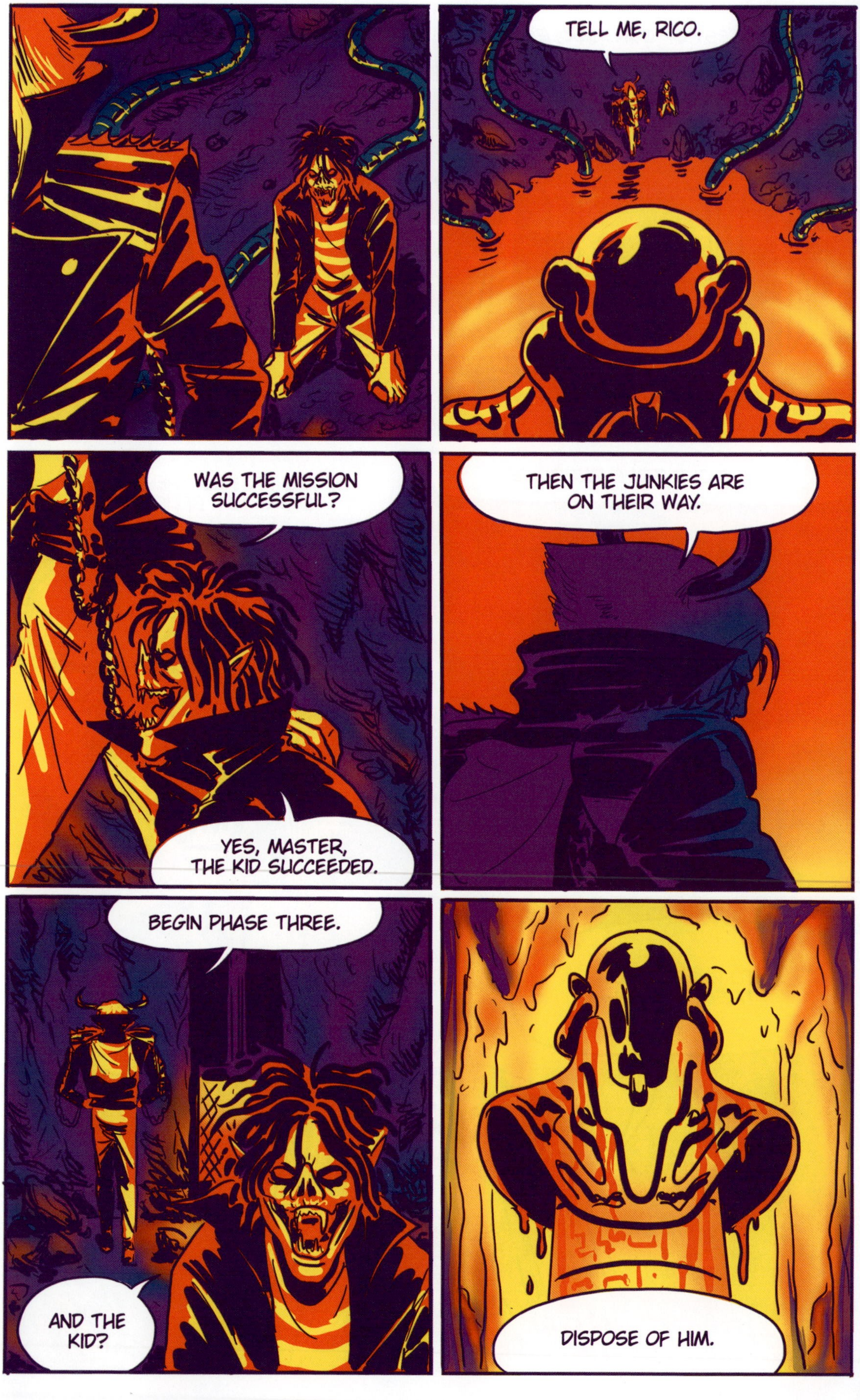
TELL ME, RICO.
WAS THE MISSION SUCCESSFUL?
YES, MASTER, THE KID SUCCEEDED.
THEN THE JUNKIES ARE ON THEIR WAY.
BEGIN PHASE THREE.
AND THE KID?
DISPOSE OF HIM.

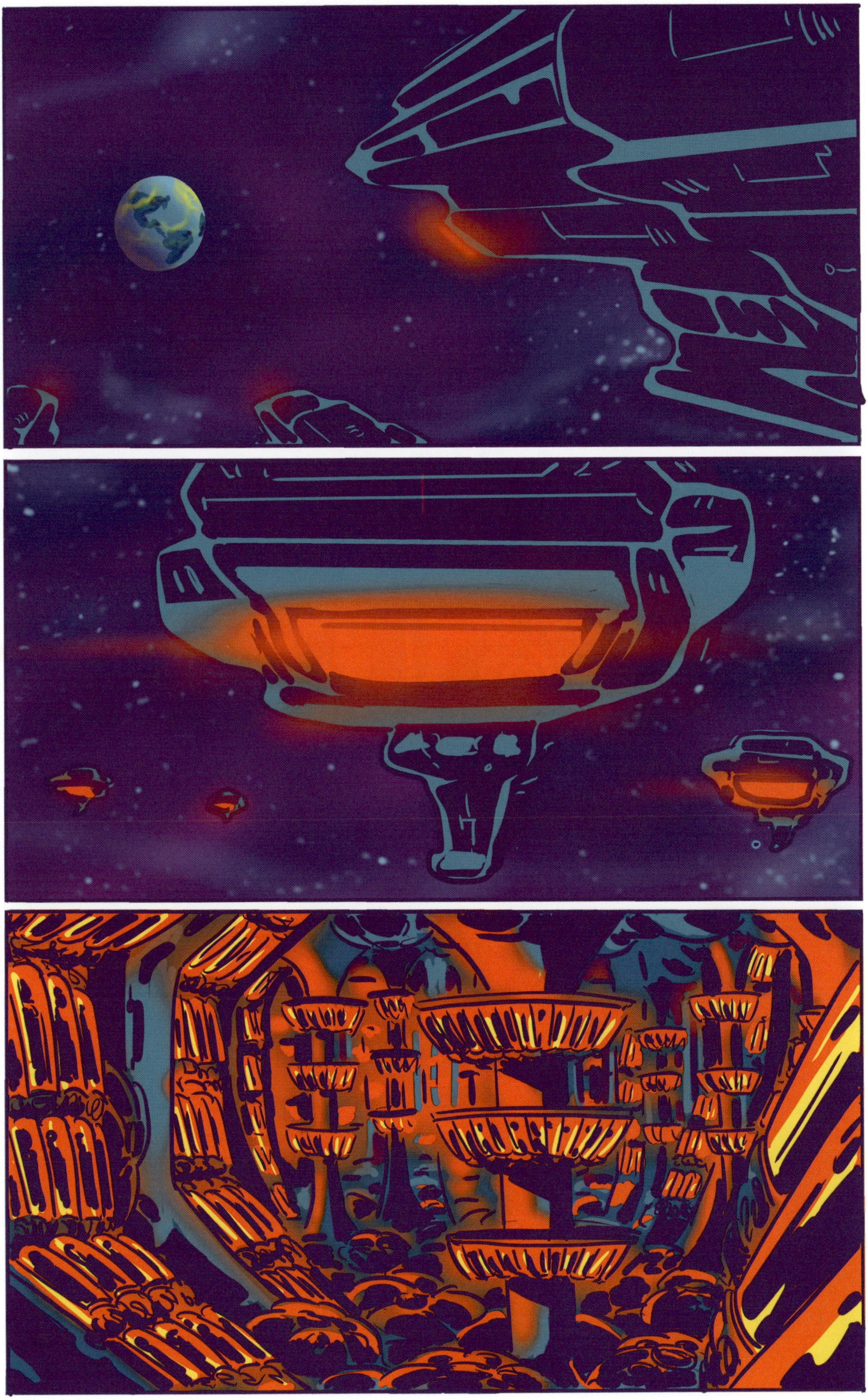

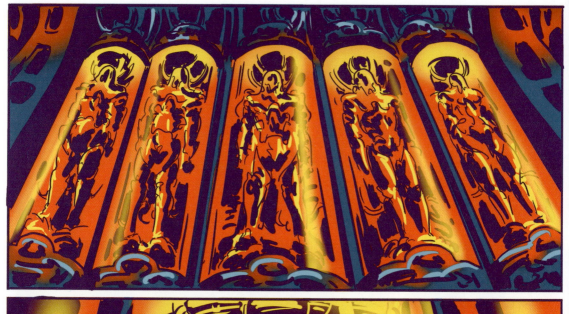

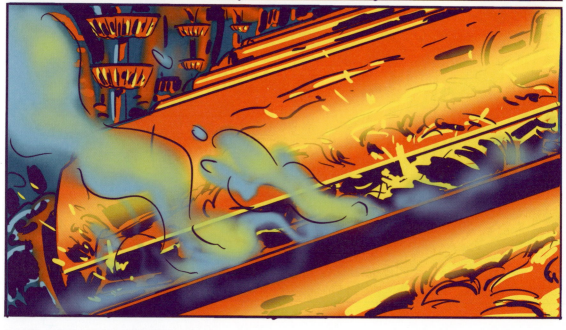

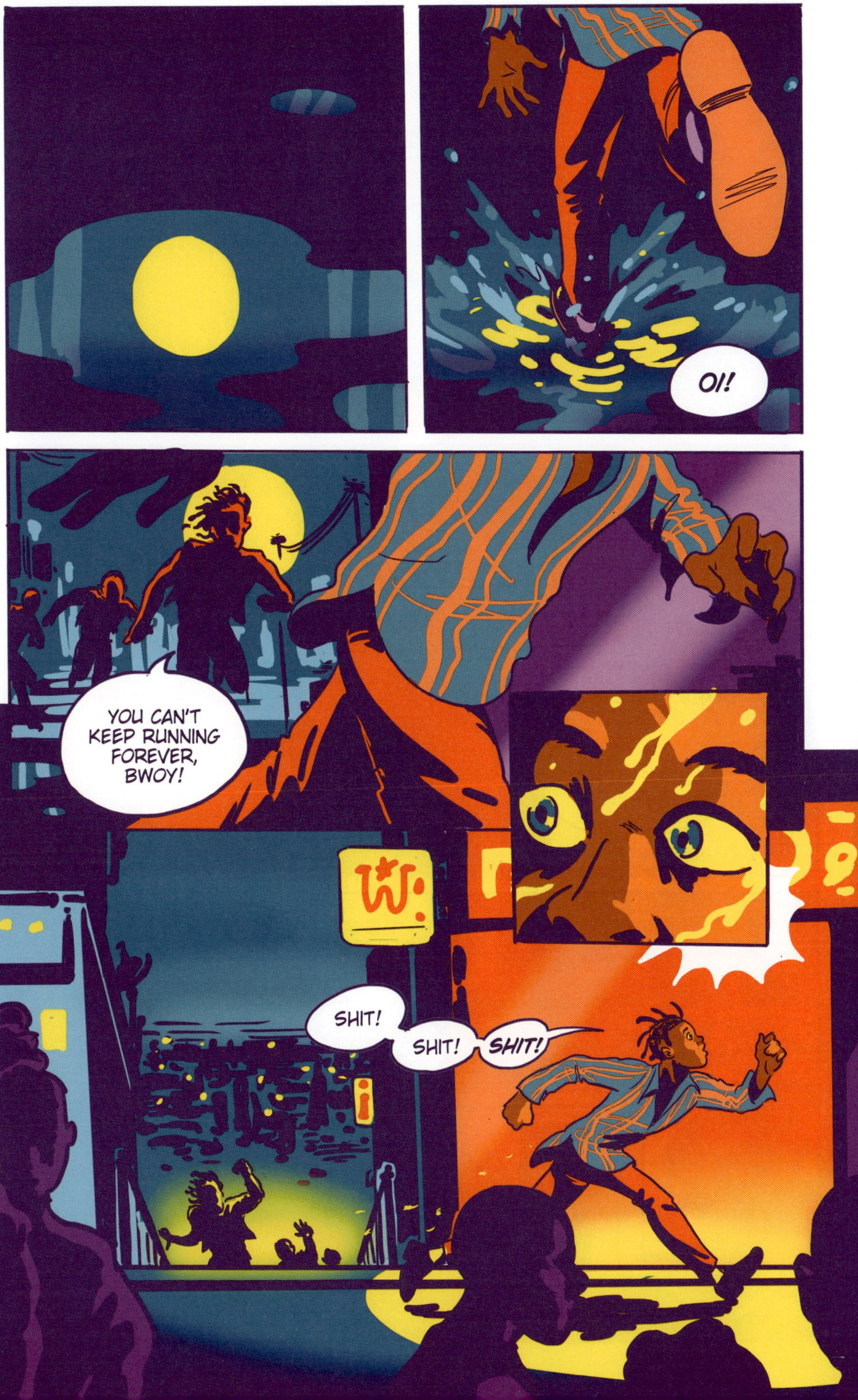
OI!
YOU CAN'T KEEP RUNNING FOREVER, BWOY!
SHIT!
SHIT!
SHIT!

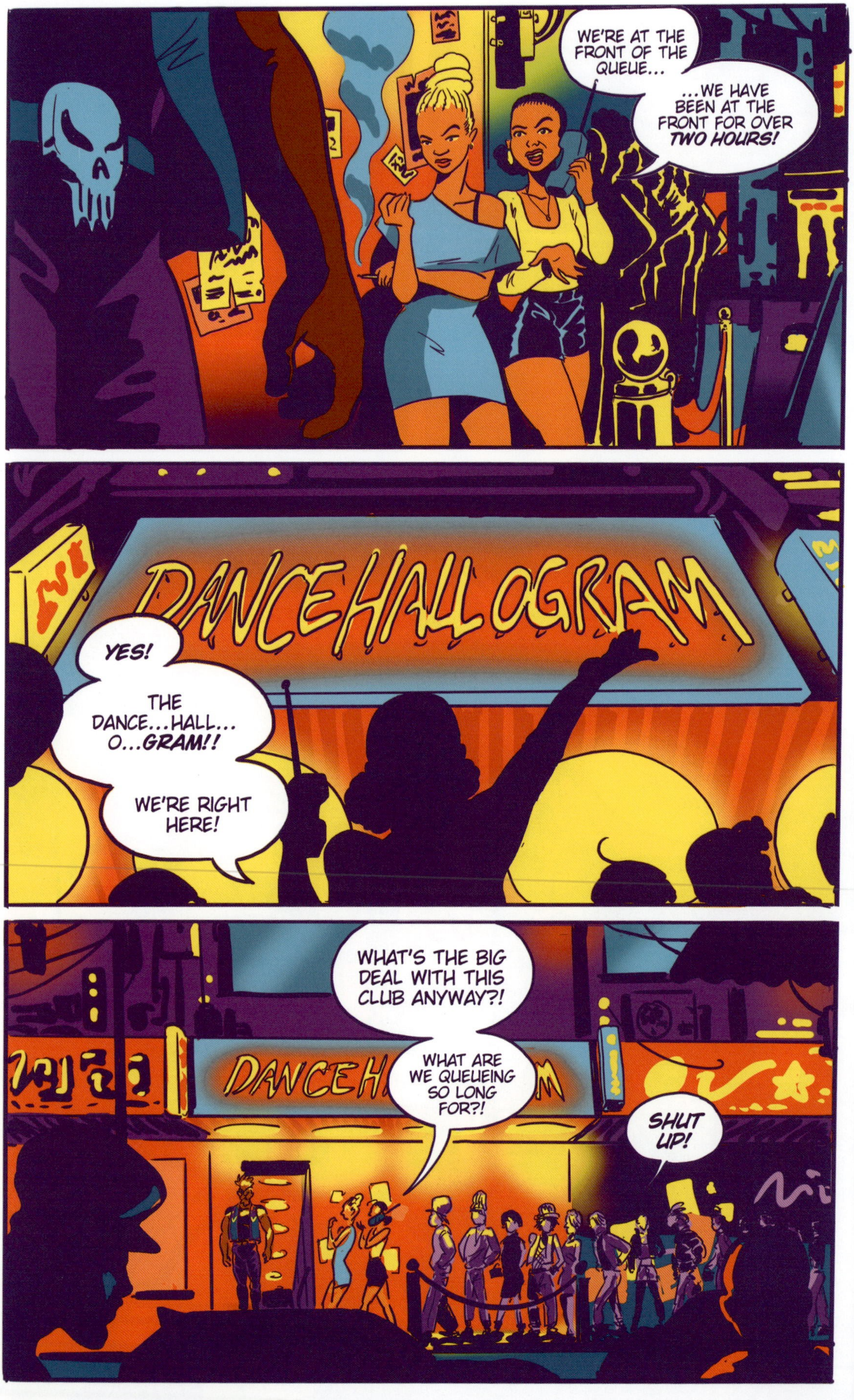
WE'RE AT THE FRONT OF THE QUEUE...
...WE HAVE BEEN AT THE FRONT FOR OVER TWO HOURS!
DANCEHALLOGRAM
YES!
THE DANCE...HALL... O...GRAM!!
WE'RE RIGHT HERE!
WHAT'S THE BIG DEAL WITH THIS CLUB ANYWAY?!
WHAT ARE WE QUEUEING SO LONG FOR?!
SHUT UP!

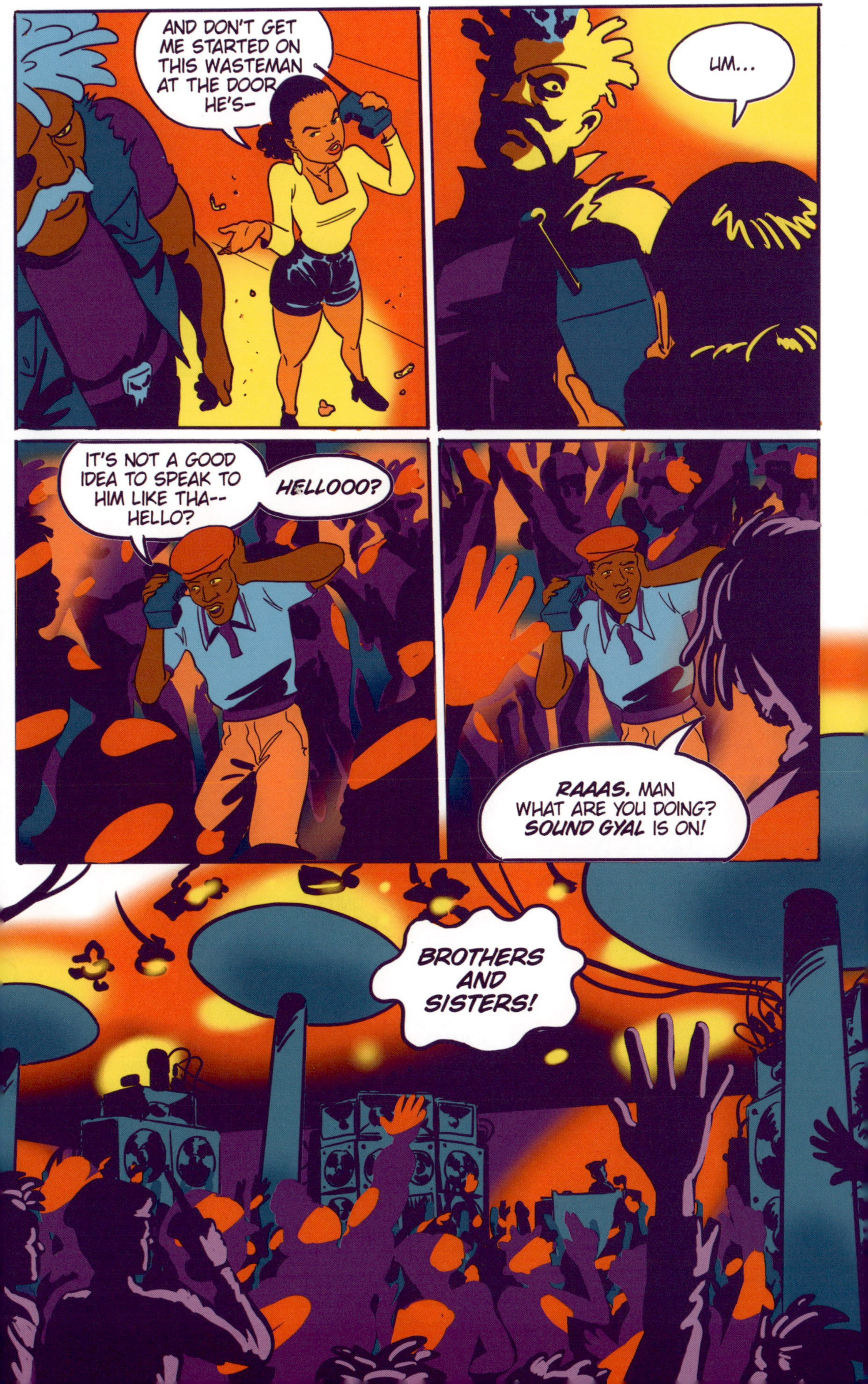
AND DON'T GET ME STARTED ON THIS WASTEMAN AT THE DOOR HE'S-
UM...
IT'S NOT A GOOD IDEA TO SPEAK TO HIM LIKE THA-- HELLO?
HELLOOO?
RAAAS. MAN WHAT ARE YOU DOING? SOUND GYAL IS ON!
BROTHERS AND SISTERS!

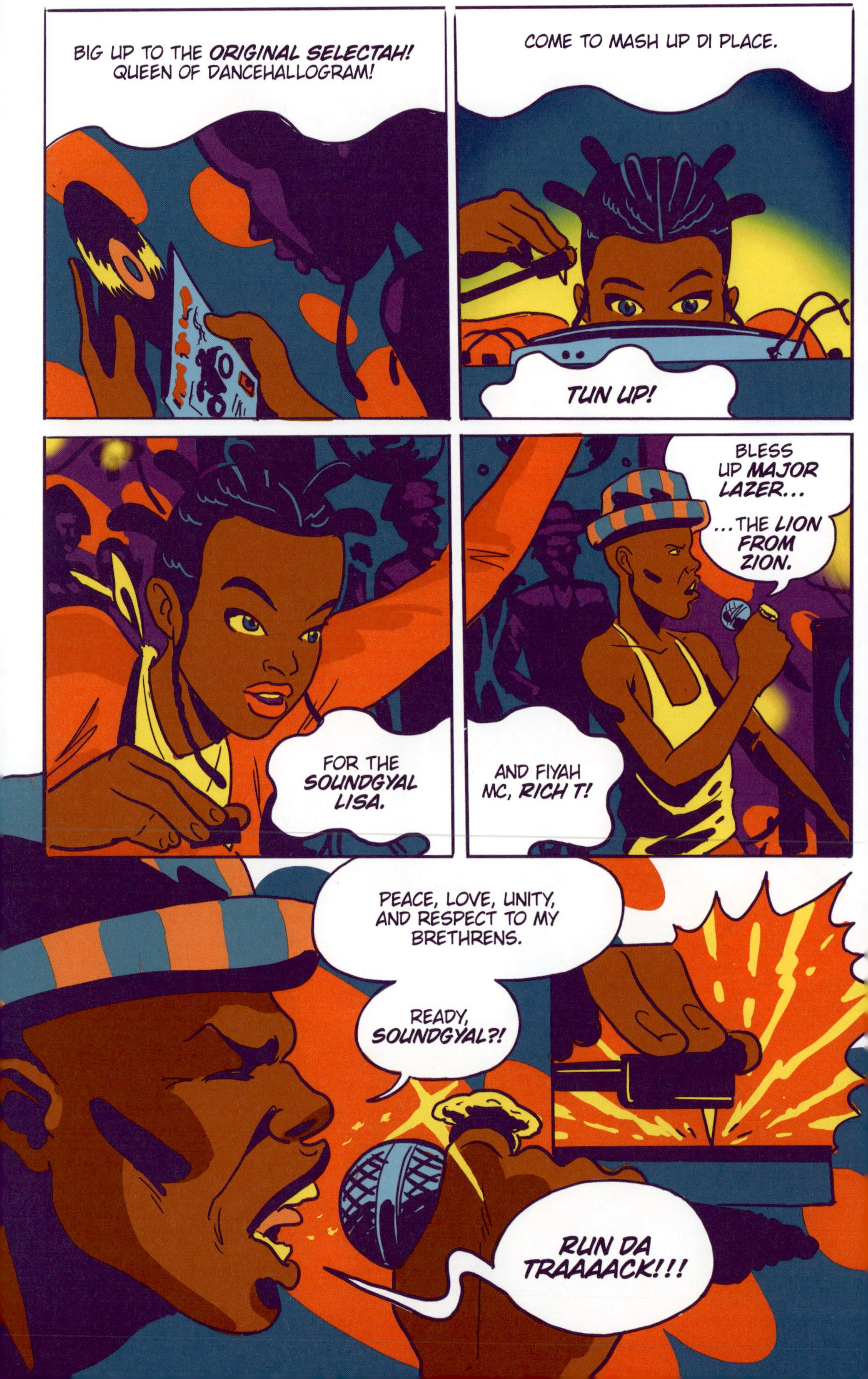
BIG UP TO THE ORIGINAL SELECTAH! QUEEN OF DANCEHALLOGRAM!
COME TO MASH UP DI PLACE.
TUN UP!
FOR THE SOUNDGYAL LISA.
BLESS UP MAJOR LAZER...
...THE LION FROM ZION.
AND FIYAH MC, RICH T!
PEACE, LOVE, UNITY, AND RESPECT TO MY BRETHRENS.
READY, SOUNDGYAL?!
RUN DA TRAAAACK!!!

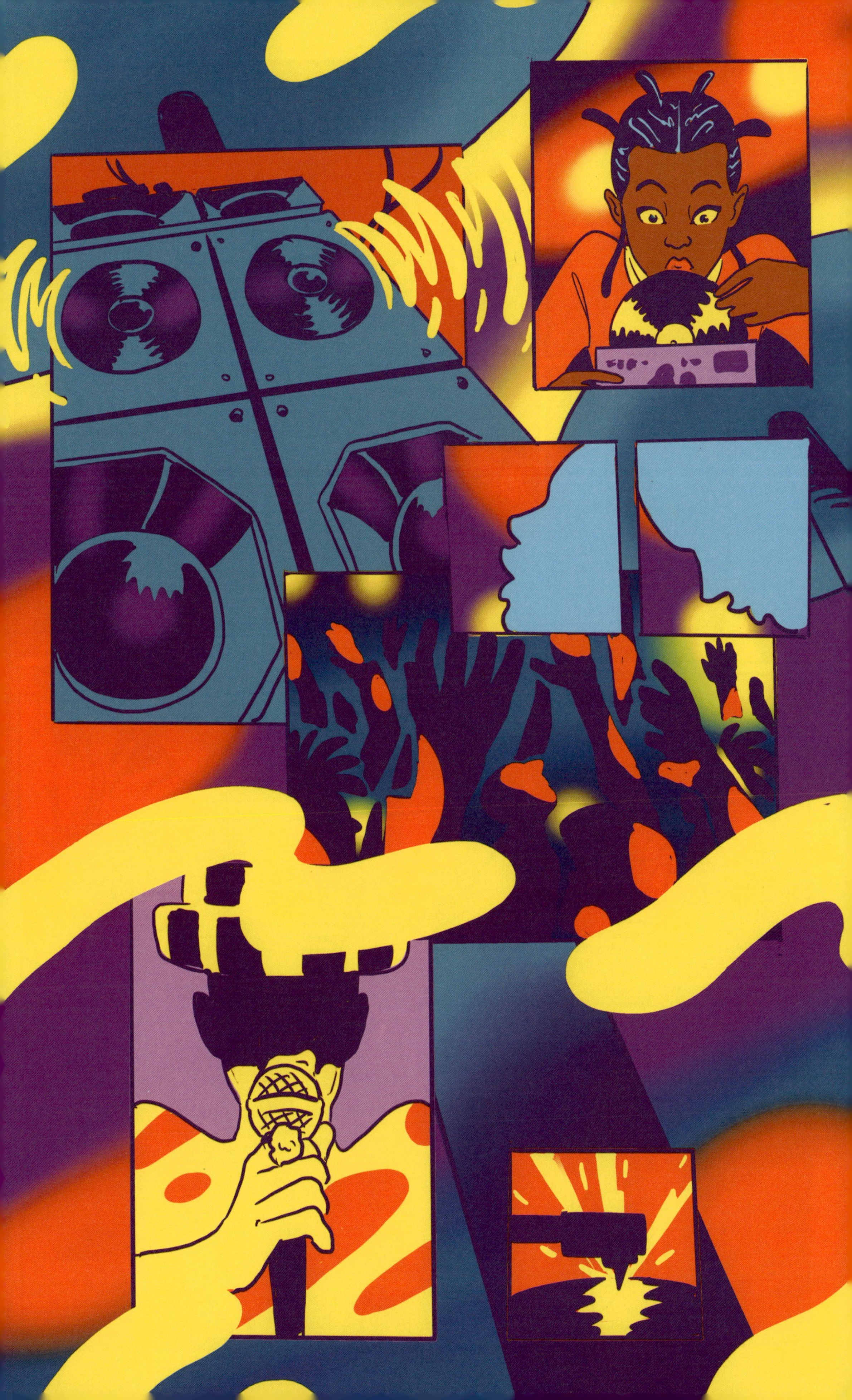

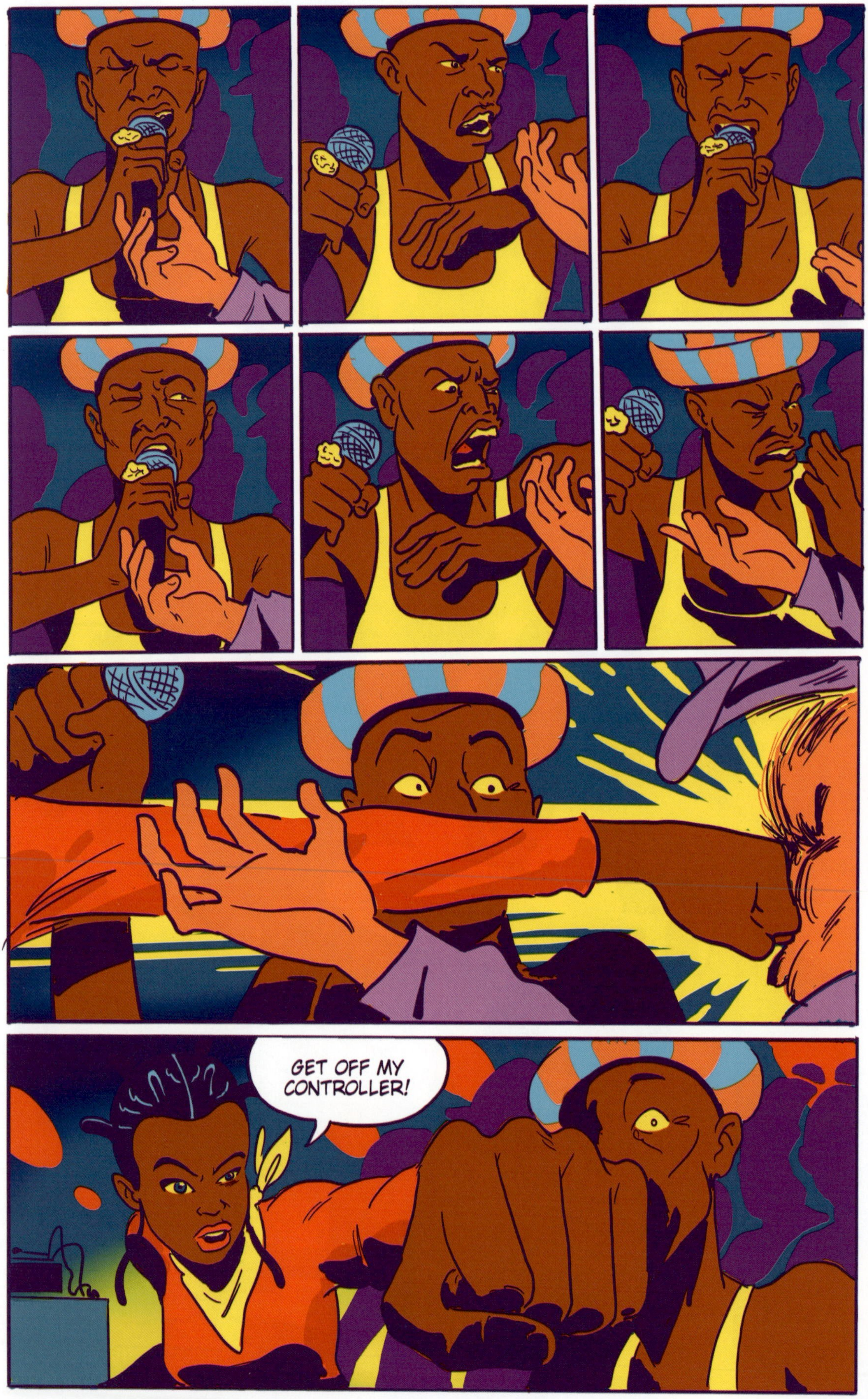
GET OFF MY CONTROLLER!

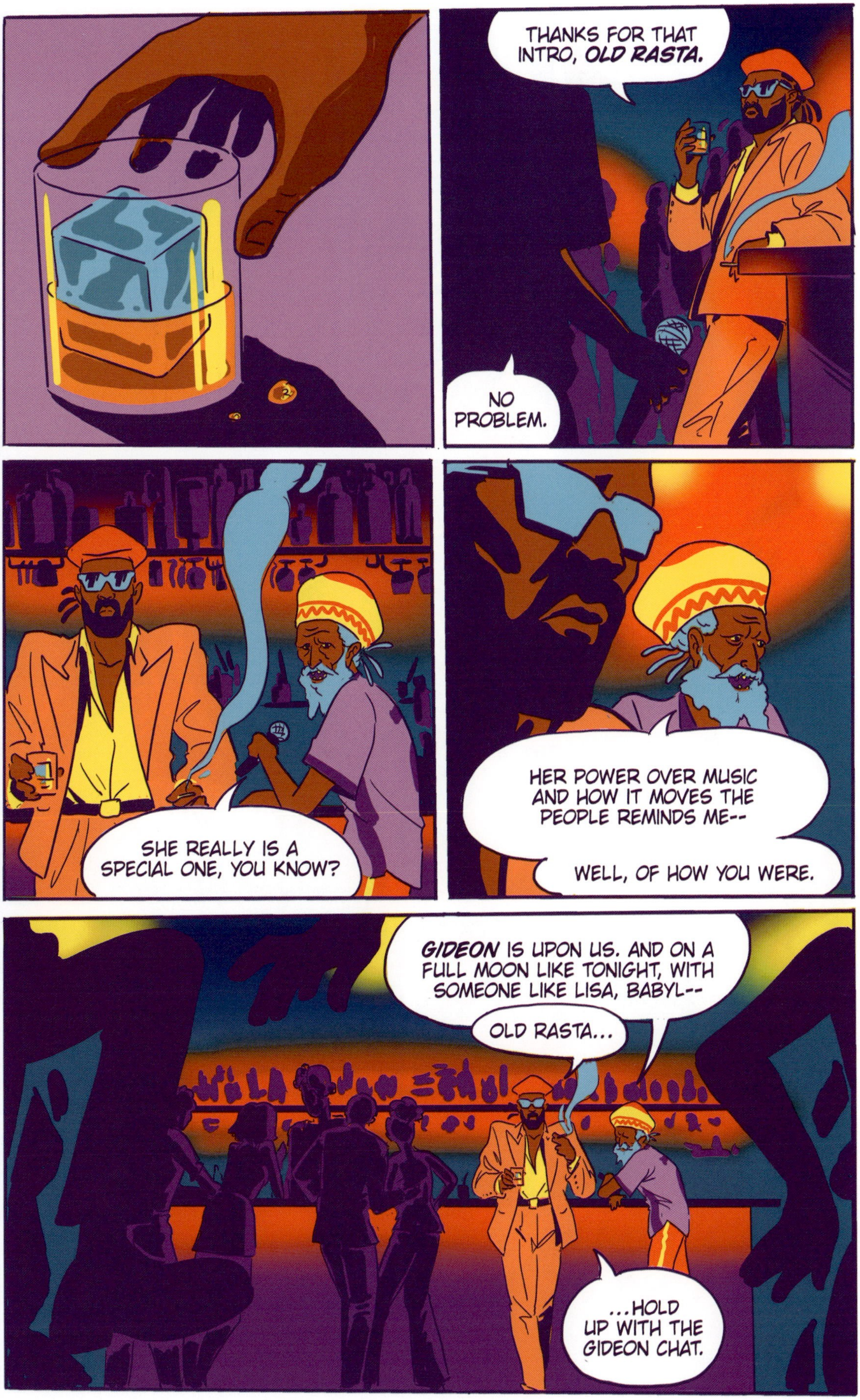
THANKS FOR THAT INTRO, OLD RASTA.
NO PROBLEM.
SHE REALLY IS A SPECIAL ONE, YOU KNOW?
HER POWER OVER MUSIC AND HOW IT MOVES THE PEOPLE REMINDS ME--
WELL, OF HOW YOU WERE.
GIDEON IS UPON US. AND ON A FULL MOON LIKE TONIGHT, WITH SOMEONE LIKE LISA, BABYL--
OLD RASTA...
...HOLD UP WITH THE GIDEON CHAT.

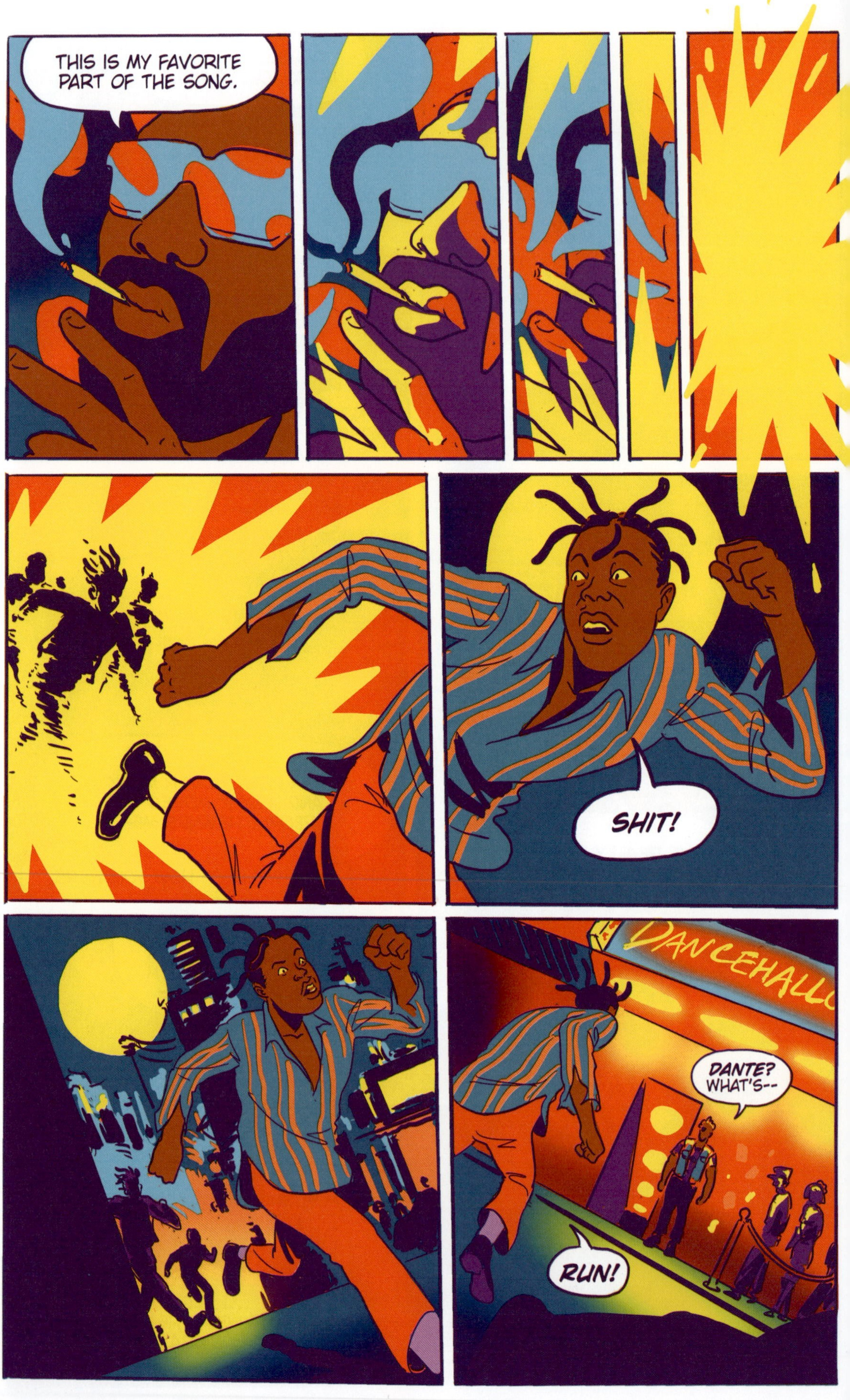
THIS IS MY FAVORITE PART OF THE SONG.
SHIT!
DANTE? WHAT'S--
RUN!
DANCEHALL

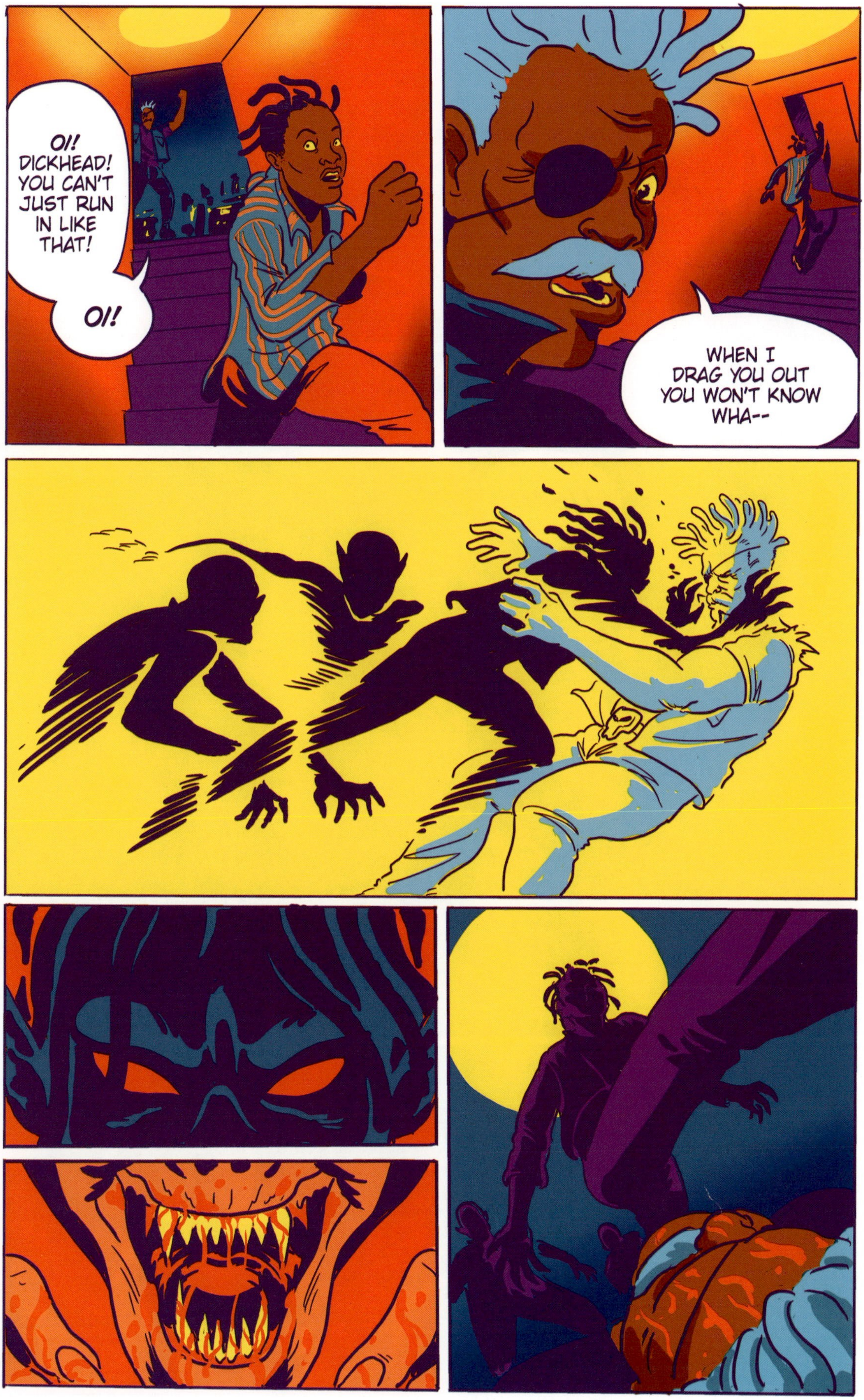
OI! DICKHEAD! YOU CAN'T JUST RUN IN LIKE THAT!
OI!
WHEN I DRAG YOU OUT YOU WON'T KNOW WHA--

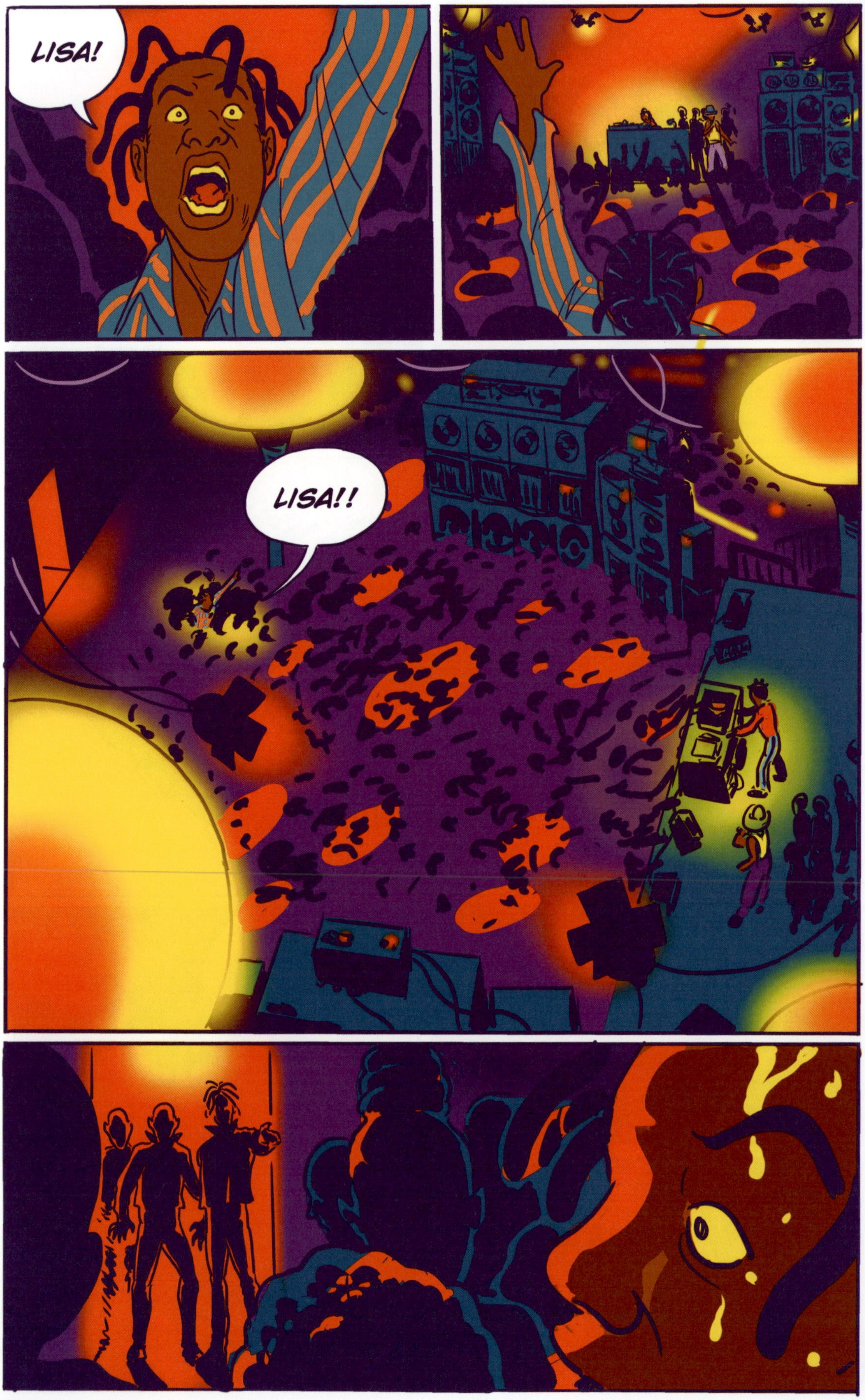
LISA!
LISA!!

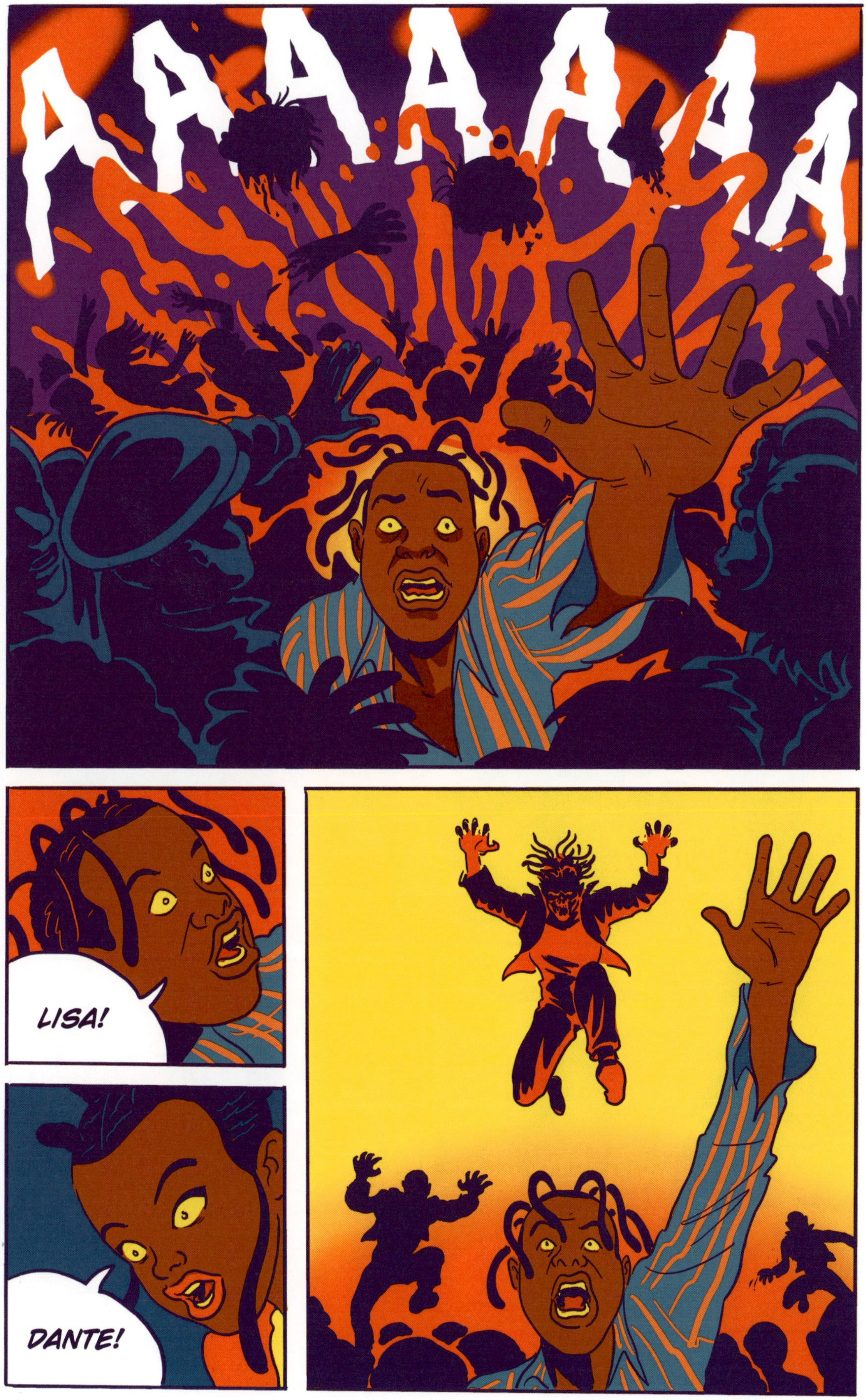
AAAAAAA
LISA!
DANTE!

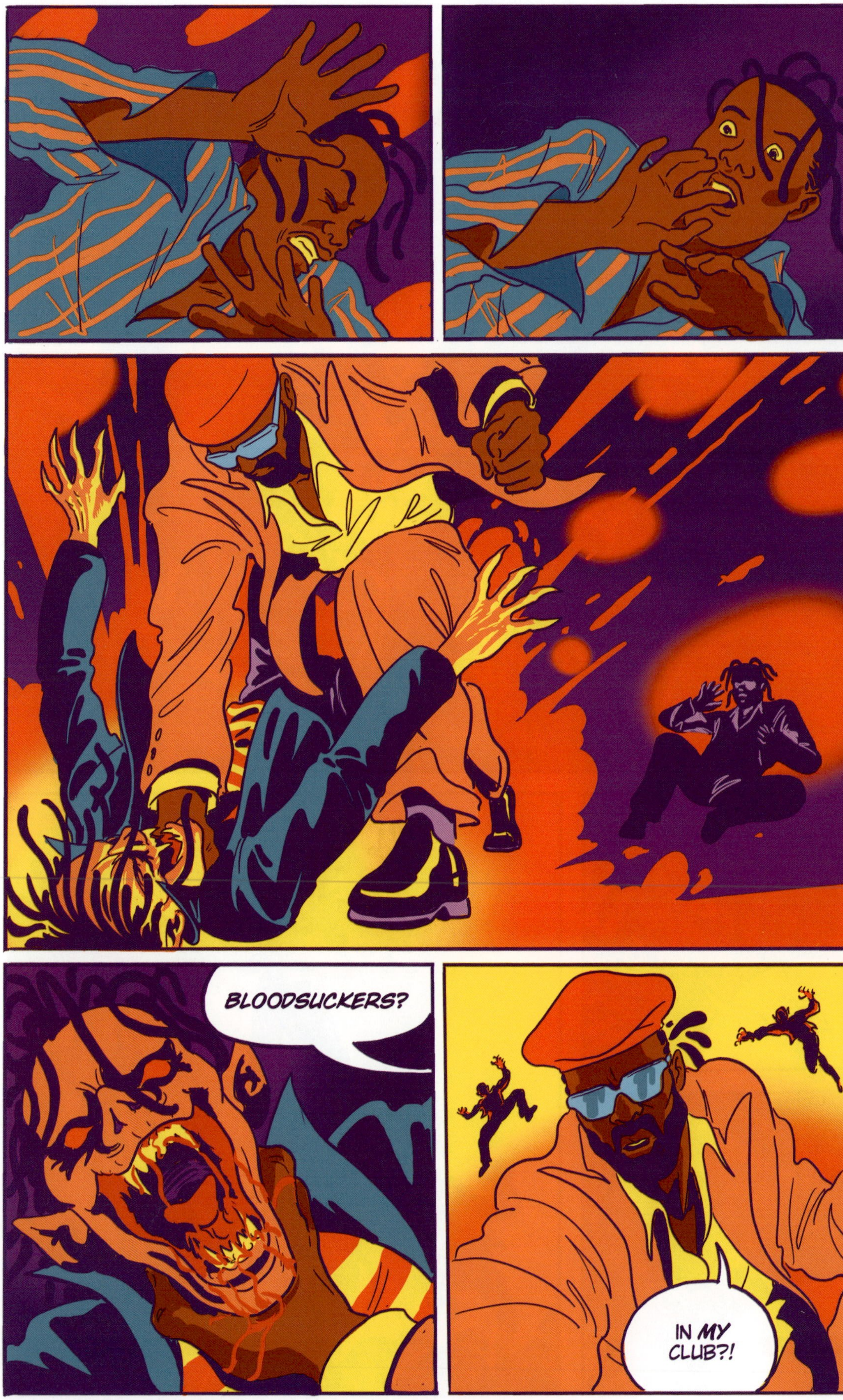
BLOODSUCKERS?
IN MY CLUB?!

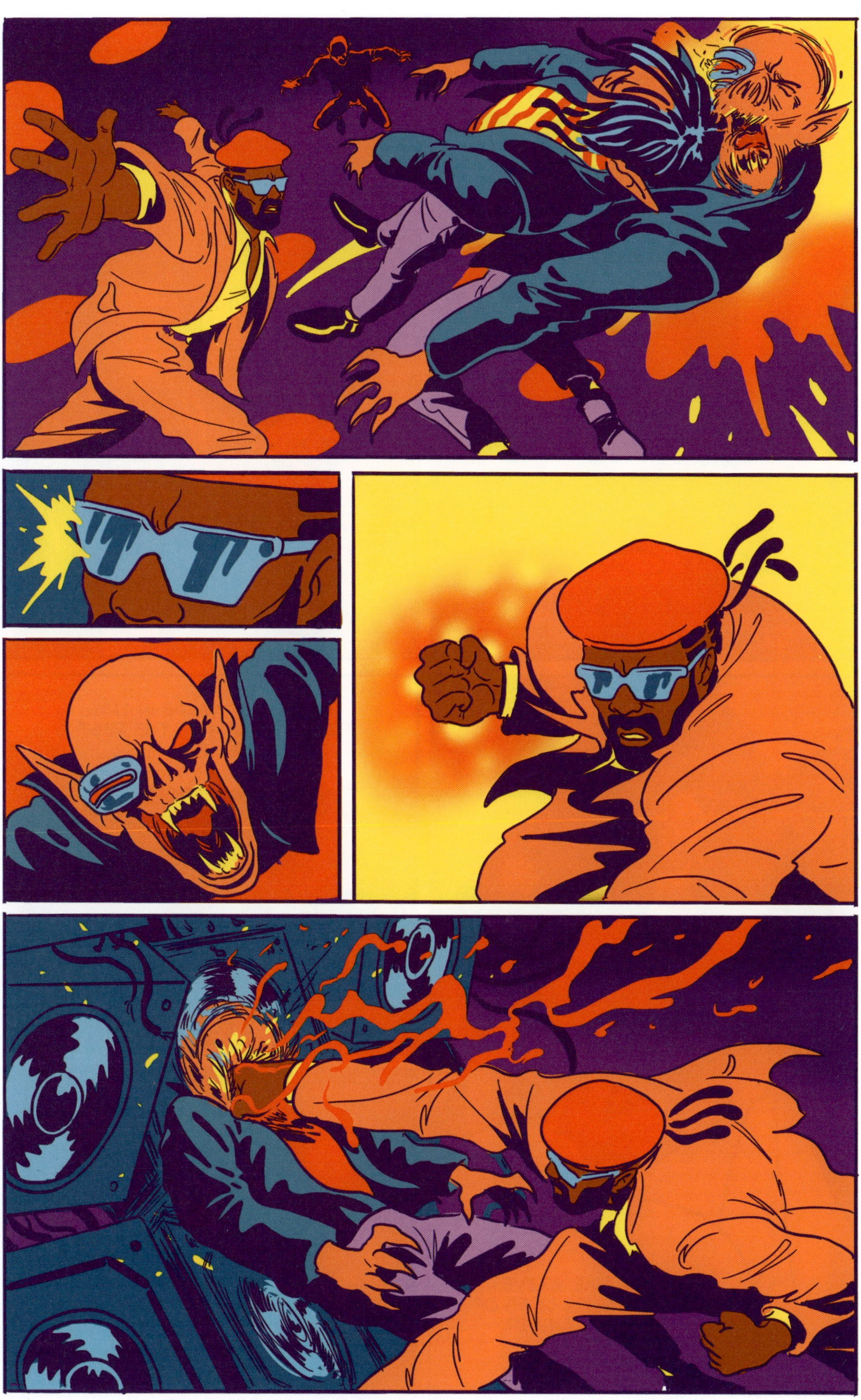

YOU'VE CROSSED THE LINE.
YOU KNOW THERE'S NO GANG BUSINESS IN DANCEHALLOGRAM.
WELL--
LOOKS LIKE YOU'VE CROSSED SOME LINES OF YOUR OWN, *LAZER.*
LOOKS LIKE YOU'RE IN THIS *FILTH* AS MUCH AS THE REST OF US.

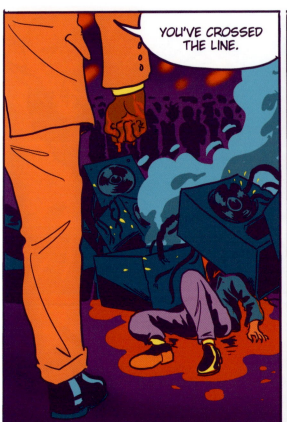

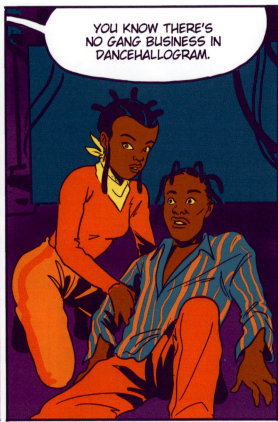

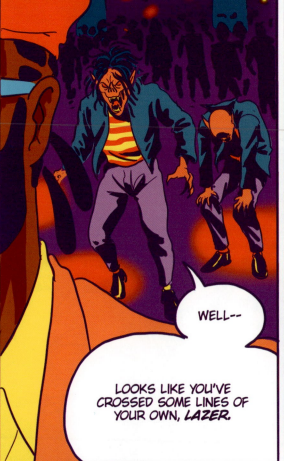

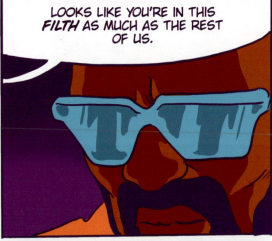

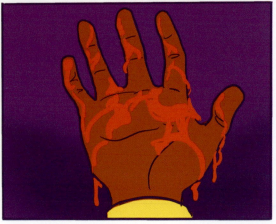

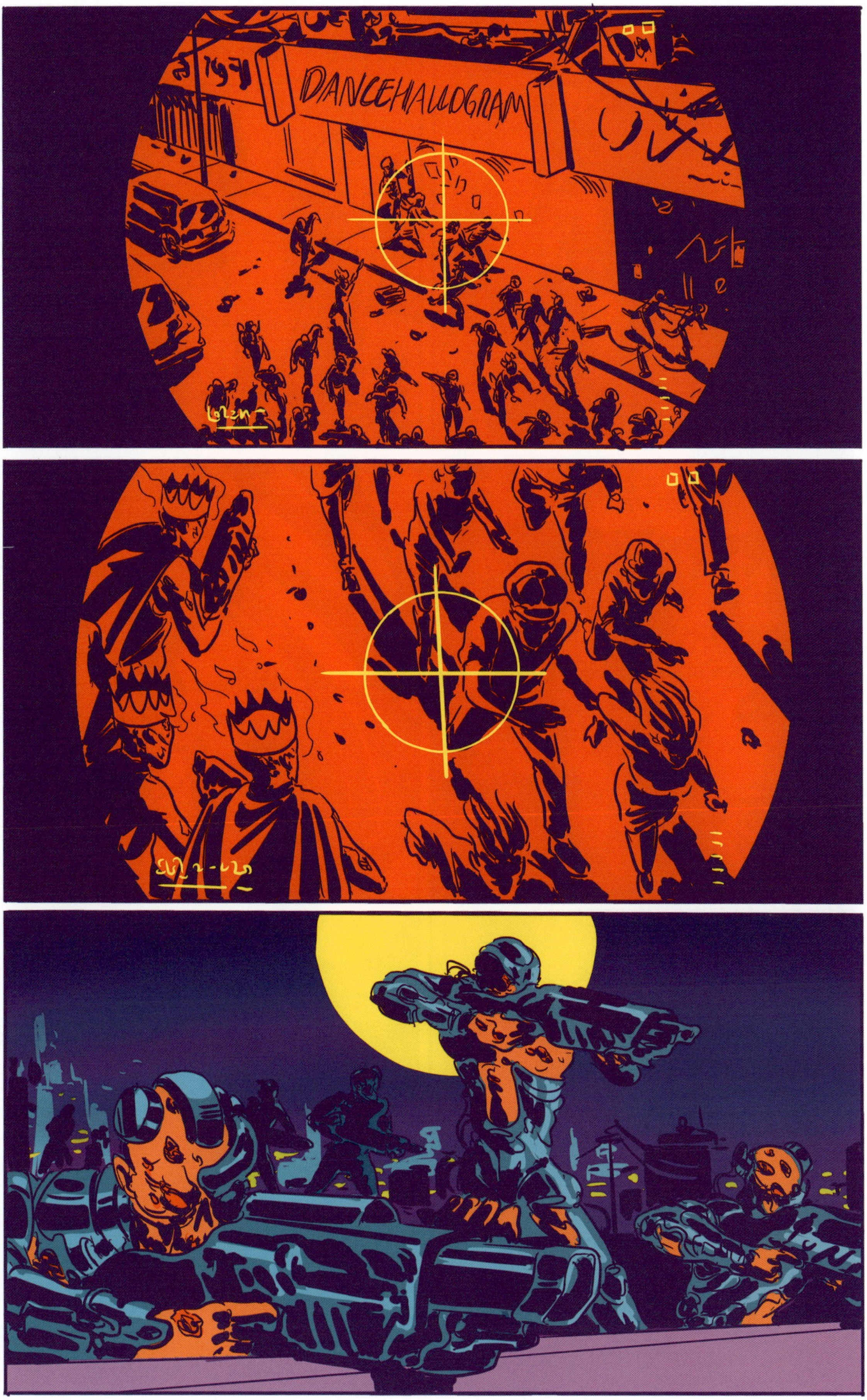
DANCEHALLOGRAM

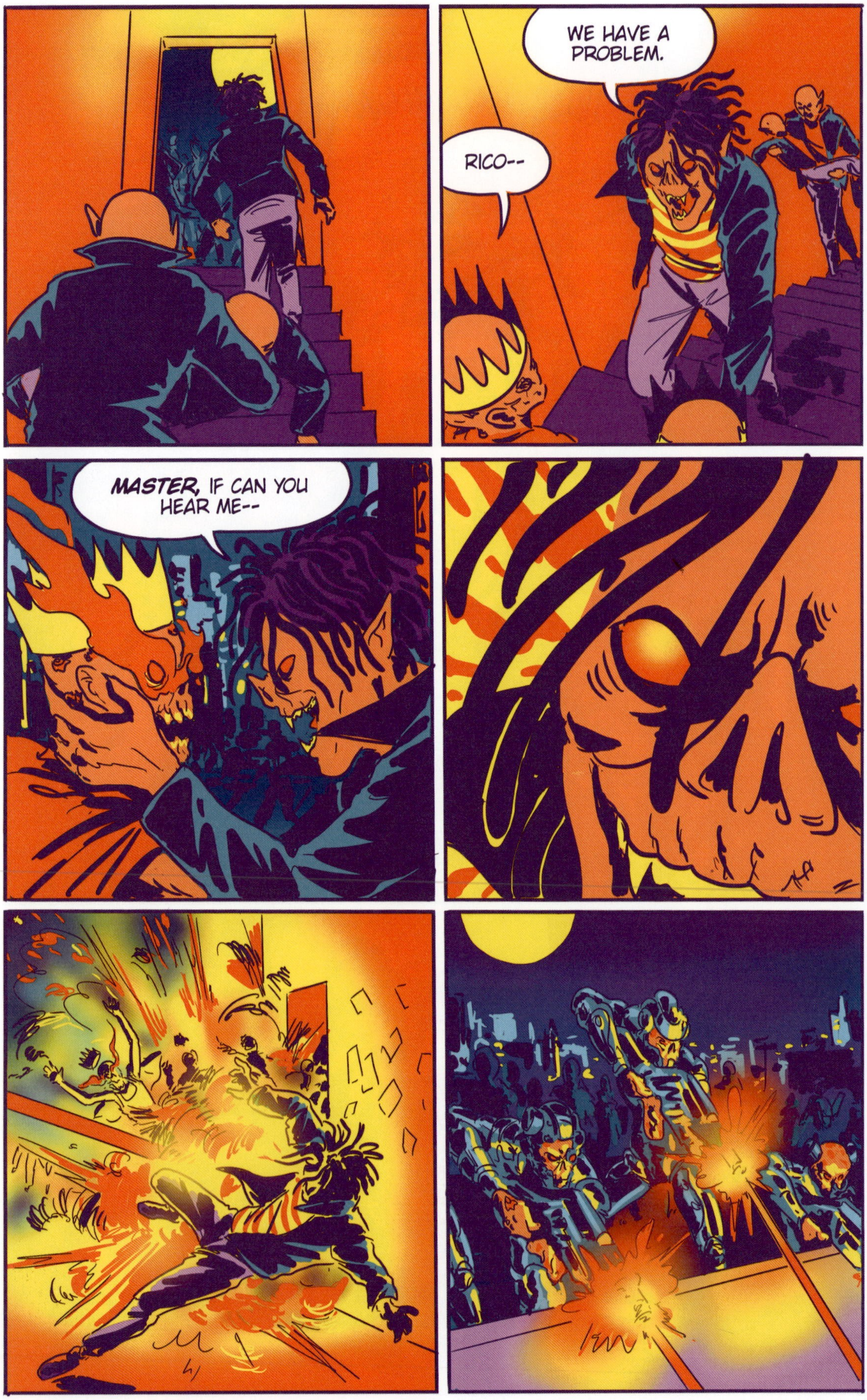
WE HAVE A PROBLEM.
RICO--
MASTER, IF CAN YOU HEAR ME--

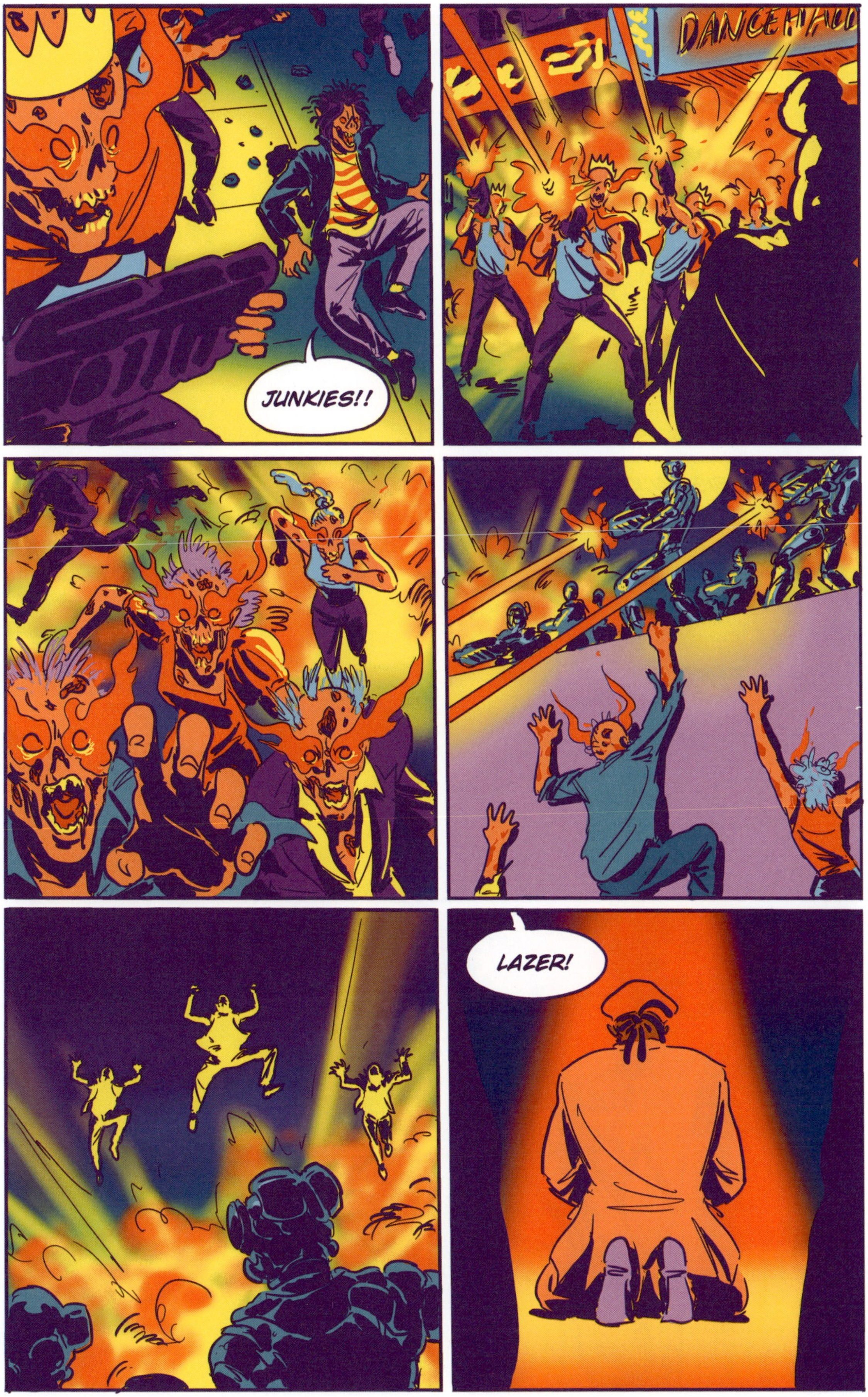
JUNKIES!!
DANCEHALL
LAZER!

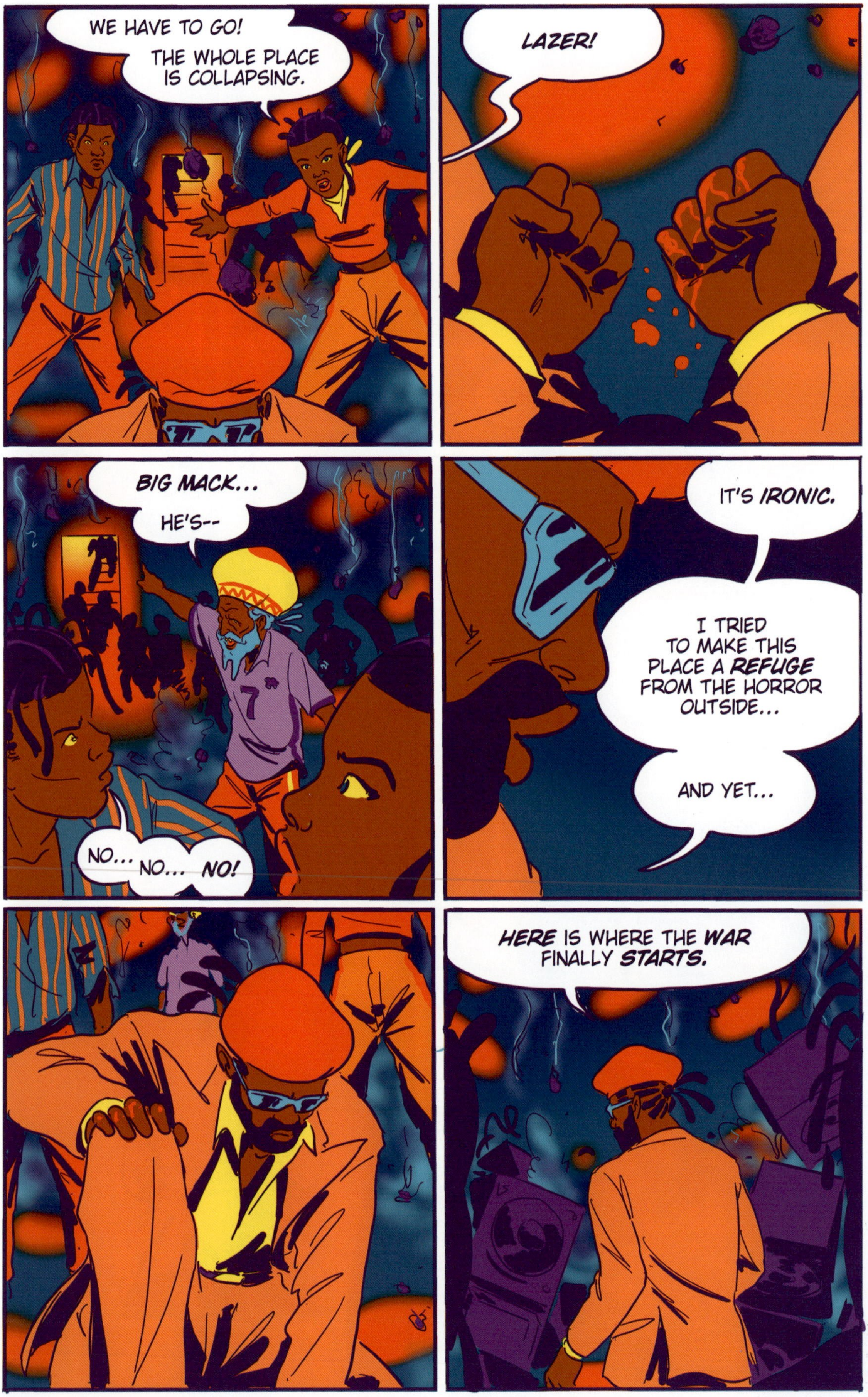
WE HAVE TO GO!
THE WHOLE PLACE IS COLLAPSING.
LAZER!
BIG MACK...
HE'S--
NO... NO... NO!
IT'S IRONIC.
I TRIED TO MAKE THIS PLACE A REFUGE FROM THE HORROR OUTSIDE...
AND YET...
HERE IS WHERE THE WAR FINALLY STARTS.

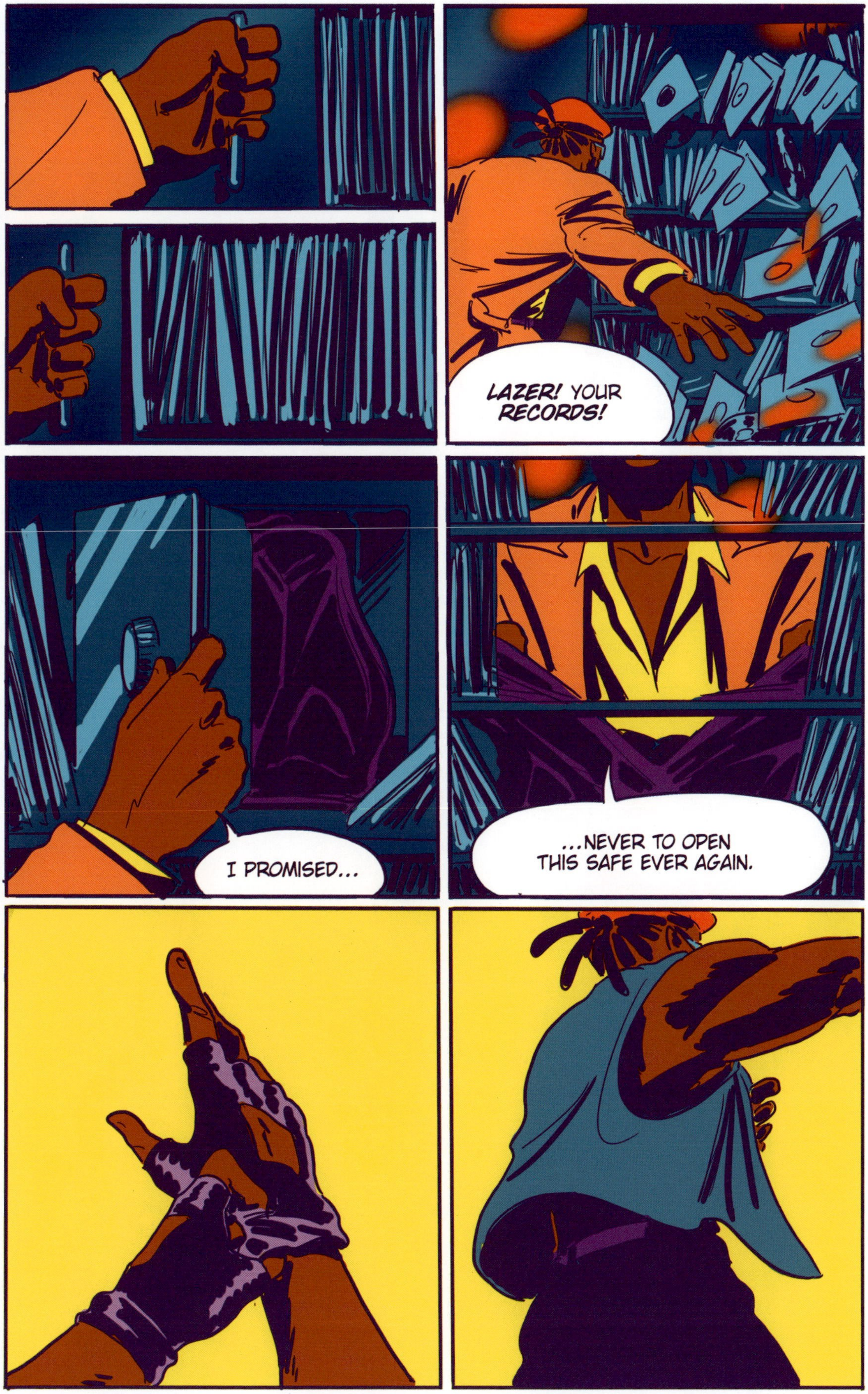
LAZER! YOUR RECORDS!
I PROMISED...
...NEVER TO OPEN THIS SAFE EVER AGAIN.

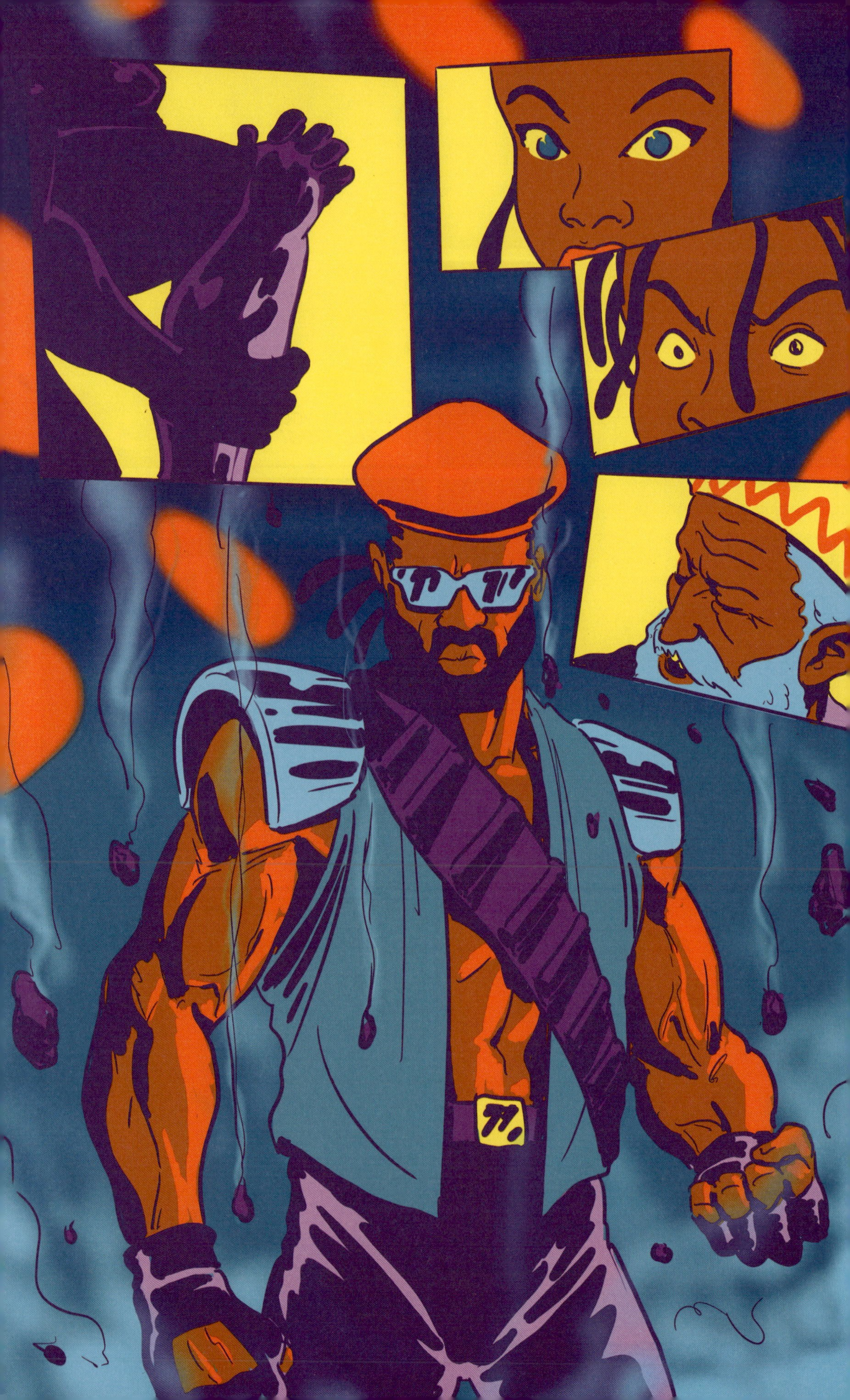

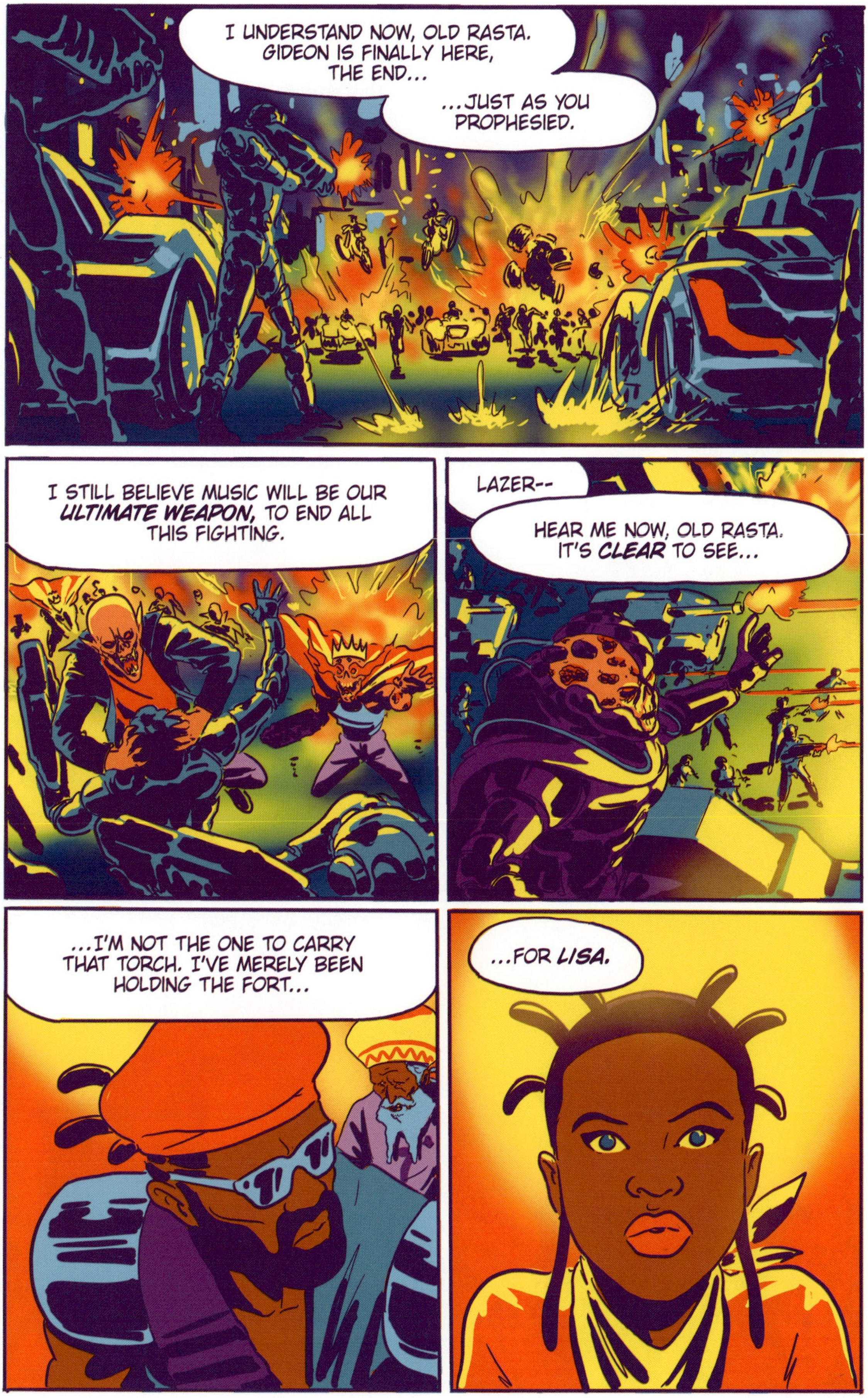
I UNDERSTAND NOW, OLD RASTA. GIDEON IS FINALLY HERE, THE END...
...JUST AS YOU PROPHESIED.
I STILL BELIEVE MUSIC WILL BE OUR ***ULTIMATE WEAPON,*** TO END ALL THIS FIGHTING.
LAZER--
HEAR ME NOW, OLD RASTA. IT'S ***CLEAR*** TO SEE...
...I'M NOT THE ONE TO CARRY THAT TORCH. I'VE MERELY BEEN HOLDING THE FORT...
...FOR ***LISA.***

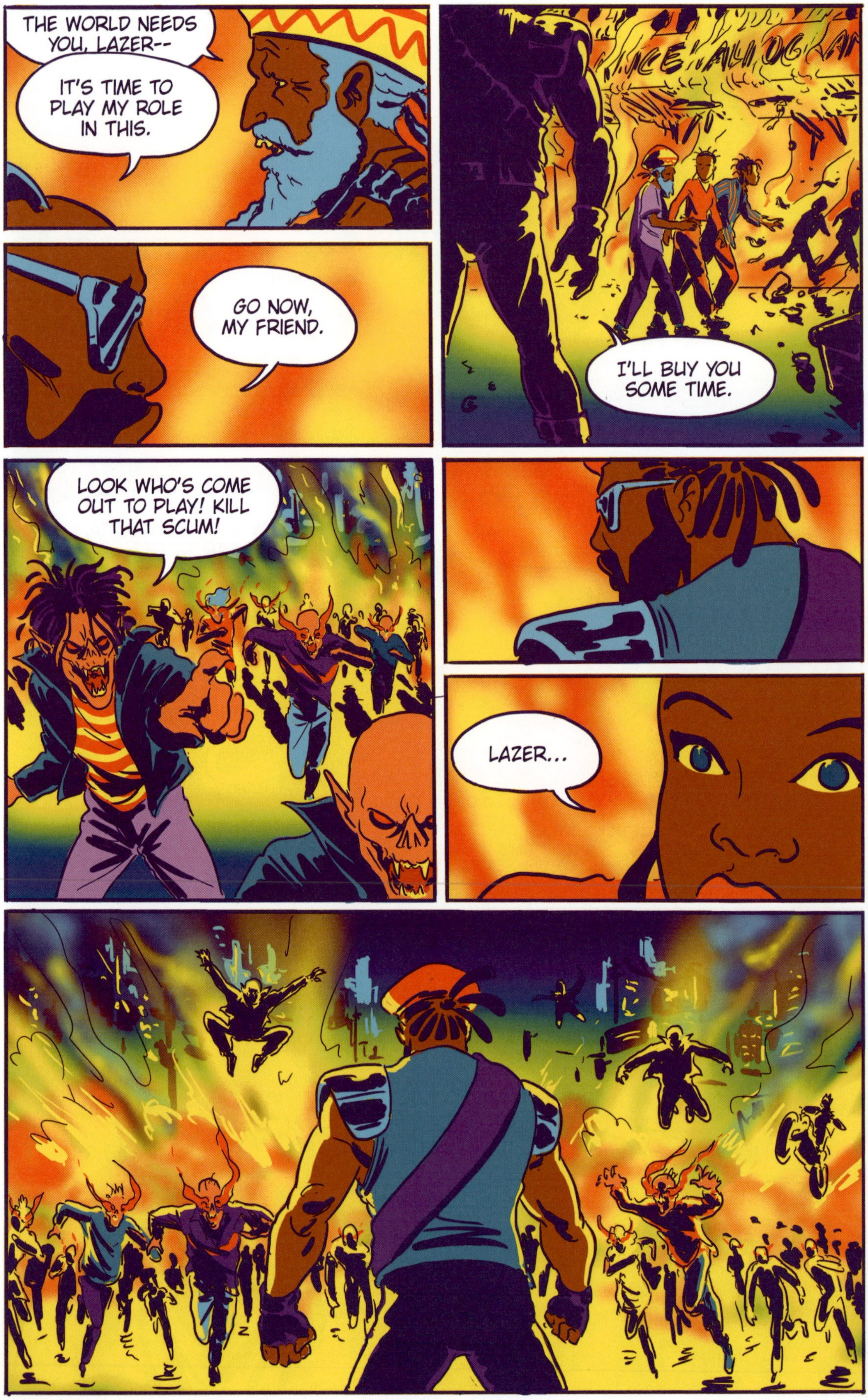
THE WORLD NEEDS YOU, LAZER--
IT'S TIME TO PLAY MY ROLE IN THIS.
GO NOW, MY FRIEND.
I'LL BUY YOU SOME TIME.
LOOK WHO'S COME OUT TO PLAY! KILL THAT SCUM!
LAZER...

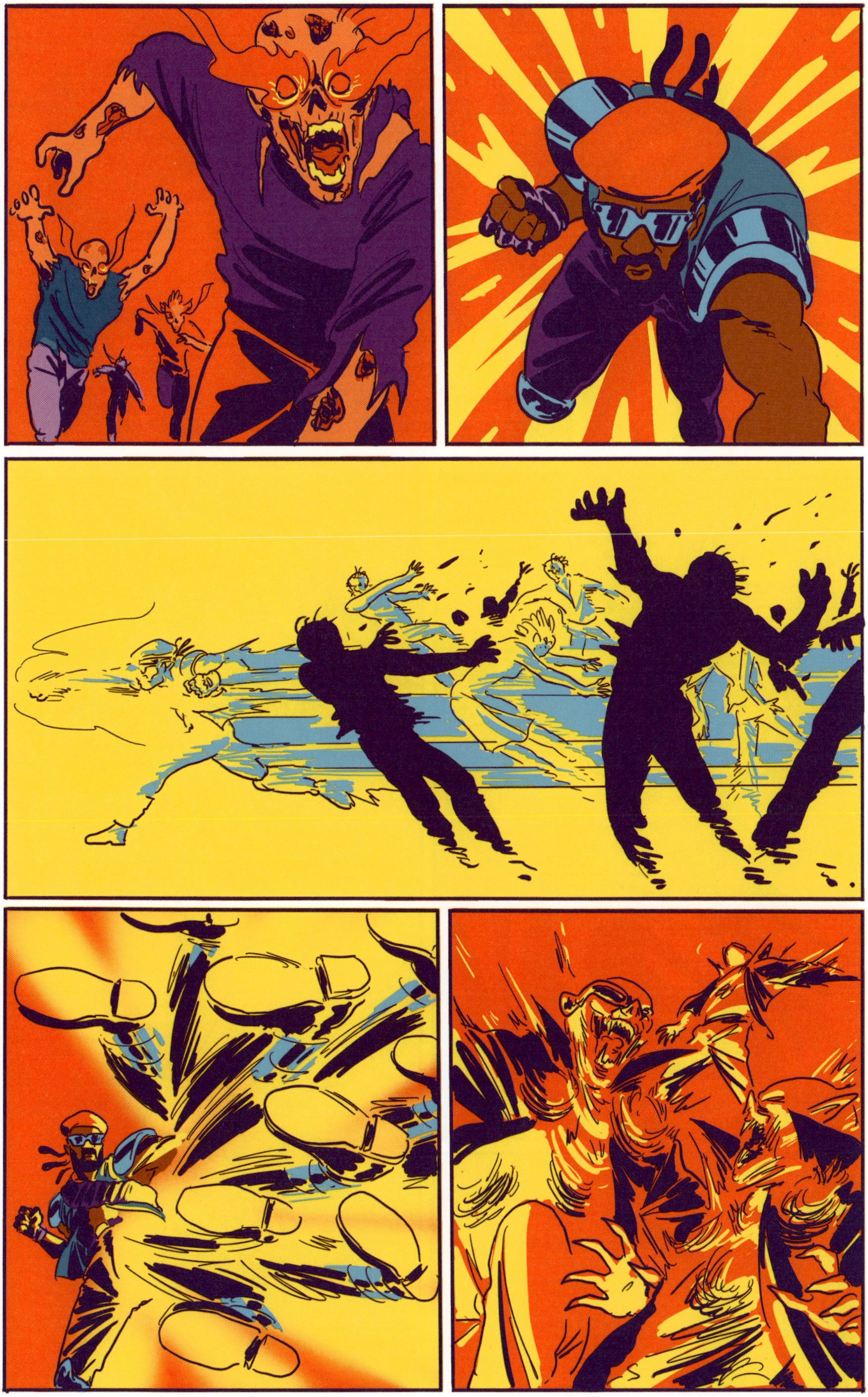

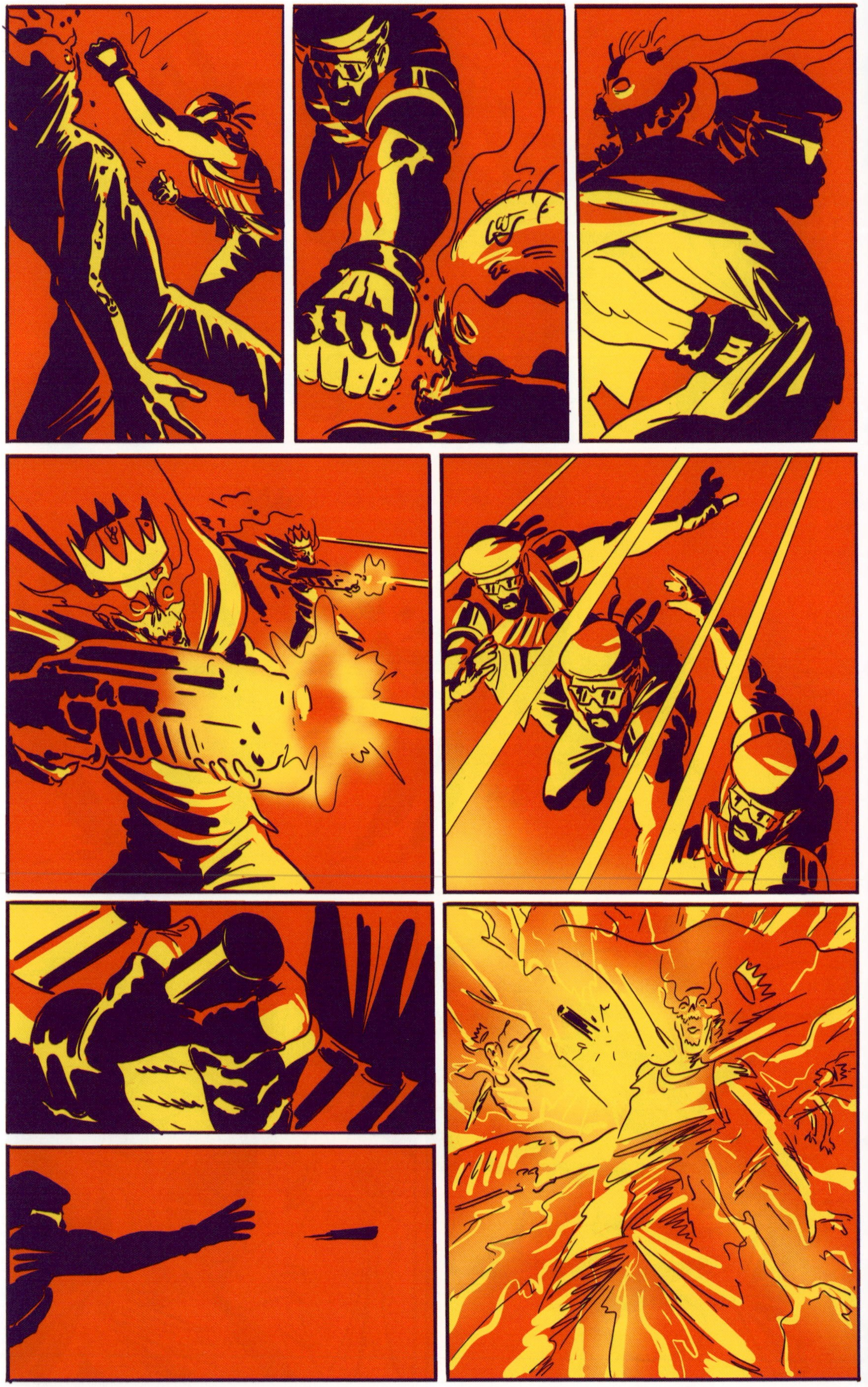

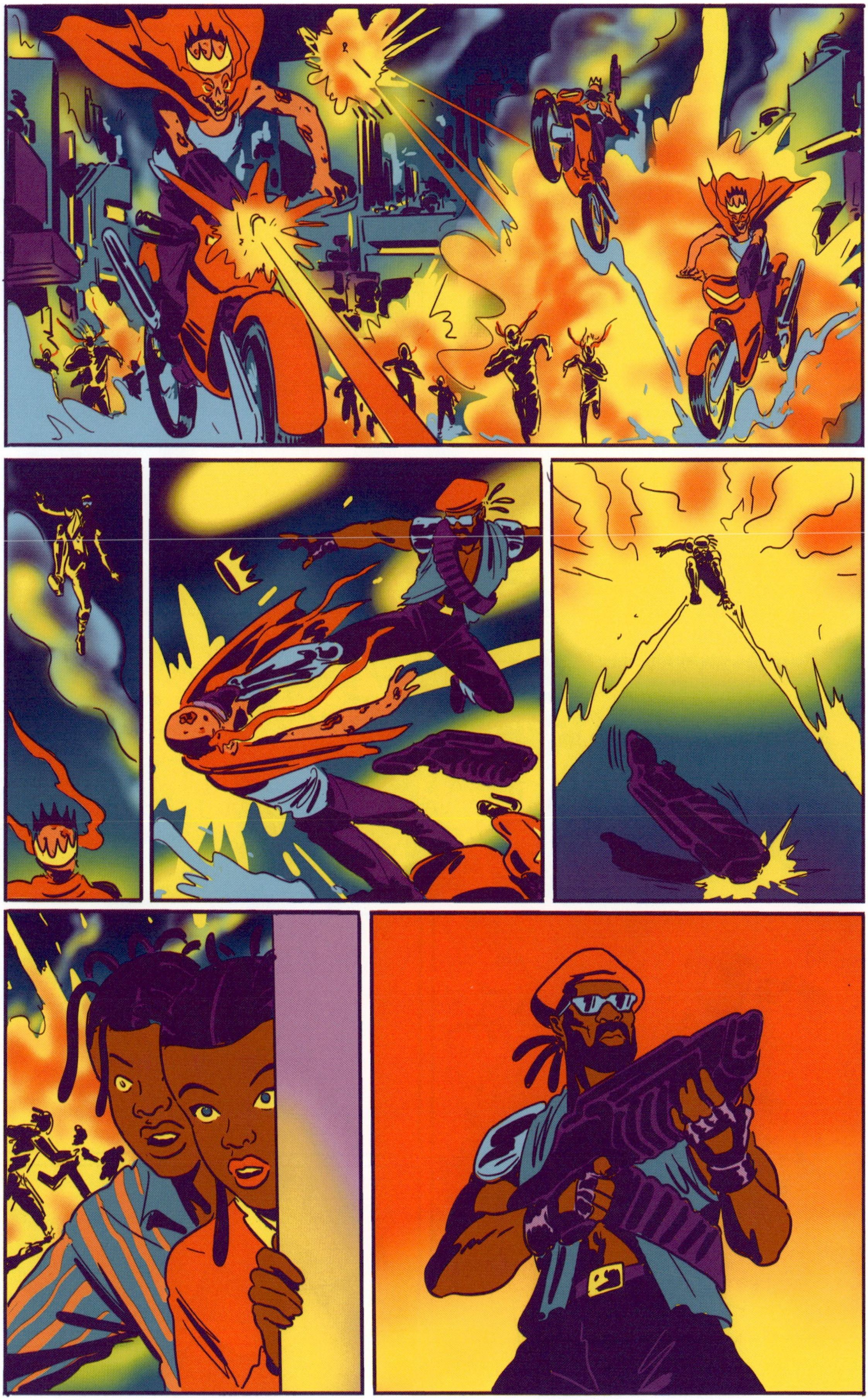

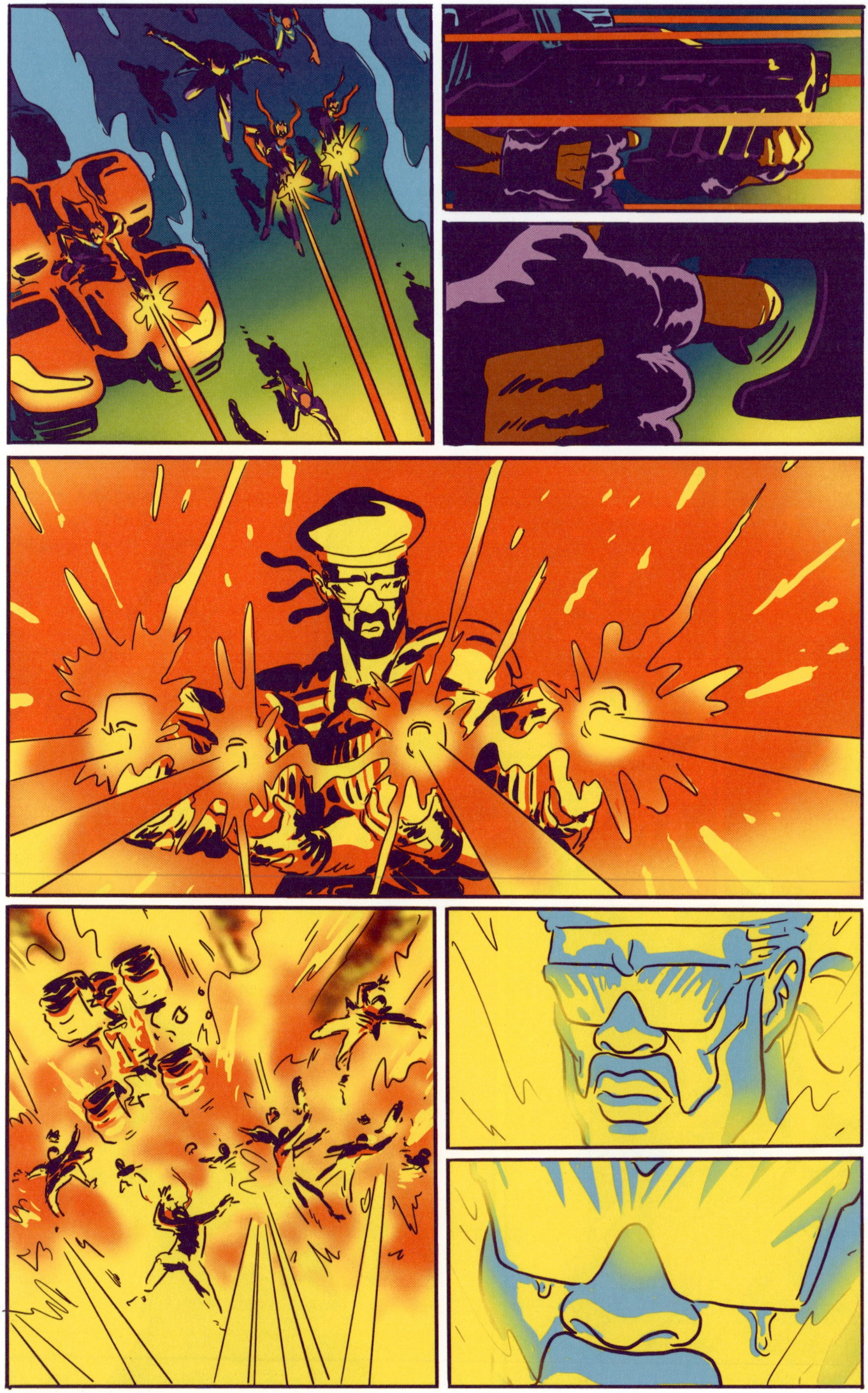

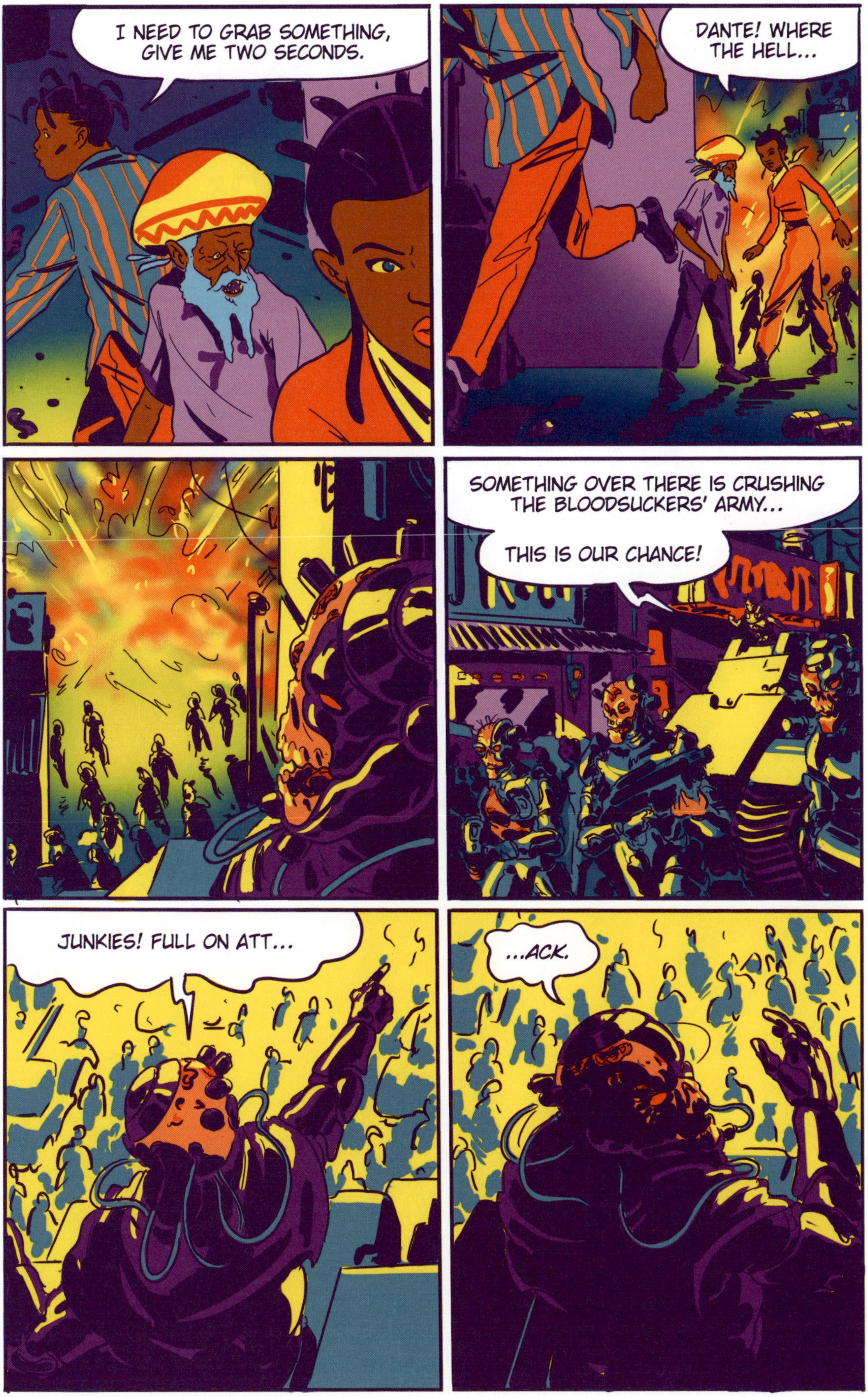
I NEED TO GRAB SOMETHING, GIVE ME TWO SECONDS.
DANTE! WHERE THE HELL...
SOMETHING OVER THERE IS CRUSHING THE BLOODSUCKERS' ARMY...
THIS IS OUR CHANCE!
JUNKIES! FULL ON ATT...
...ACK.

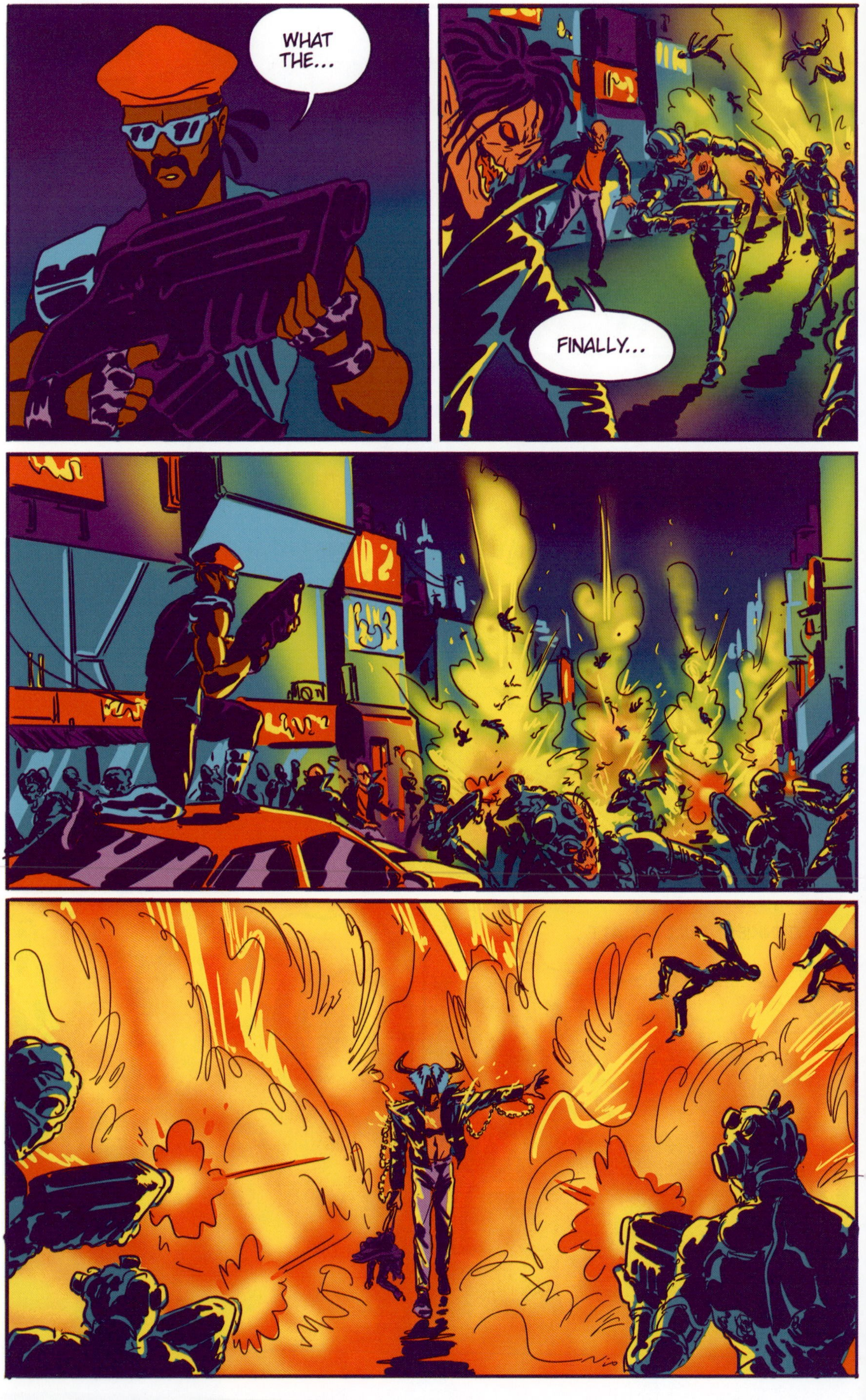
WHAT THE...
FINALLY...

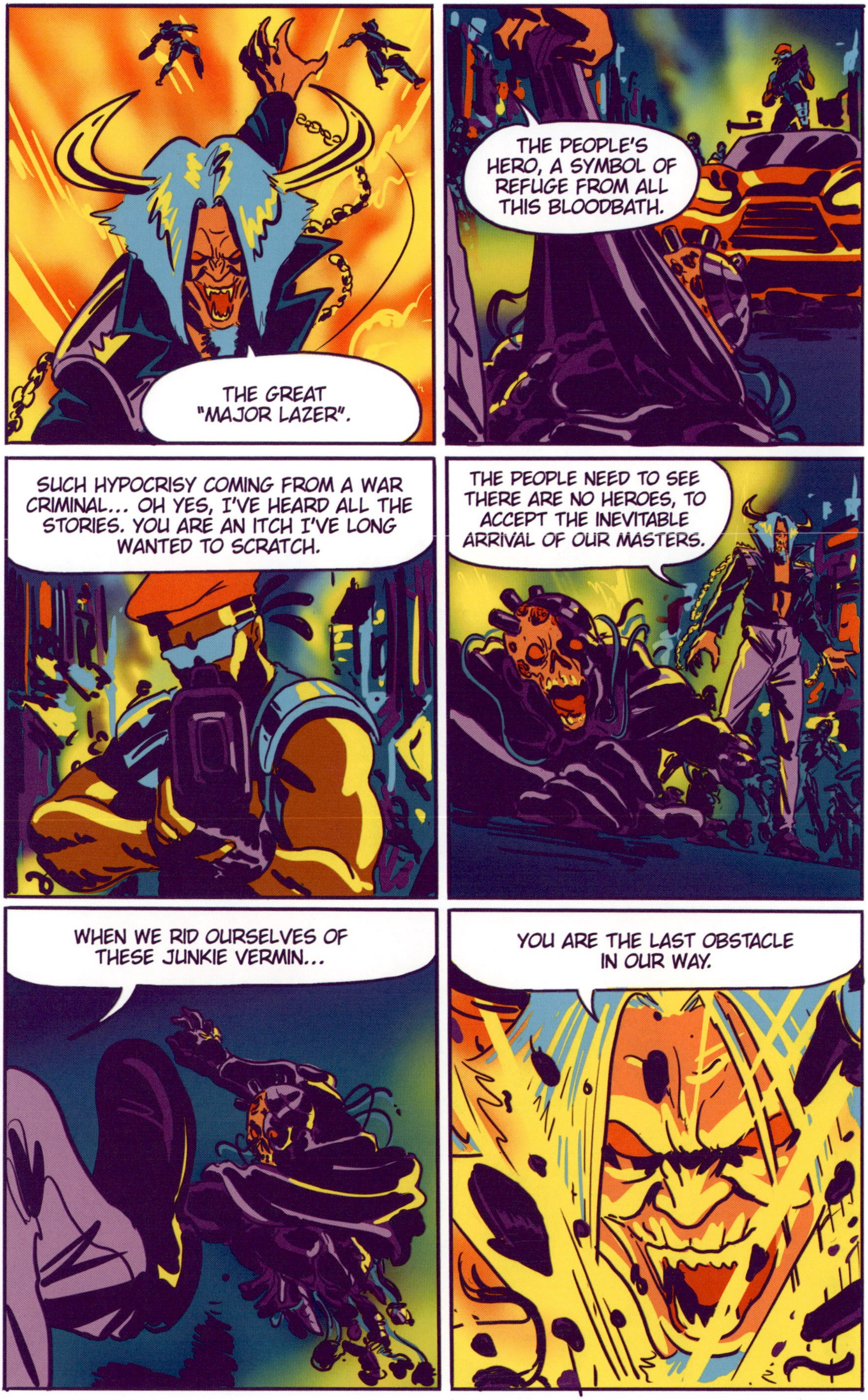
THE GREAT "MAJOR LAZER".
THE PEOPLE'S HERO, A SYMBOL OF REFUGE FROM ALL THIS BLOODBATH.
SUCH HYPOCRISY COMING FROM A WAR CRIMINAL... OH YES, I'VE HEARD ALL THE STORIES. YOU ARE AN ITCH I'VE LONG WANTED TO SCRATCH.
THE PEOPLE NEED TO SEE THERE ARE NO HEROES, TO ACCEPT THE INEVITABLE ARRIVAL OF OUR MASTERS.
WHEN WE RID OURSELVES OF THESE JUNKIE VERMIN...
YOU ARE THE LAST OBSTACLE IN OUR WAY.

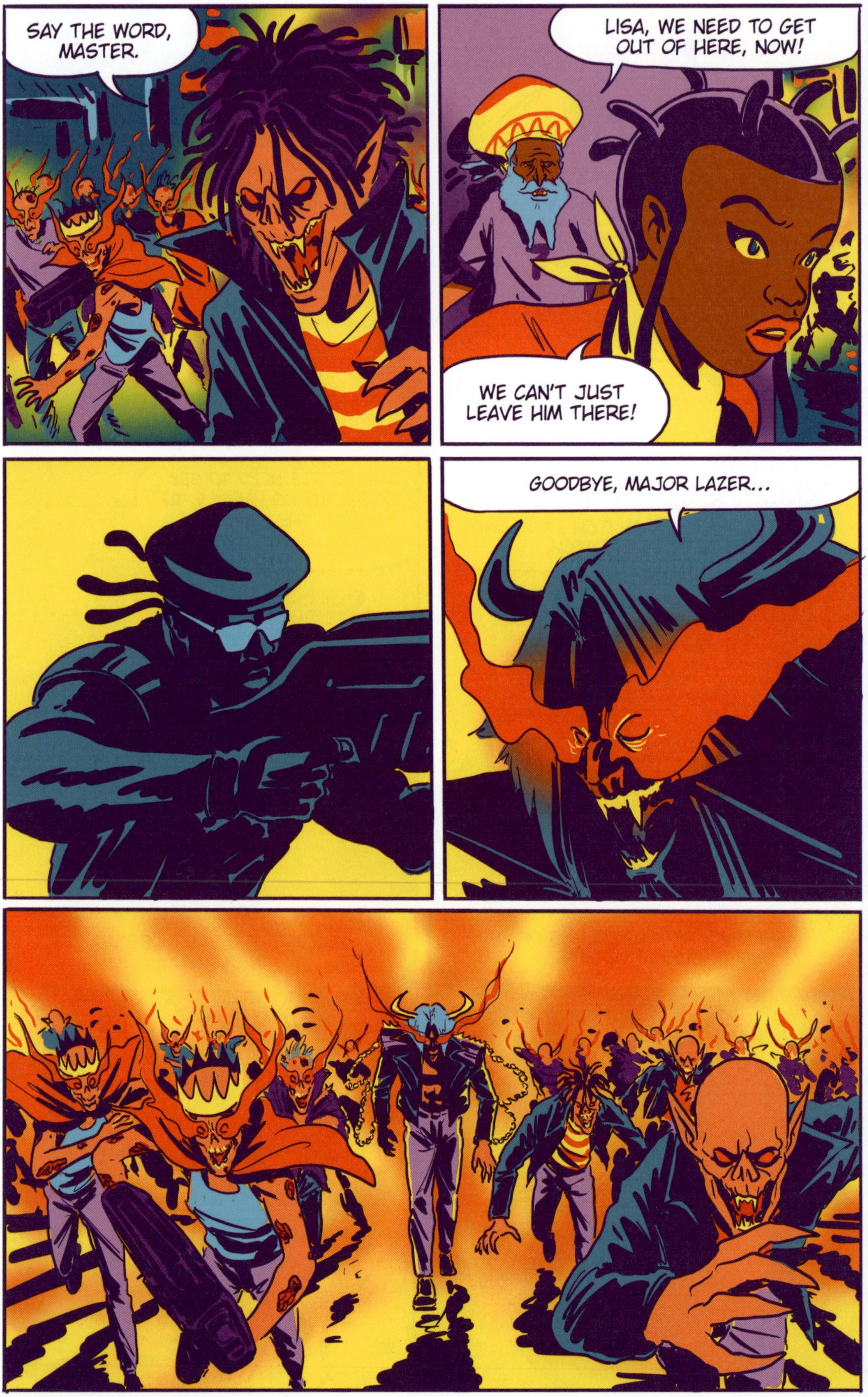
SAY THE WORD, MASTER.
LISA, WE NEED TO GET OUT OF HERE, NOW!
WE CAN'T JUST LEAVE HIM THERE!
GOODBYE, MAJOR LAZER...

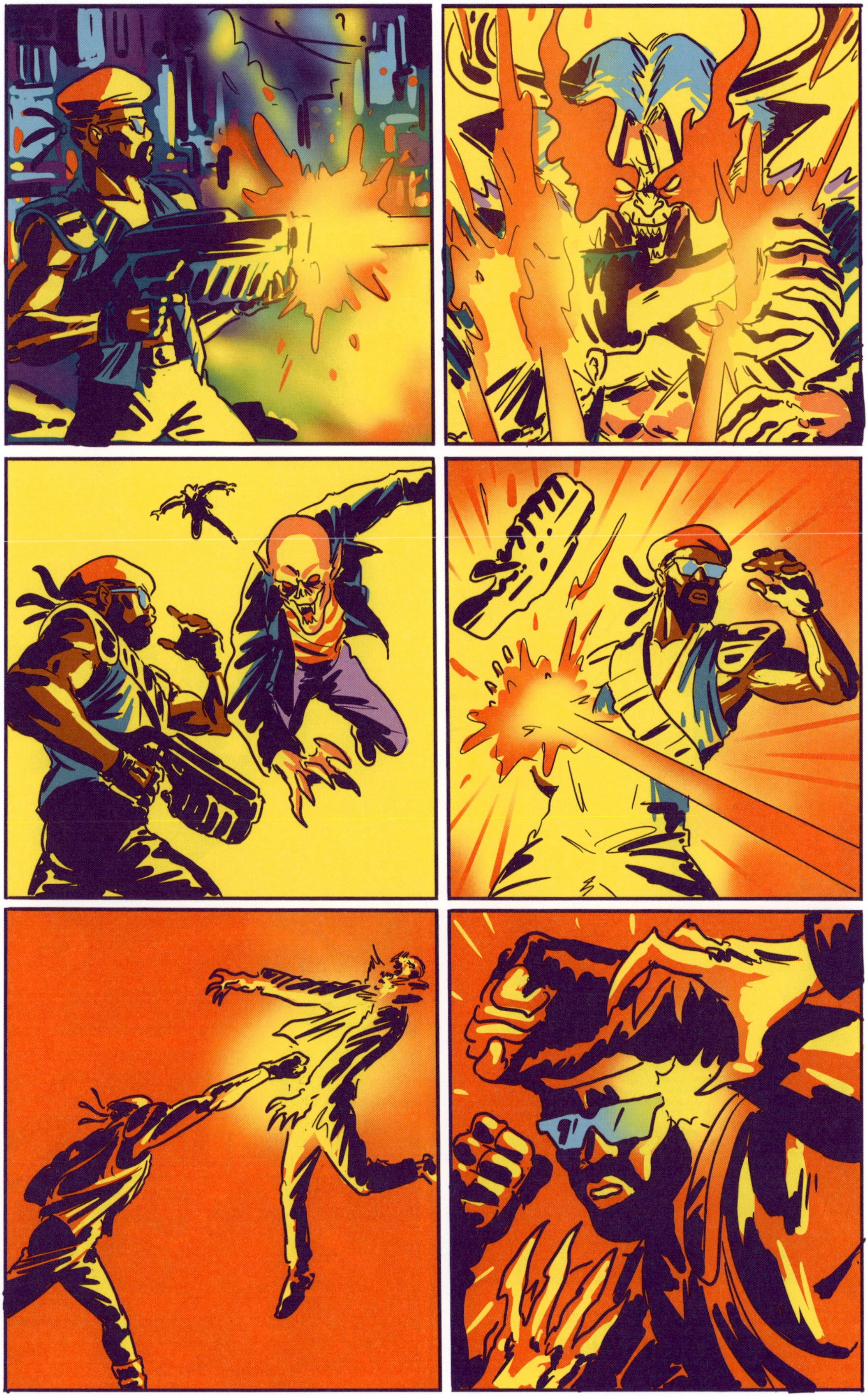

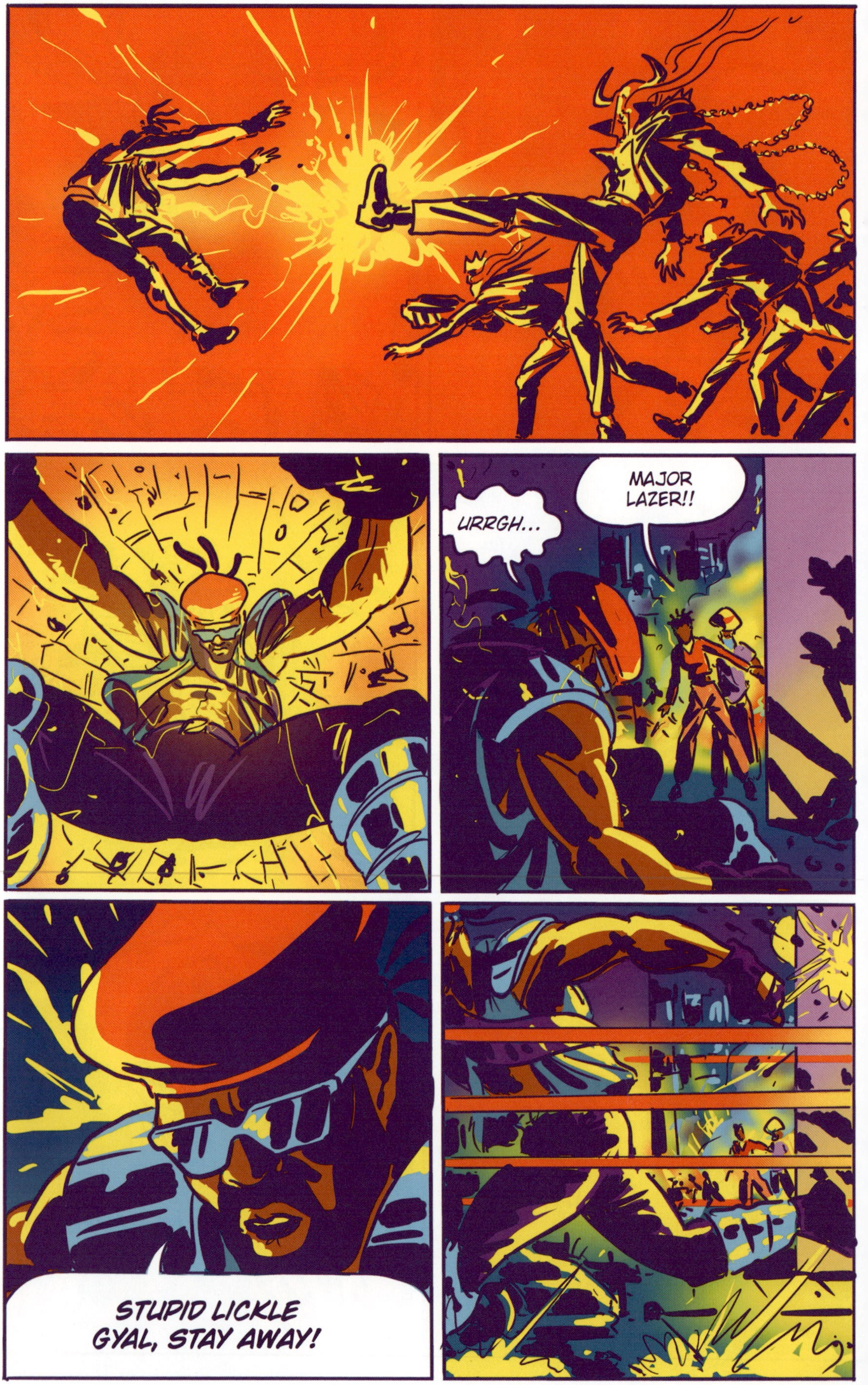
URRGH...
MAJOR LAZER!!
STUPID LICKLE GYAL, STAY AWAY!

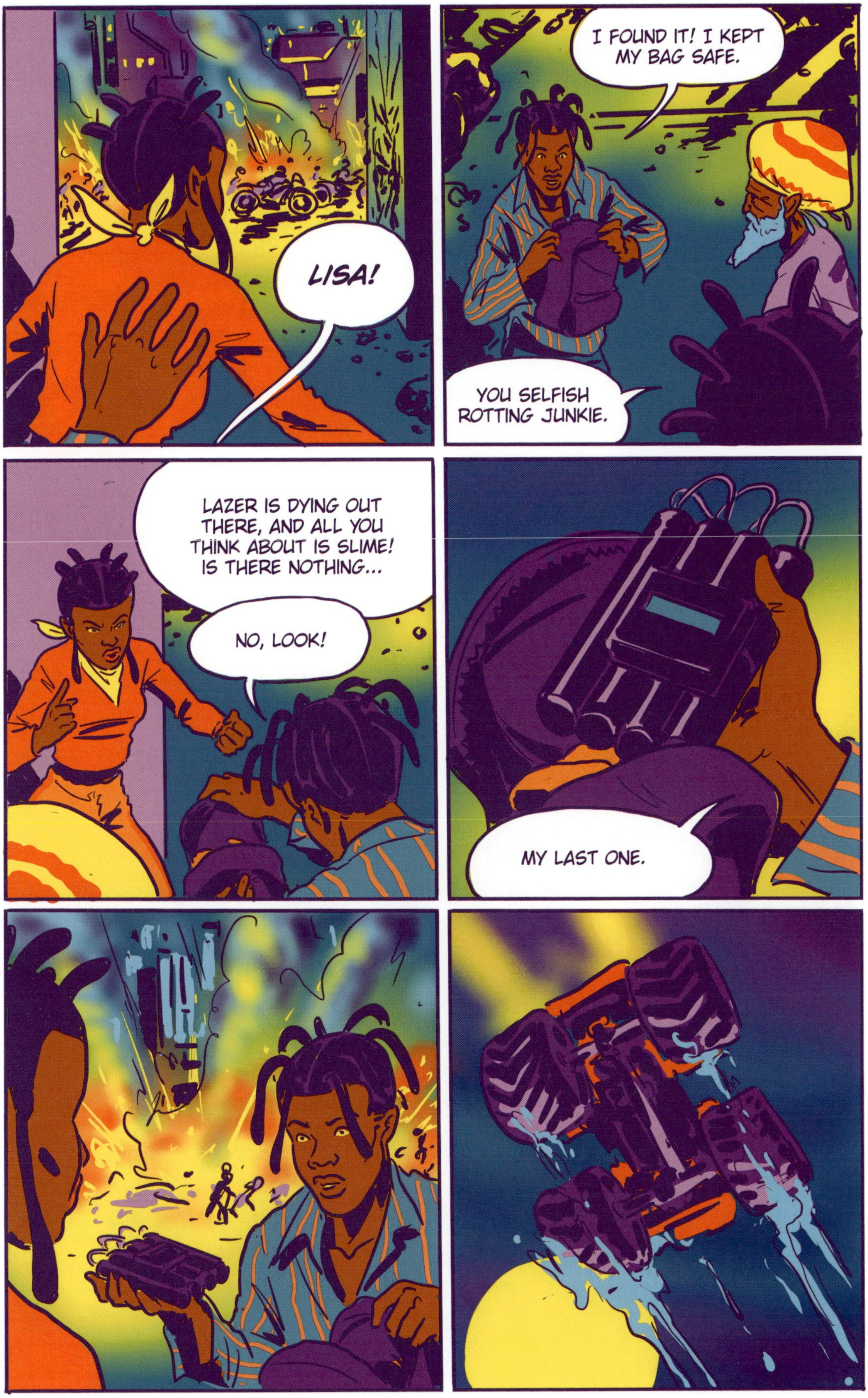
LISA!
I FOUND IT! I KEPT MY BAG SAFE.
YOU SELFISH ROTTING JUNKIE.
LAZER IS DYING OUT THERE, AND ALL YOU THINK ABOUT IS SLIME! IS THERE NOTHING...
NO, LOOK!
MY LAST ONE.

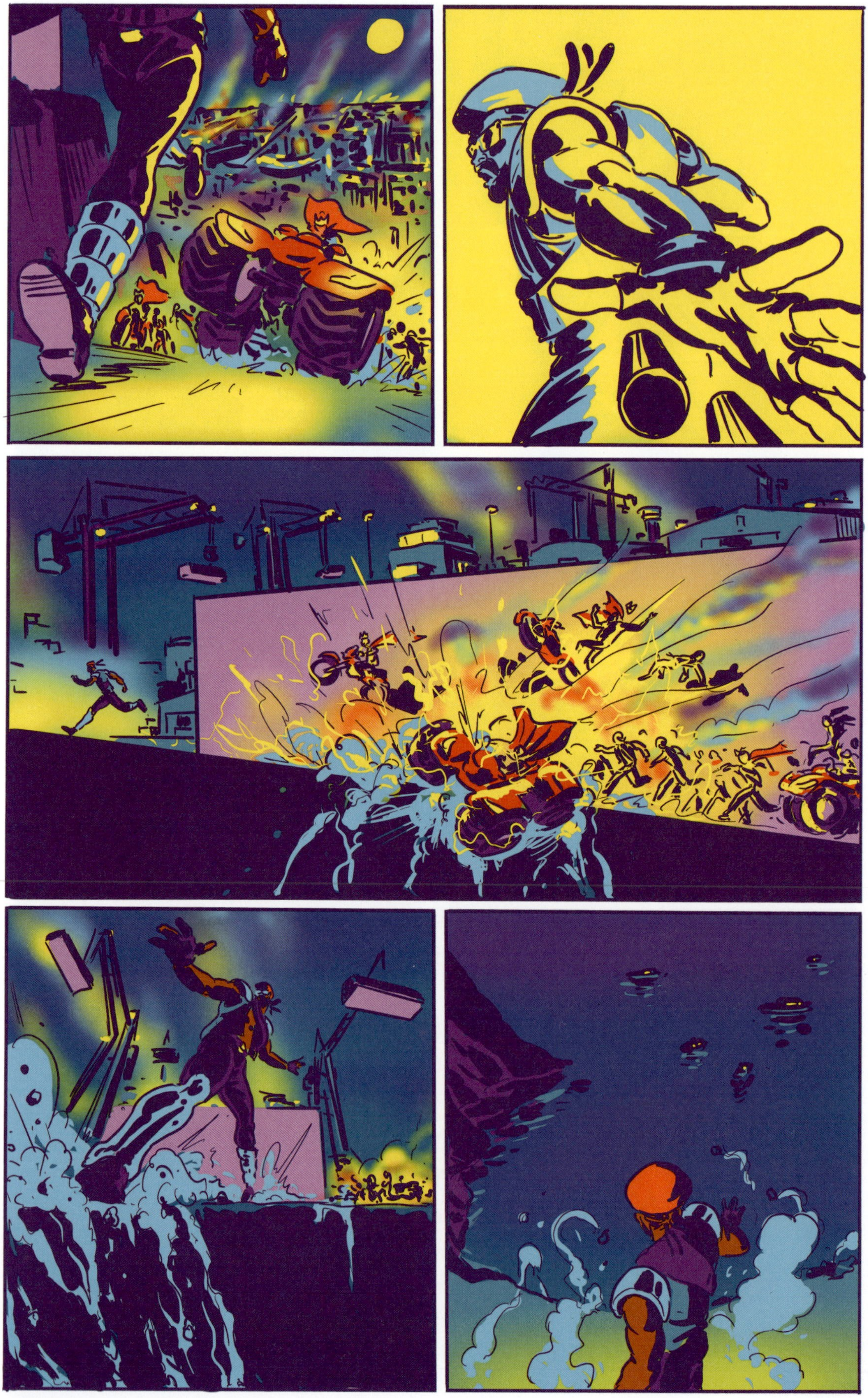

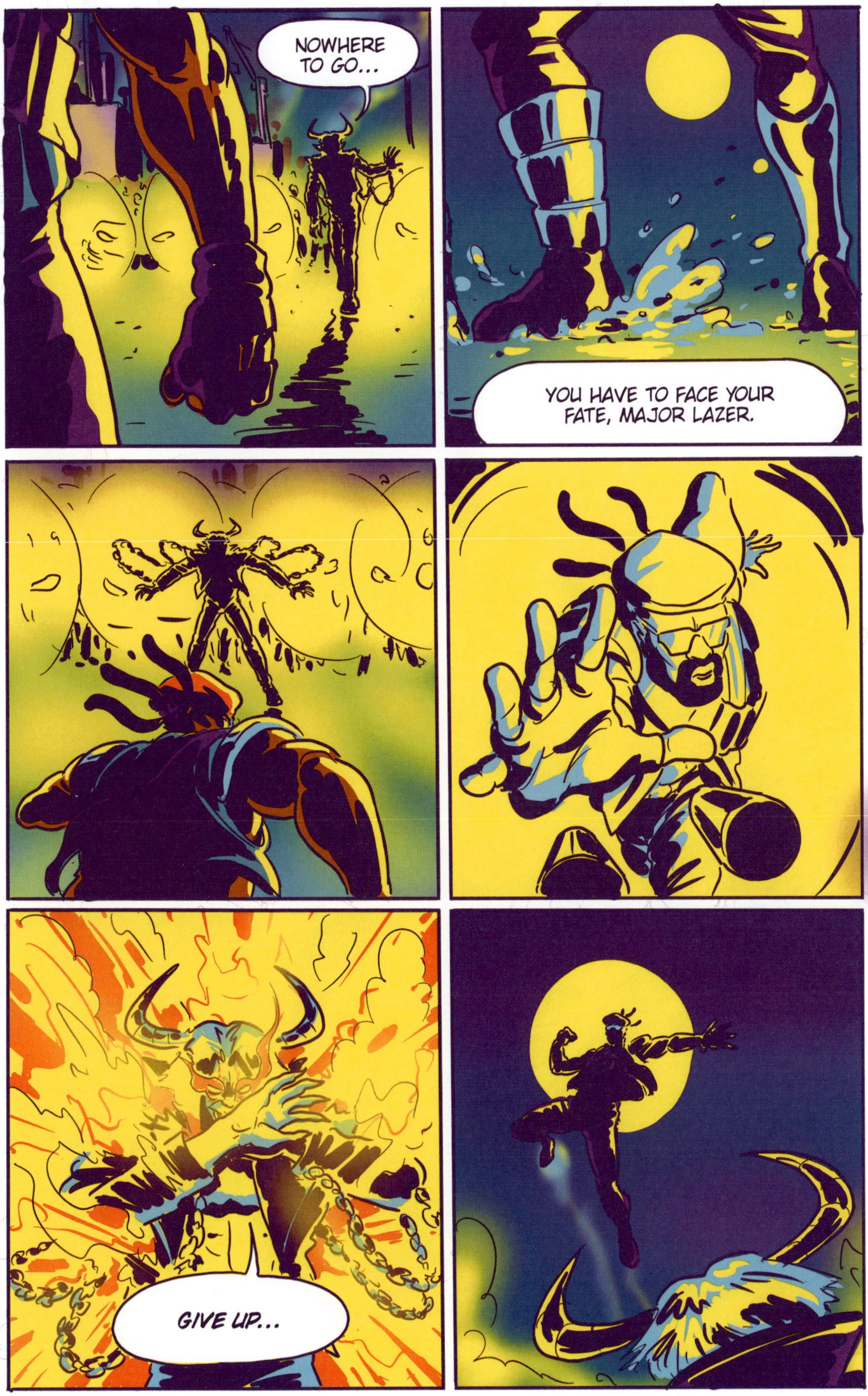
NOWHERE TO GO...
YOU HAVE TO FACE YOUR FATE, MAJOR LAZER.
GIVE UP...

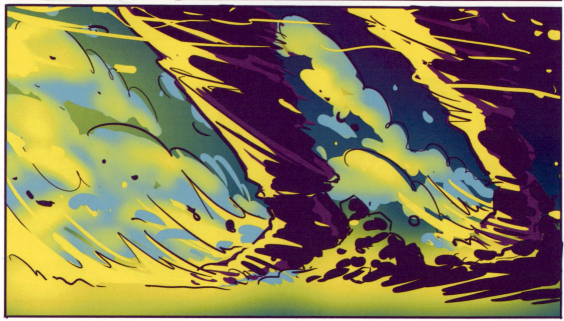

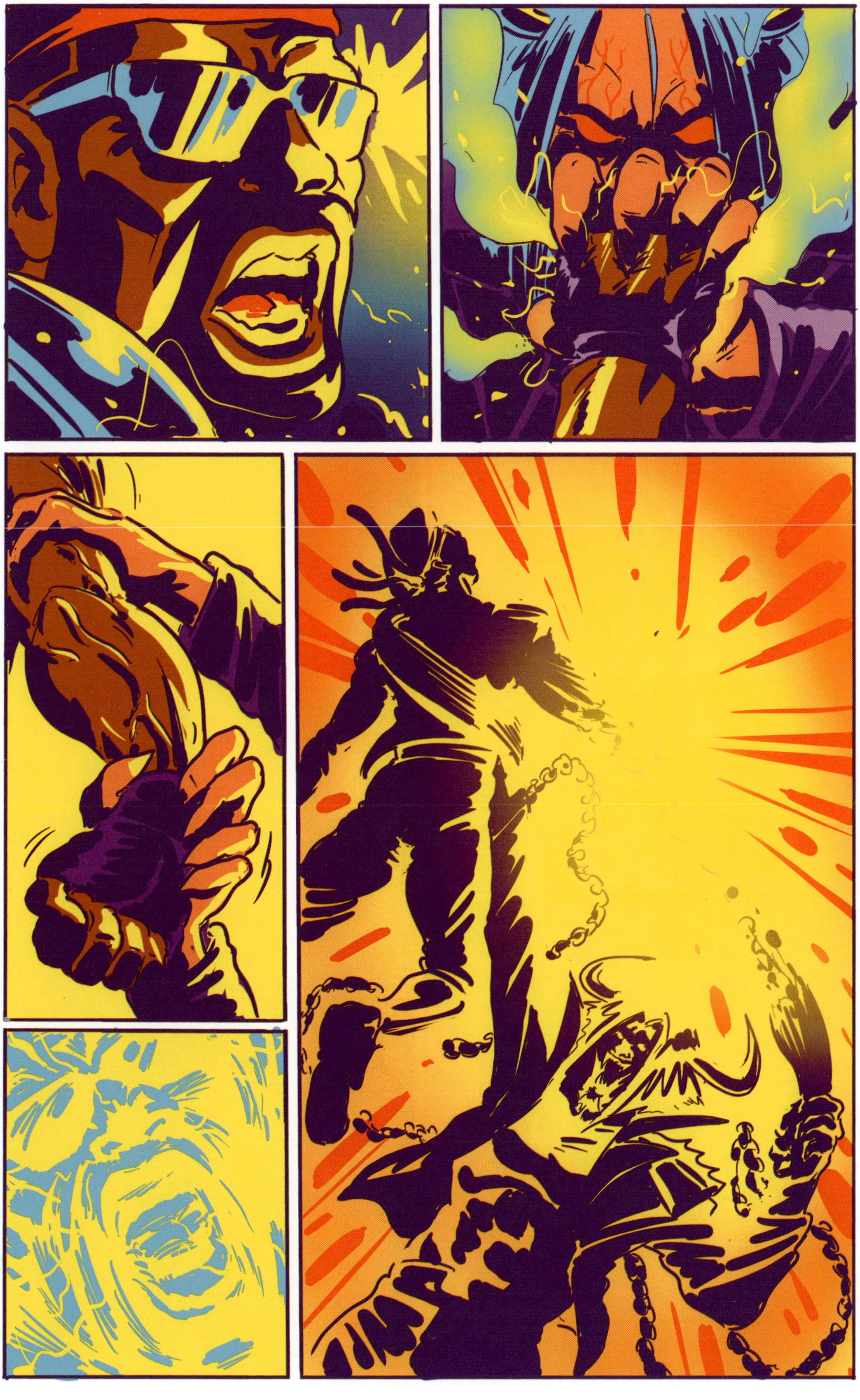

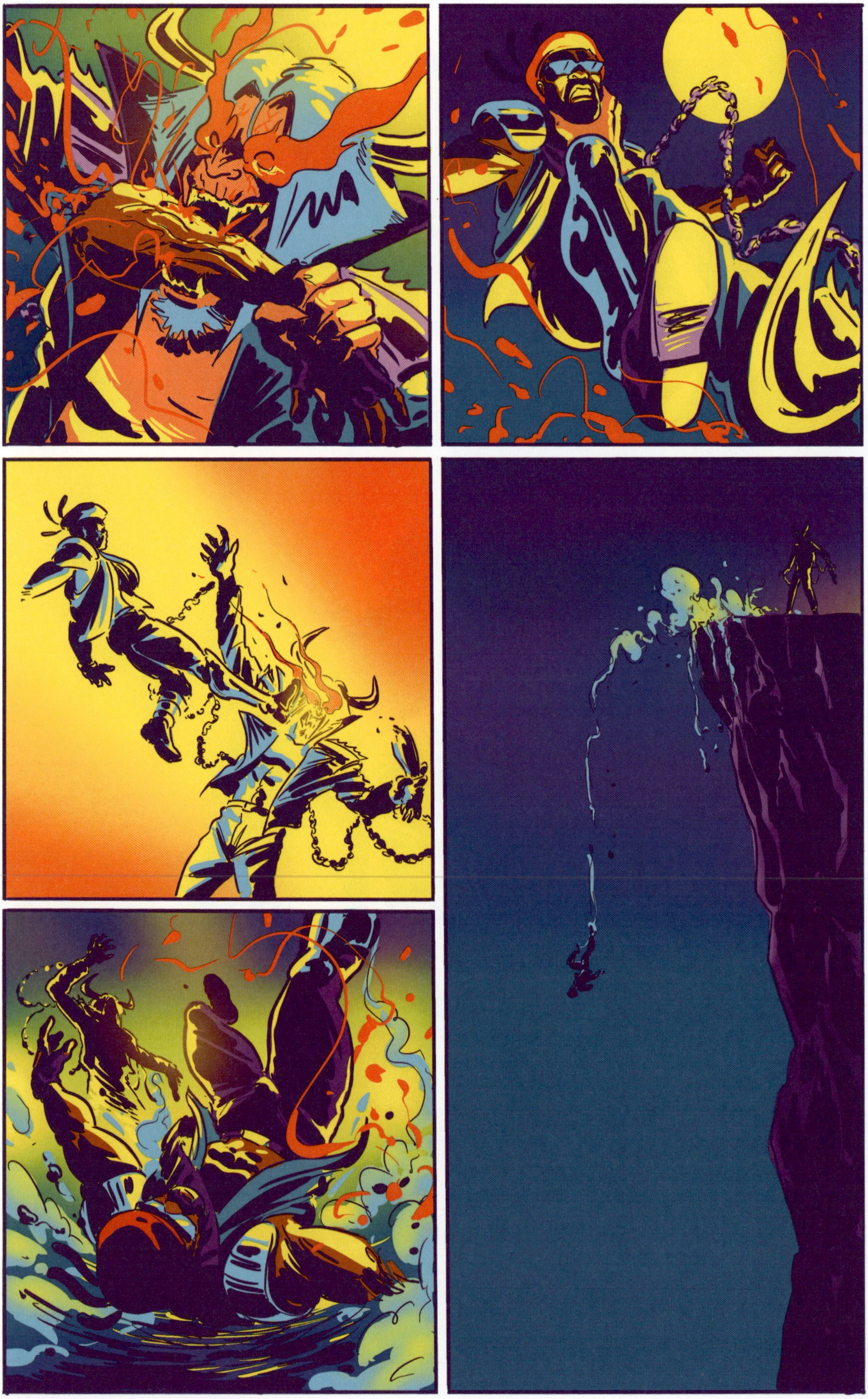

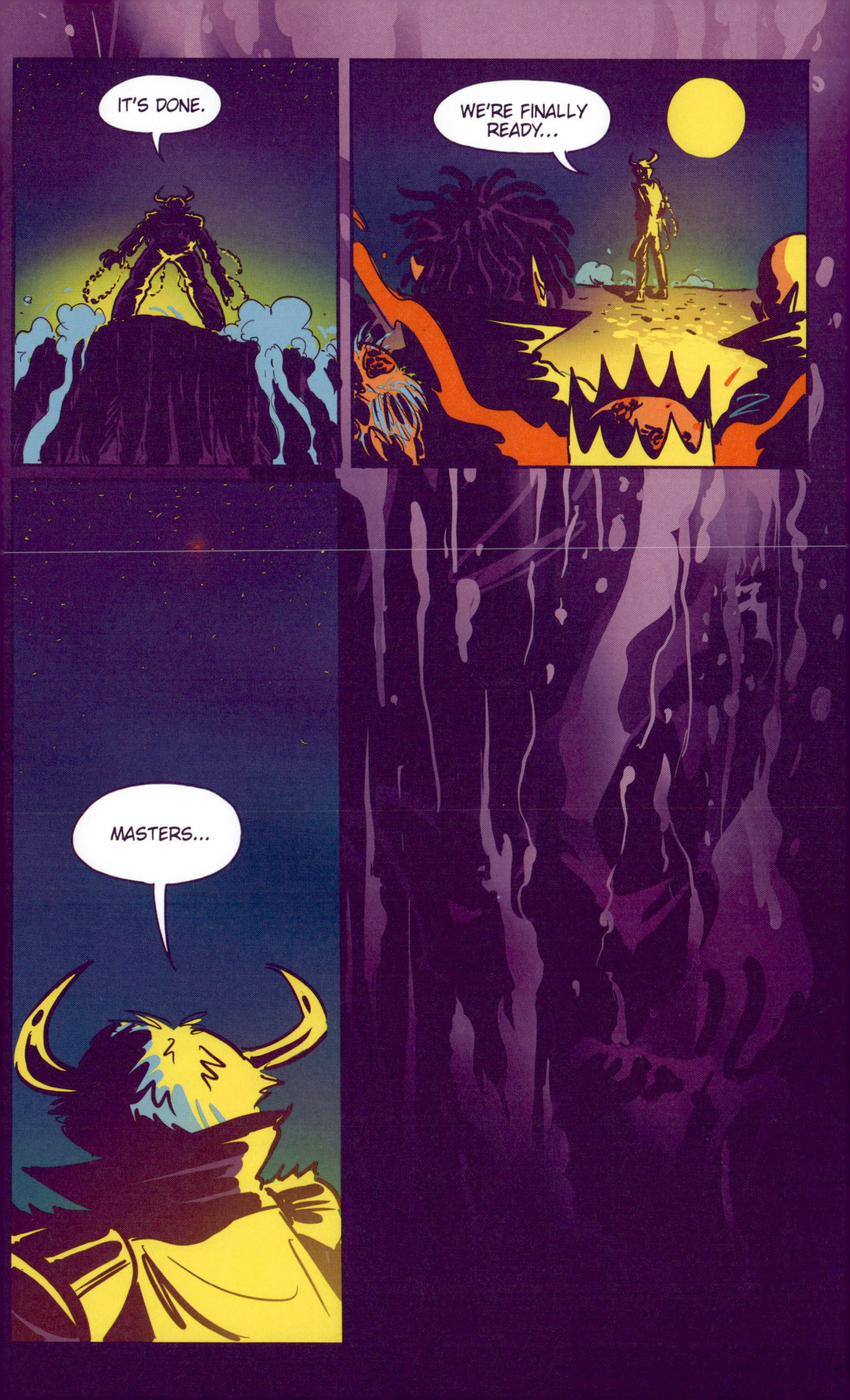
IT'S DONE.
WE'RE FINALLY READY...
MASTERS...

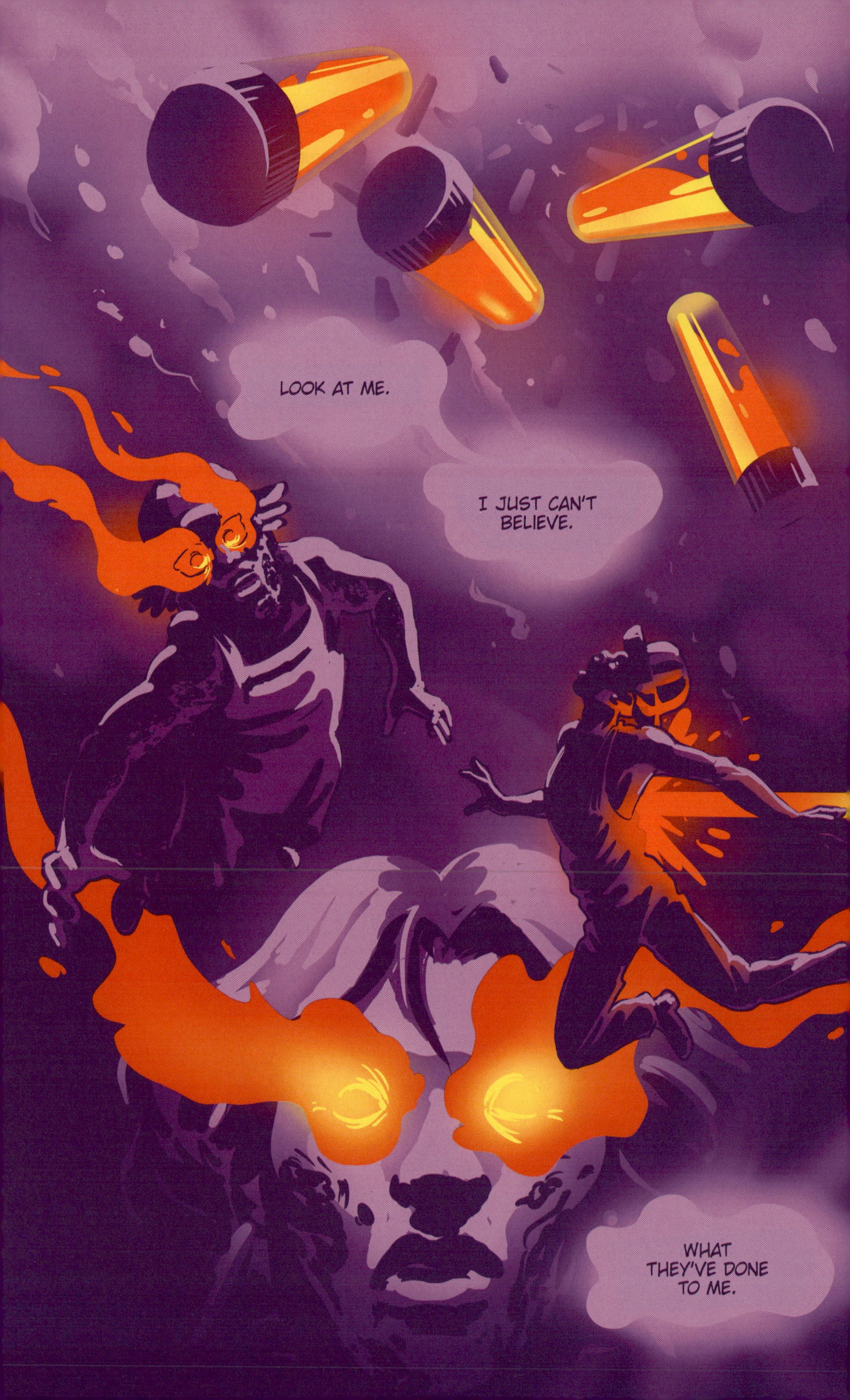
LOOK AT ME.
I JUST CAN'T BELIEVE.
WHAT THEY'VE DONE TO ME.

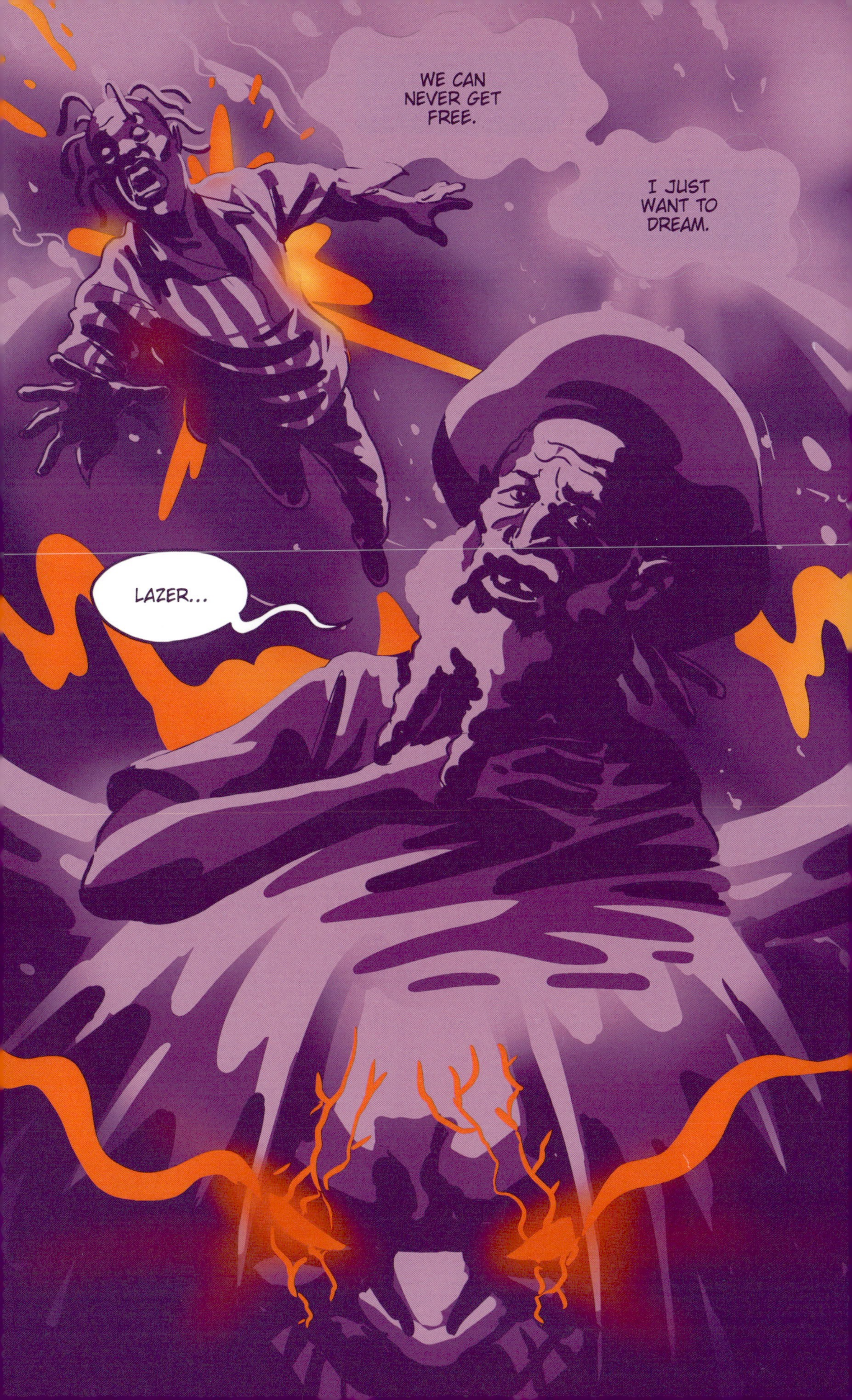
WE CAN NEVER GET FREE.
I JUST WANT TO DREAM.
LAZER...

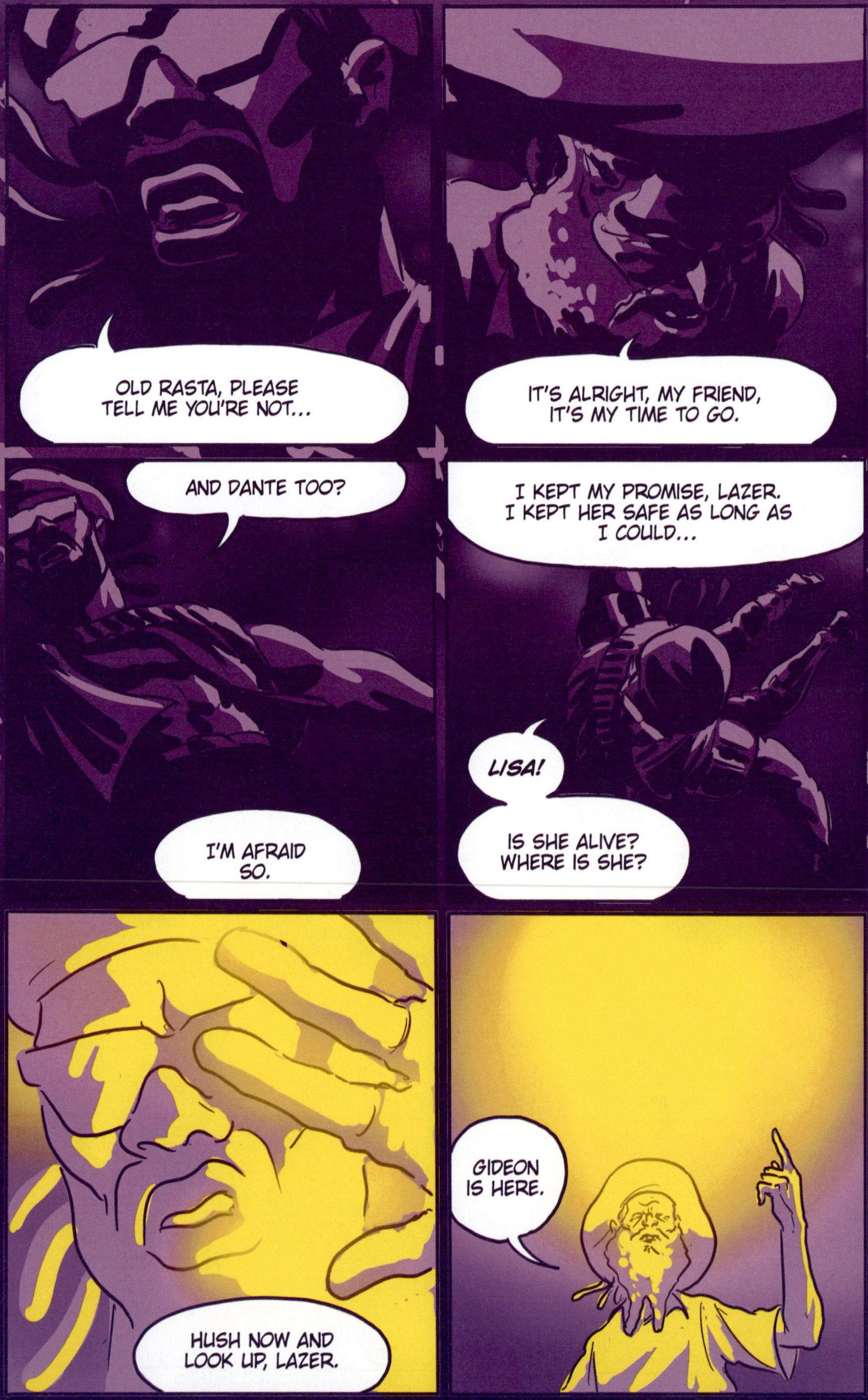
OLD RASTA, PLEASE TELL ME YOU'RE NOT...
IT'S ALRIGHT, MY FRIEND, IT'S MY TIME TO GO.
AND DANTE TOO?
I'M AFRAID SO.
I KEPT MY PROMISE, LAZER. I KEPT HER SAFE AS LONG AS I COULD...
LISA!
IS SHE ALIVE? WHERE IS SHE?
HUSH NOW AND LOOK UP, LAZER.
GIDEON IS HERE.

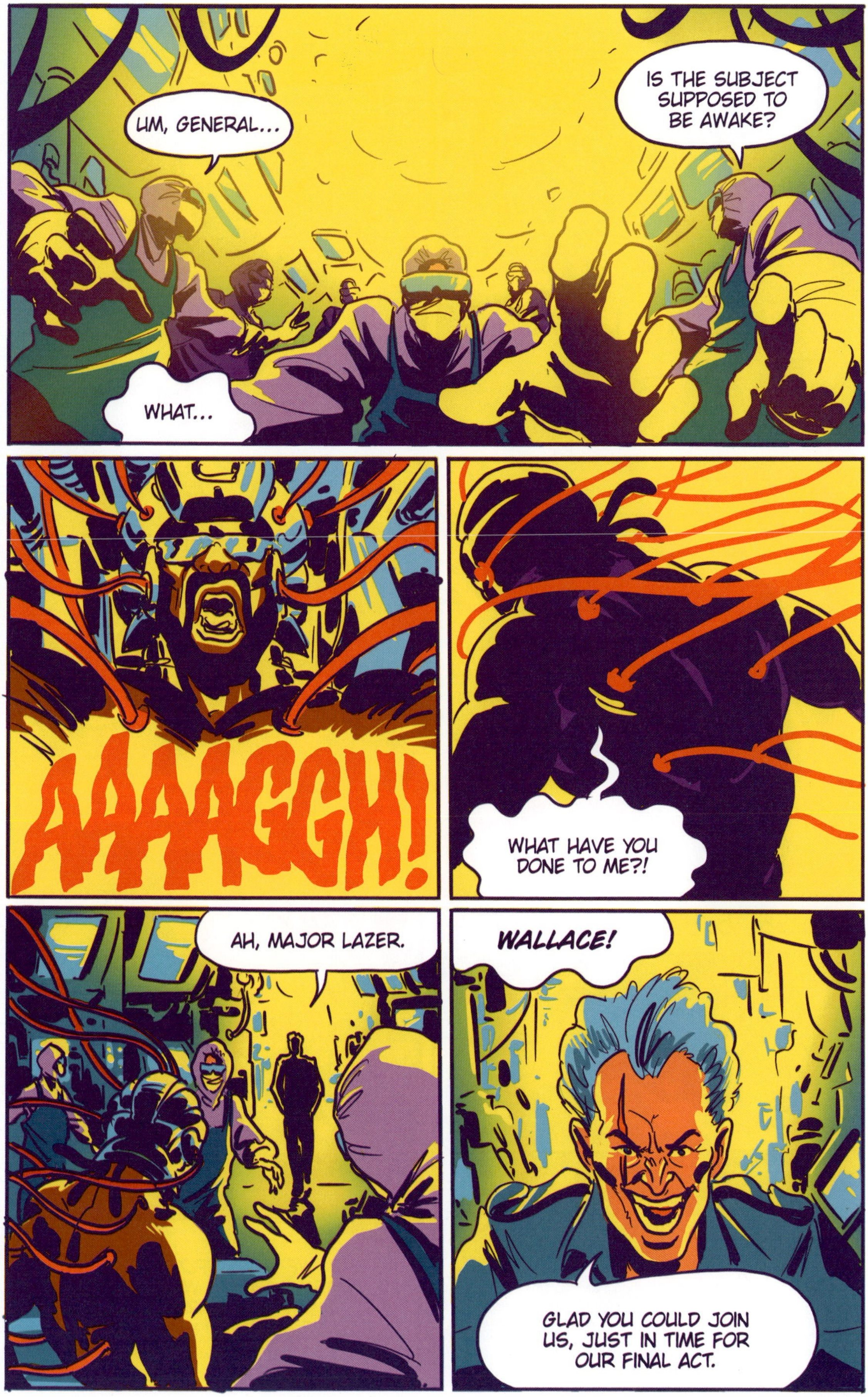
UM, GENERAL...
IS THE SUBJECT SUPPOSED TO BE AWAKE?
WHAT...
AAAAGGH!
WHAT HAVE YOU DONE TO ME?!
AH, MAJOR LAZER.
WALLACE!
GLAD YOU COULD JOIN US, JUST IN TIME FOR OUR FINAL ACT.

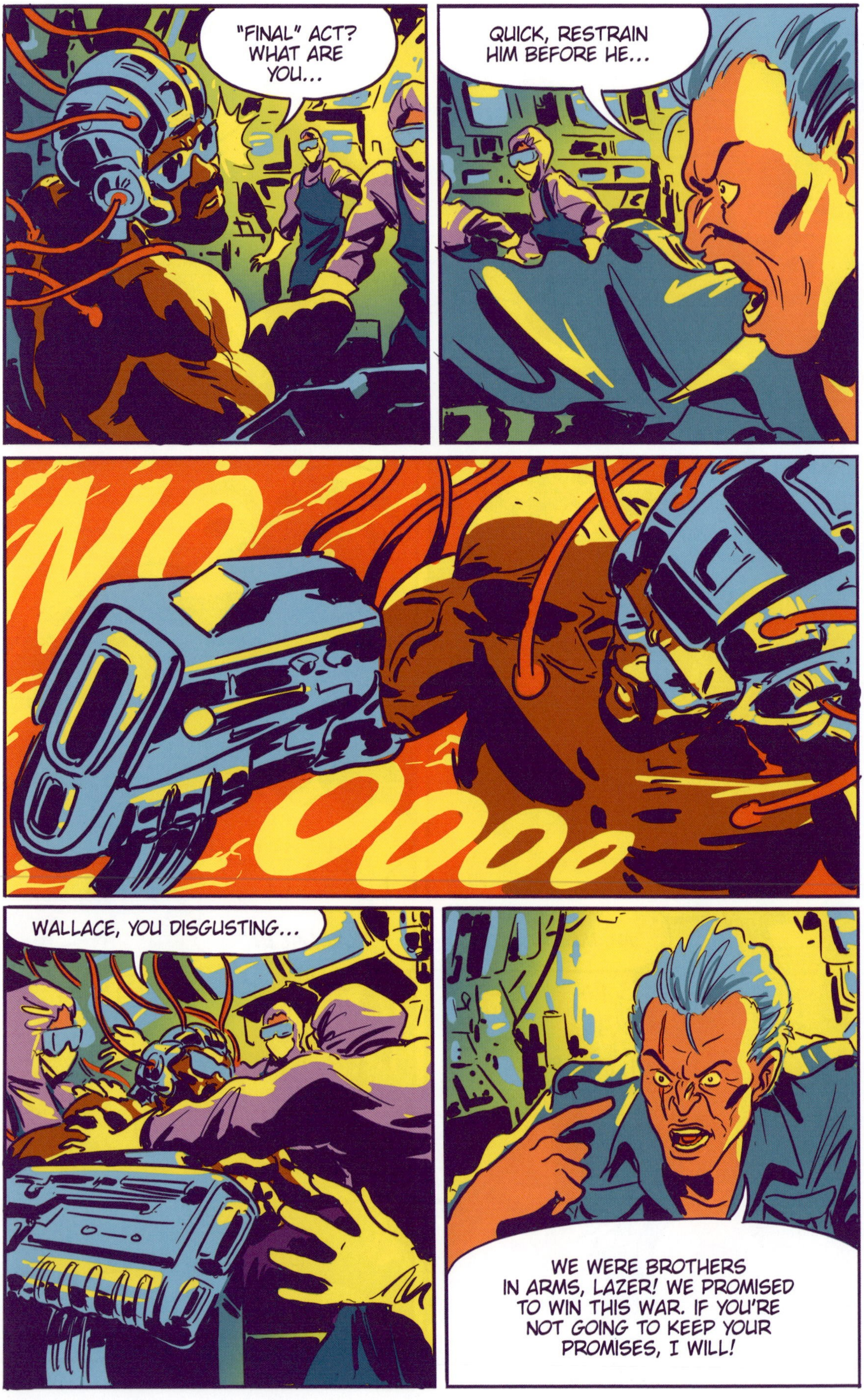
"FINAL" ACT? WHAT ARE YOU...
QUICK, RESTRAIN HIM BEFORE HE...
NOOOOOO
WALLACE, YOU DISGUSTING...
WE WERE BROTHERS IN ARMS, LAZER! WE PROMISED TO WIN THIS WAR. IF YOU'RE NOT GOING TO KEEP YOUR PROMISES, I WILL!

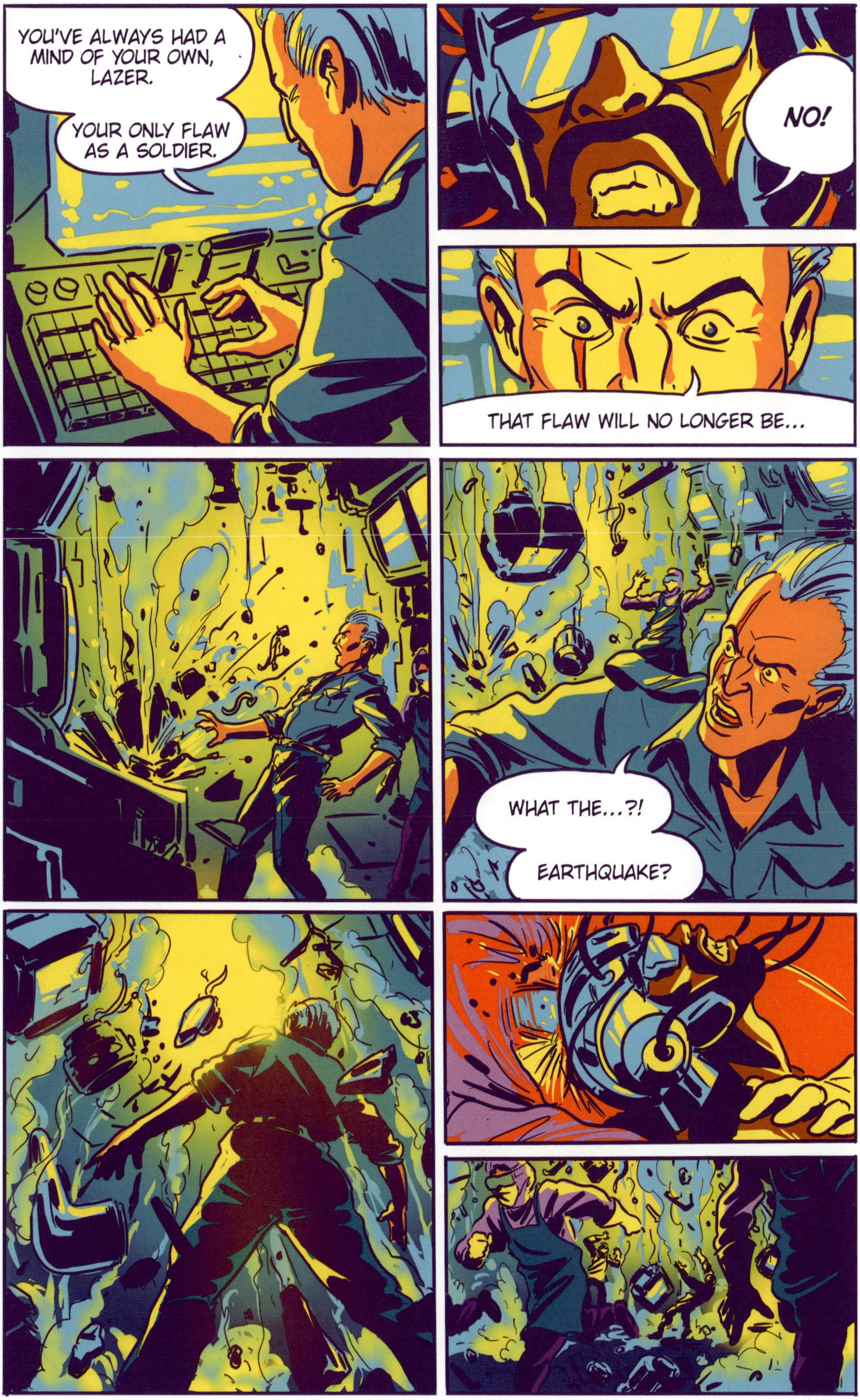
YOU'VE ALWAYS HAD A MIND OF YOUR OWN, LAZER.
YOUR ONLY FLAW AS A SOLDIER.
NO!
THAT FLAW WILL NO LONGER BE...
WHAT THE...?!
EARTHQUAKE?

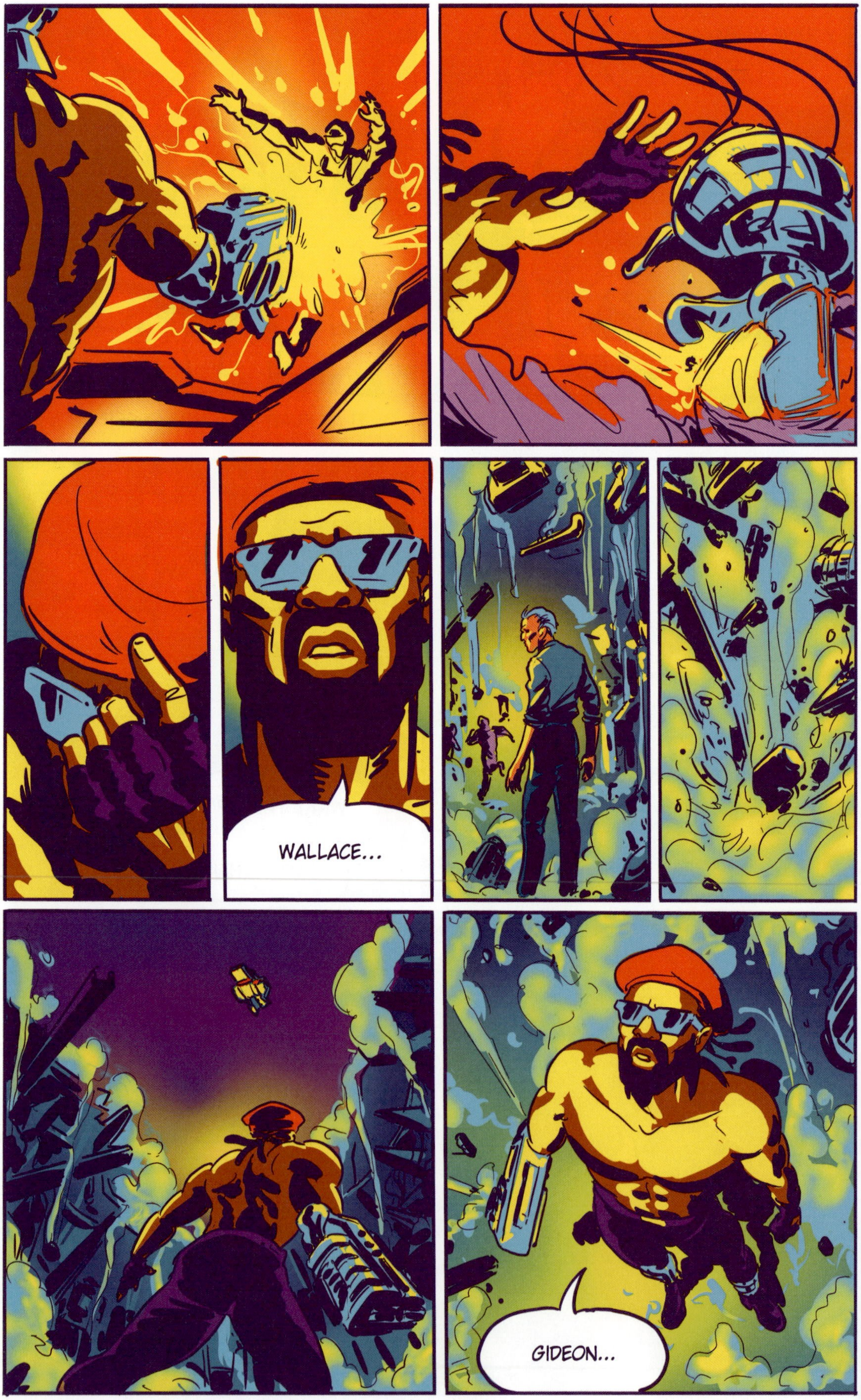
WALLACE...
GIDEON...

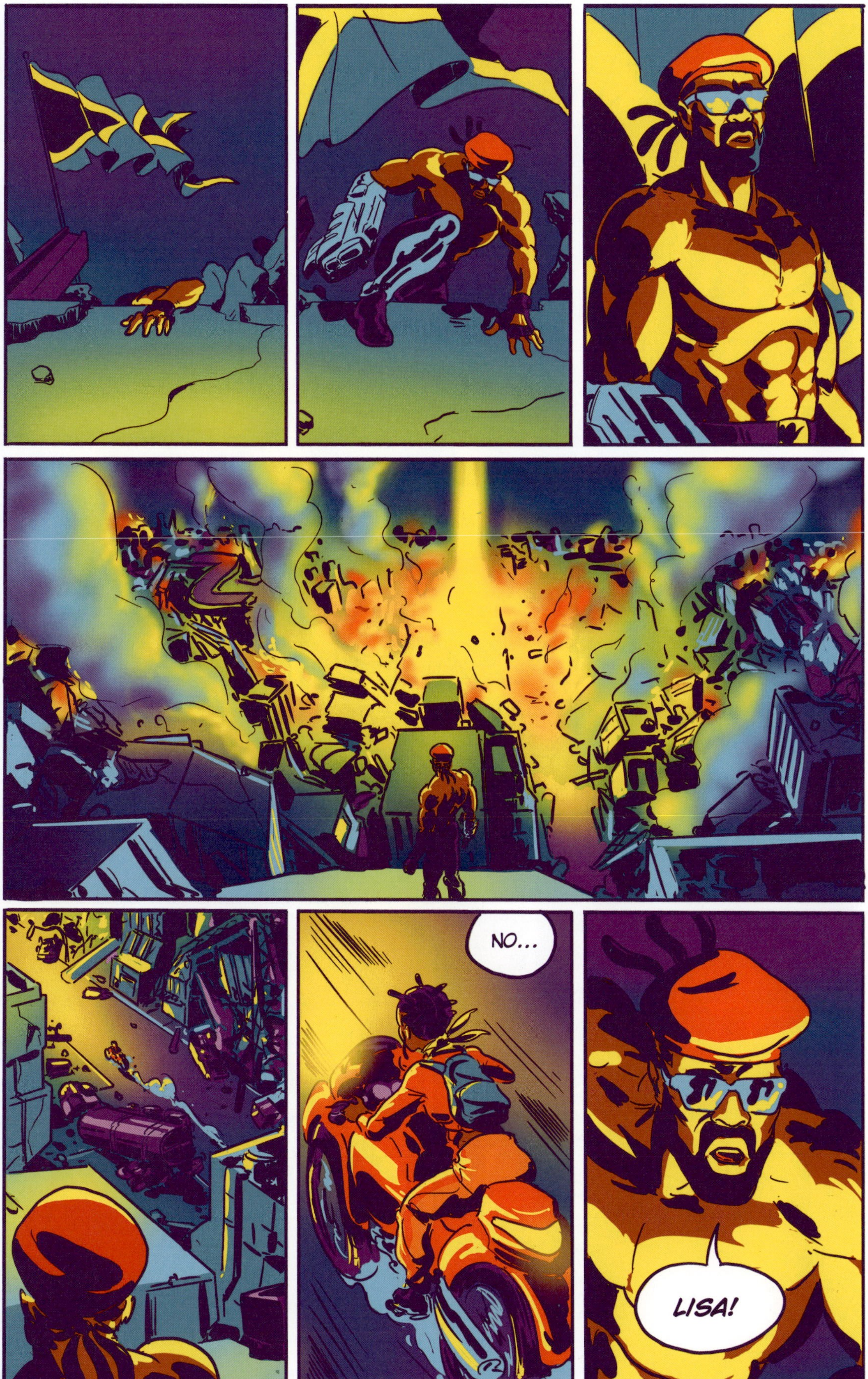
NO...
LISA!

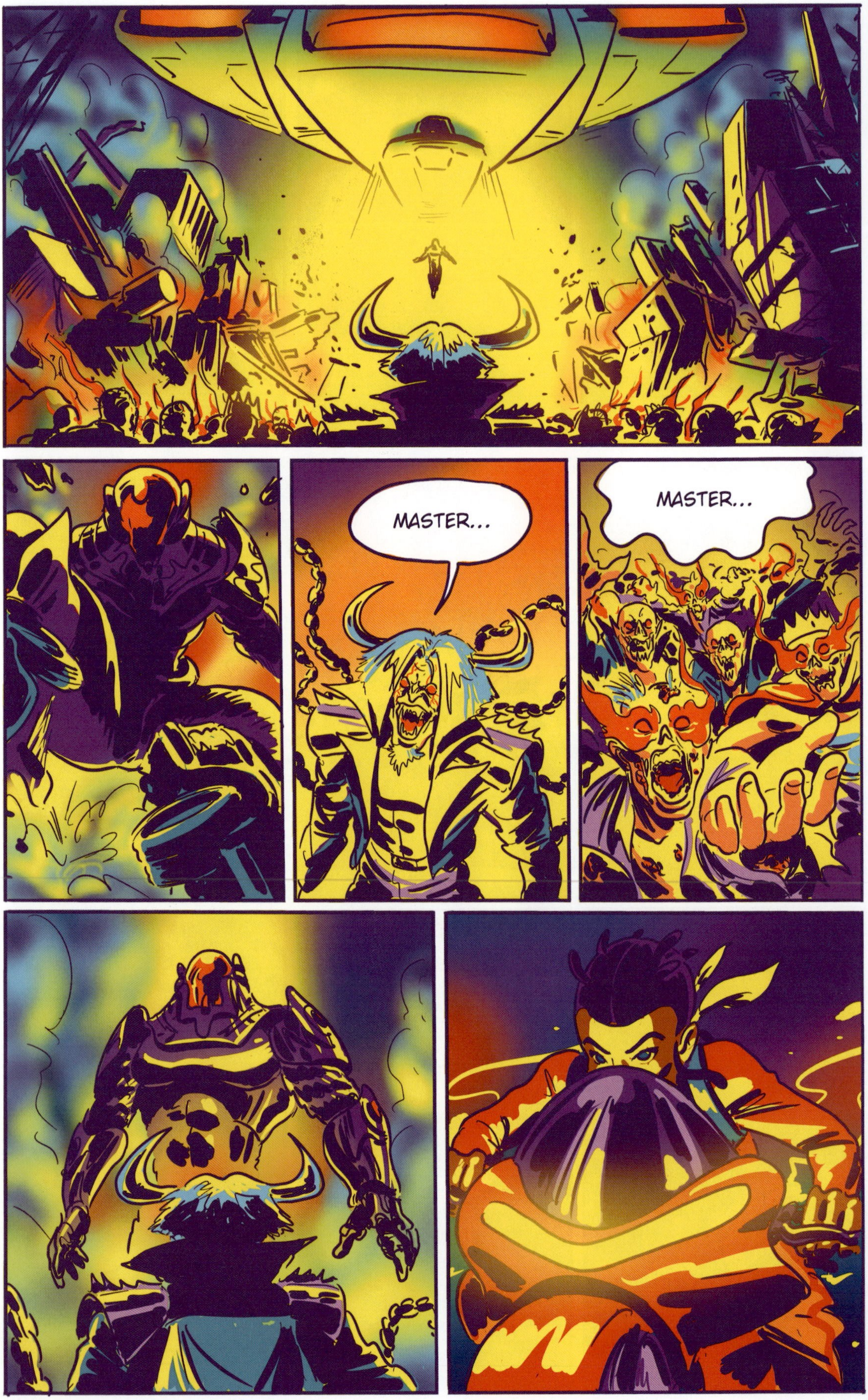

MASTER...
MASTER...

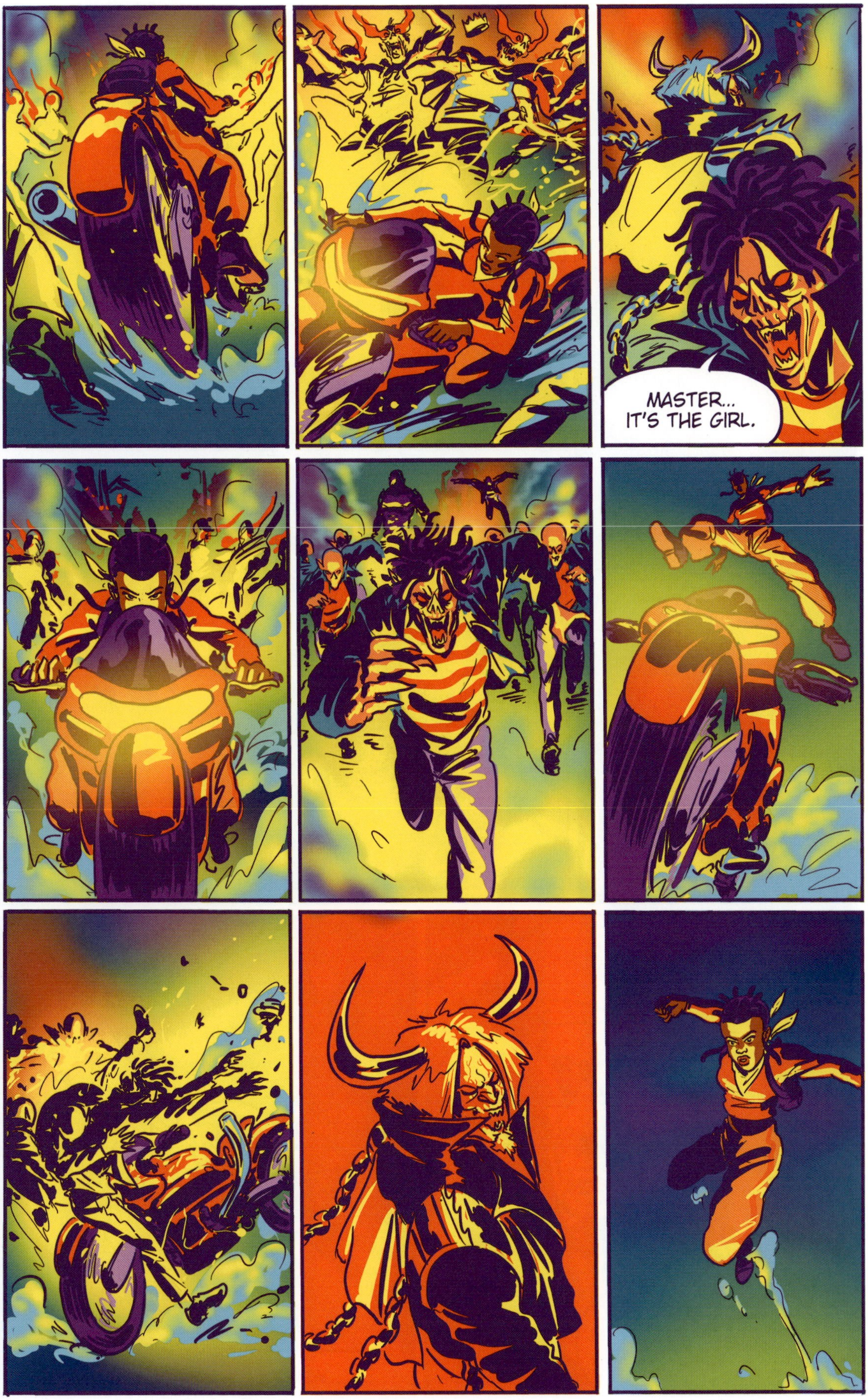
MASTER...
IT'S THE GIRL.

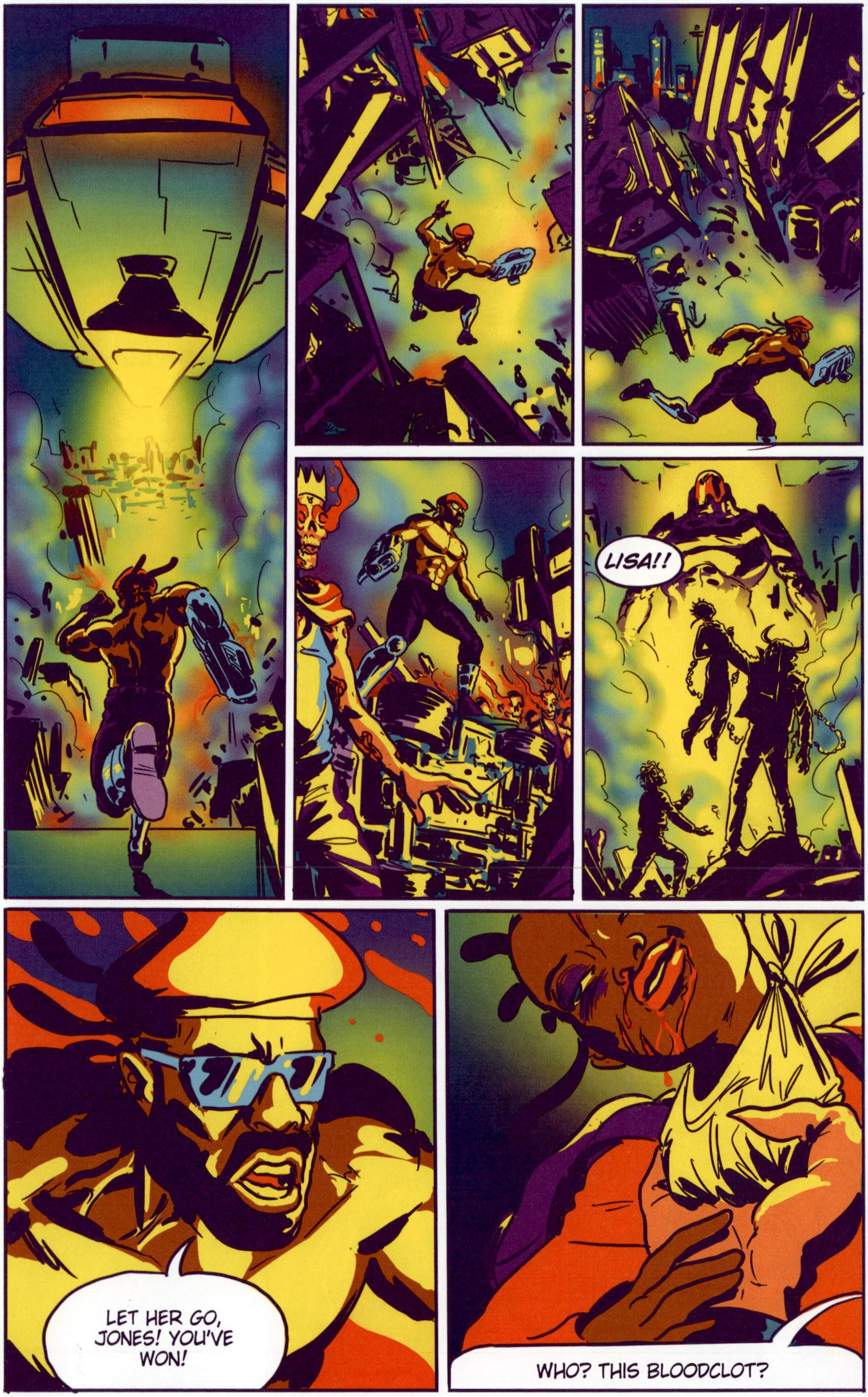
LISA!!
LET HER GO, JONES! YOU'VE WON!
WHO? THIS BLOODCLOT?

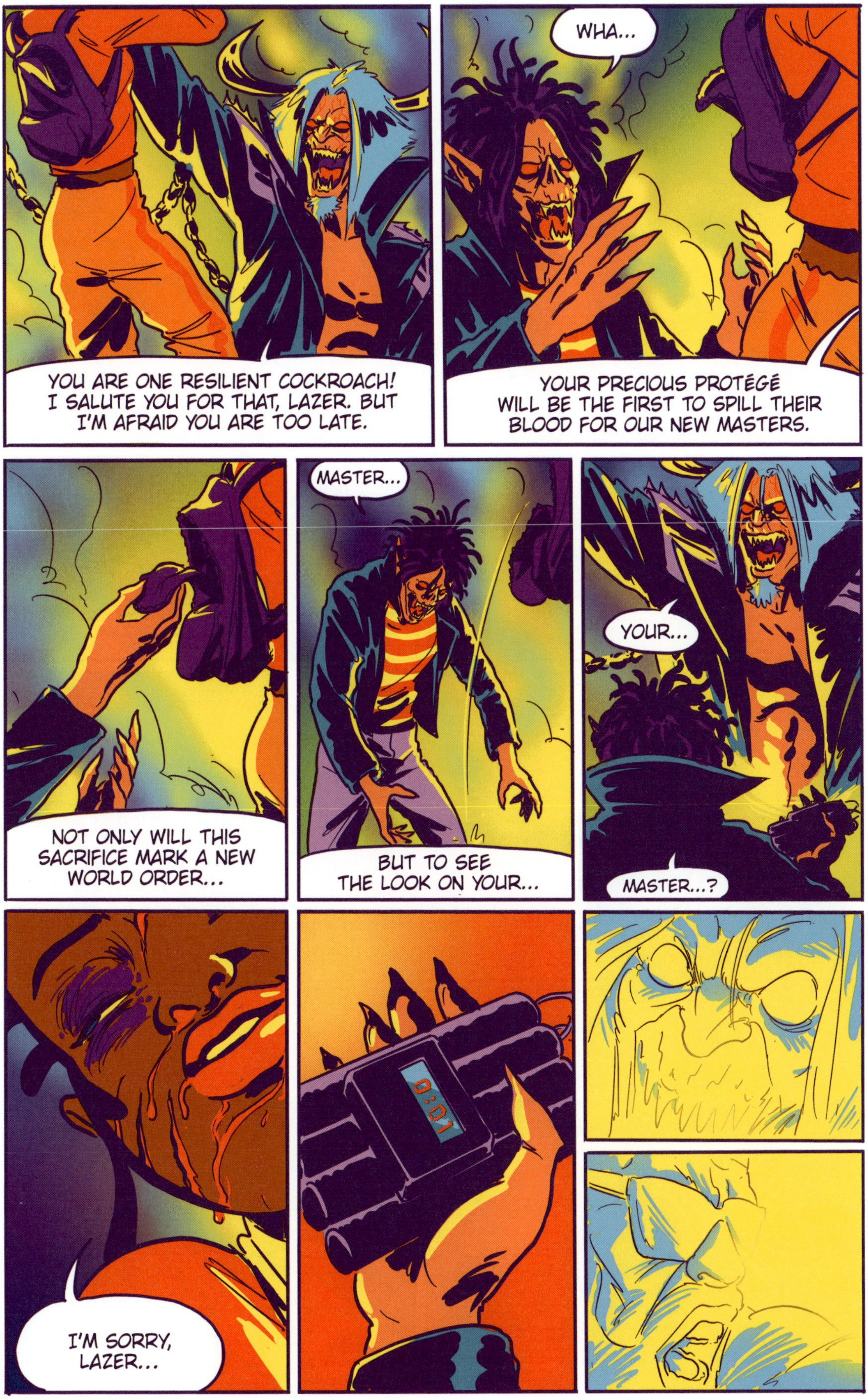
YOU ARE ONE RESILIENT COCKROACH! I SALUTE YOU FOR THAT, LAZER. BUT I'M AFRAID YOU ARE TOO LATE.
WHA...
YOUR PRECIOUS PROTÉGÉ WILL BE THE FIRST TO SPILL THEIR BLOOD FOR OUR NEW MASTERS.
NOT ONLY WILL THIS SACRIFICE MARK A NEW WORLD ORDER...
MASTER...
BUT TO SEE THE LOOK ON YOUR...
YOUR...
MASTER...?
I'M SORRY, LAZER...
0:01

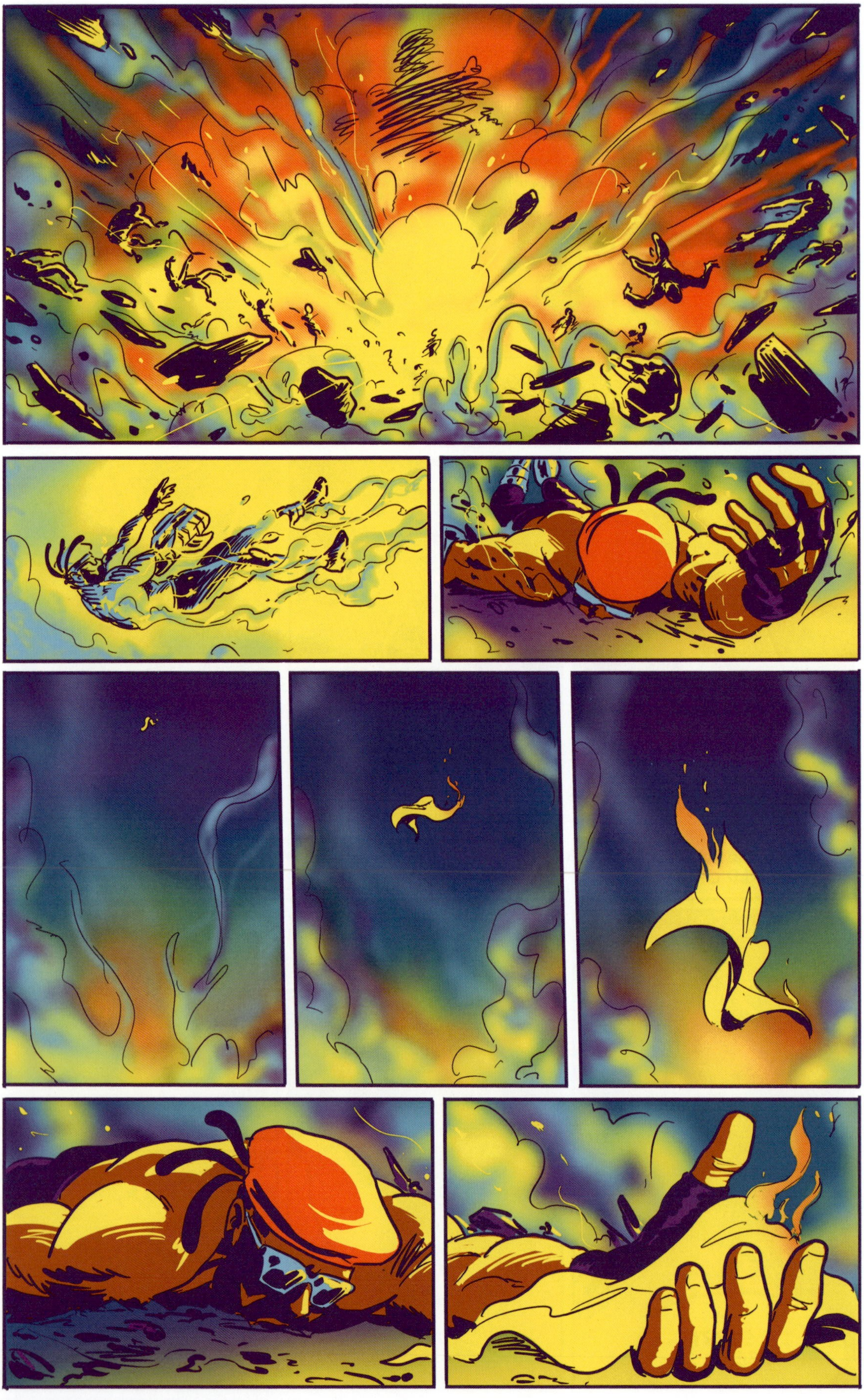

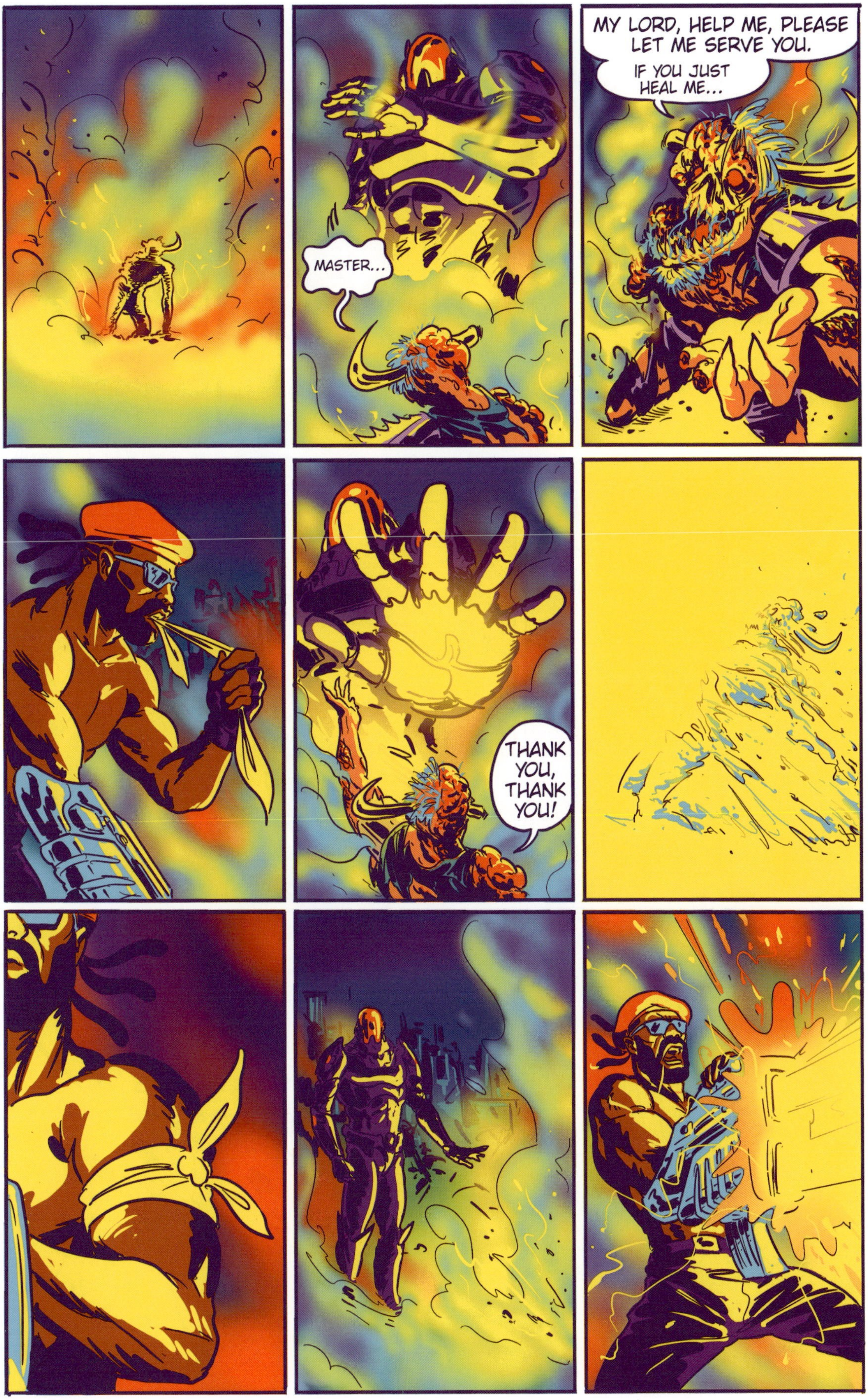
MASTER...
MY LORD, HELP ME, PLEASE LET ME SERVE YOU.
IF YOU JUST HEAL ME...
THANK YOU, THANK YOU!

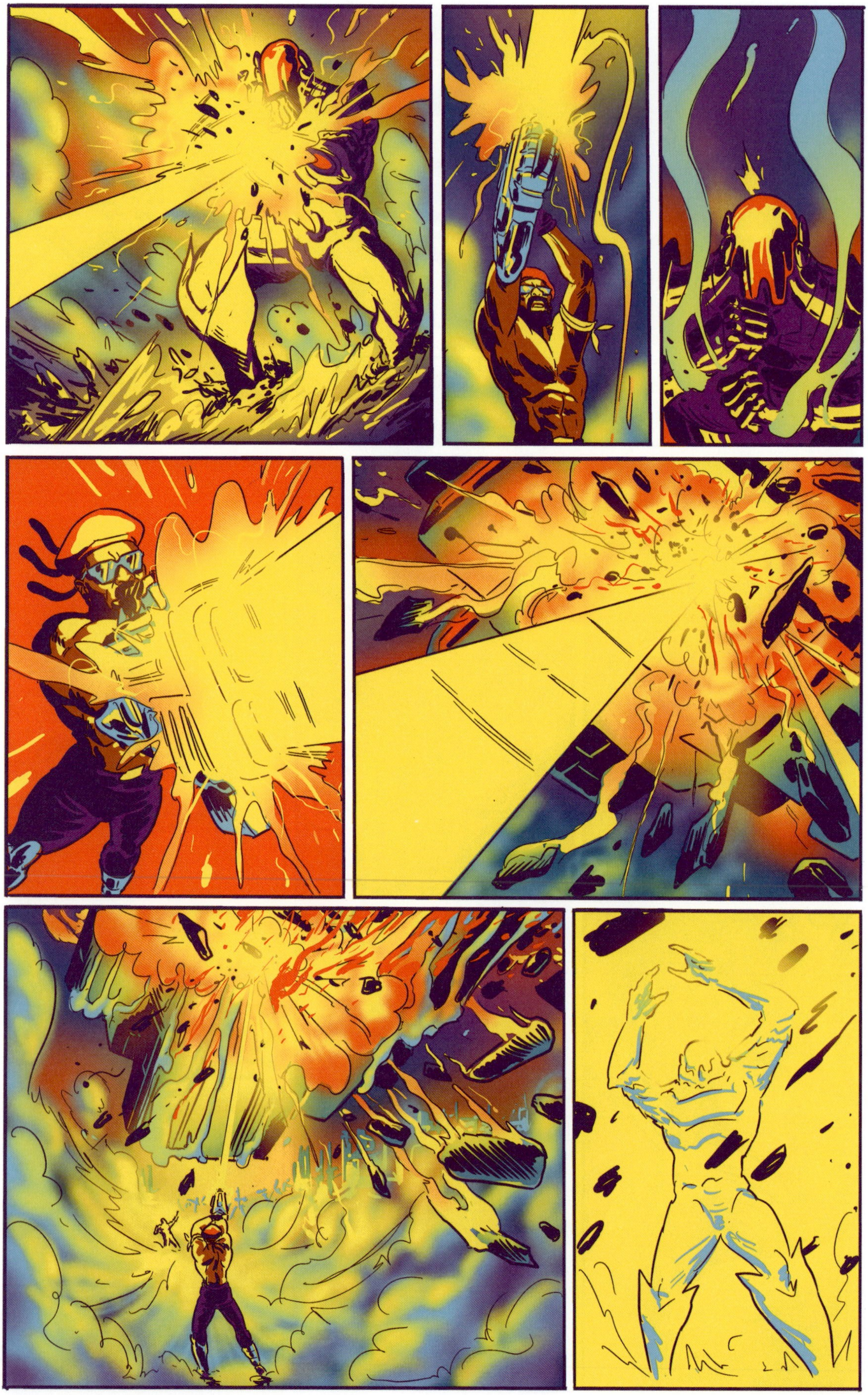

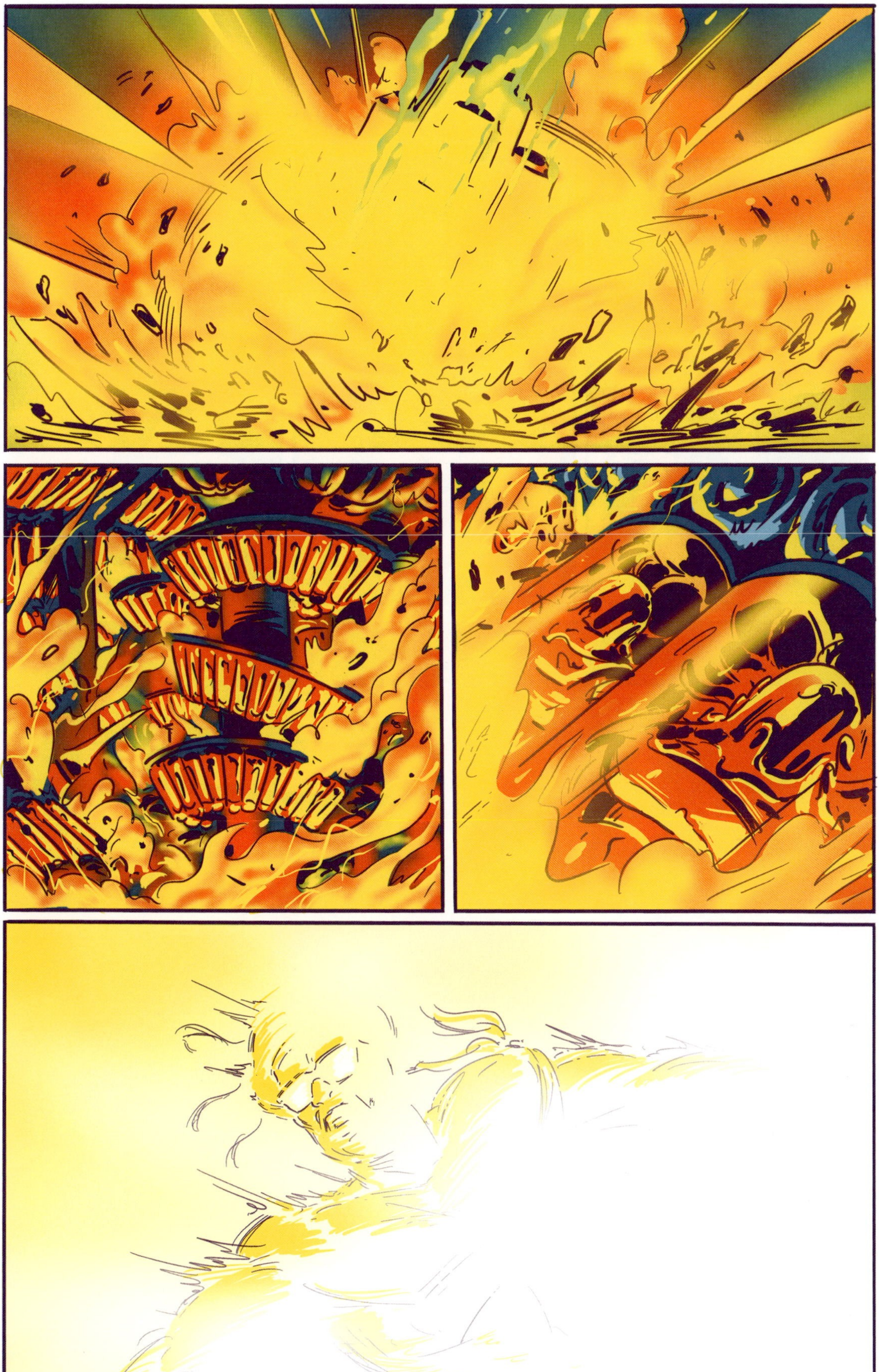

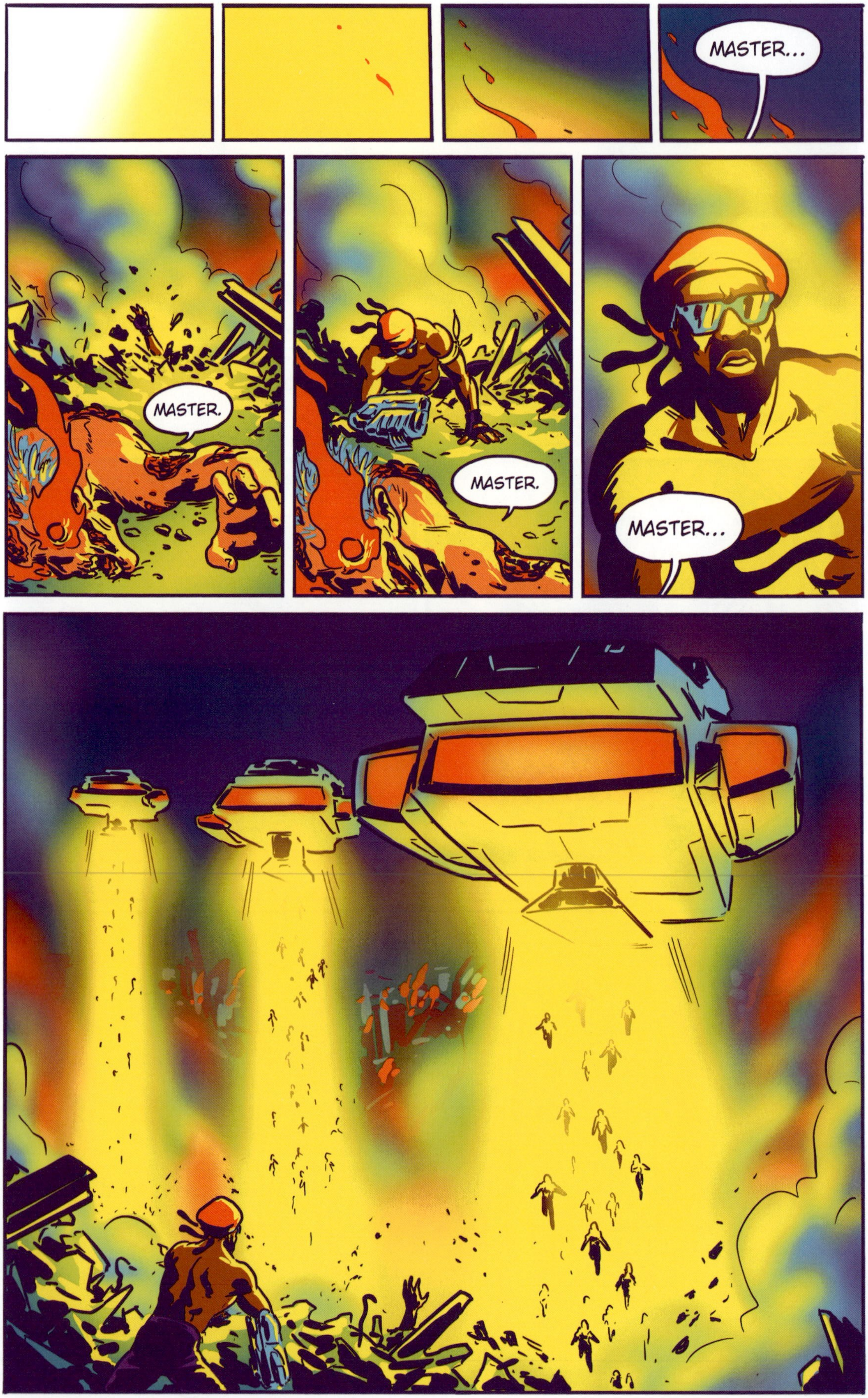
MASTER...
MASTER.
MASTER.
MASTER...

GALLERY

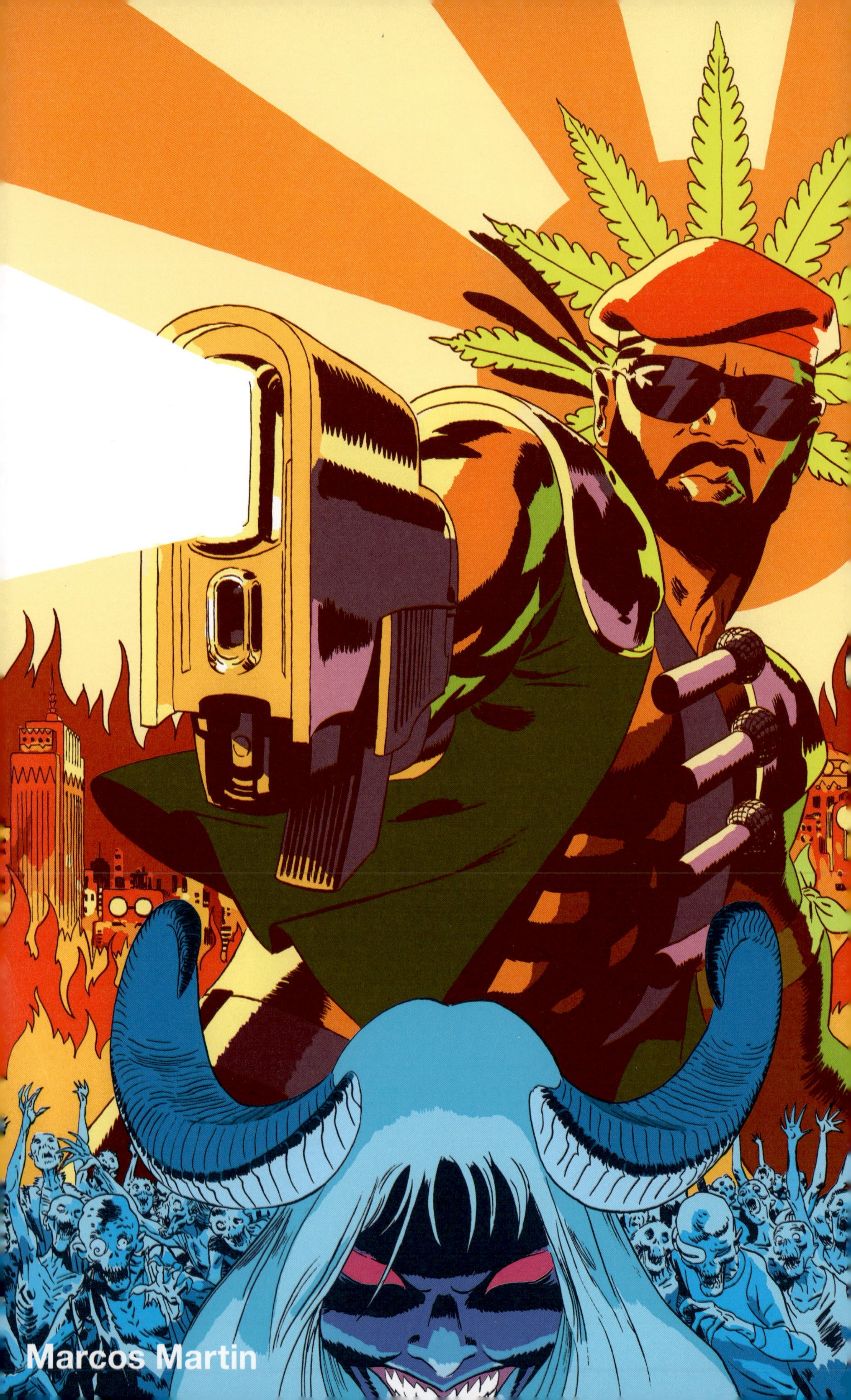
Marcos Martin

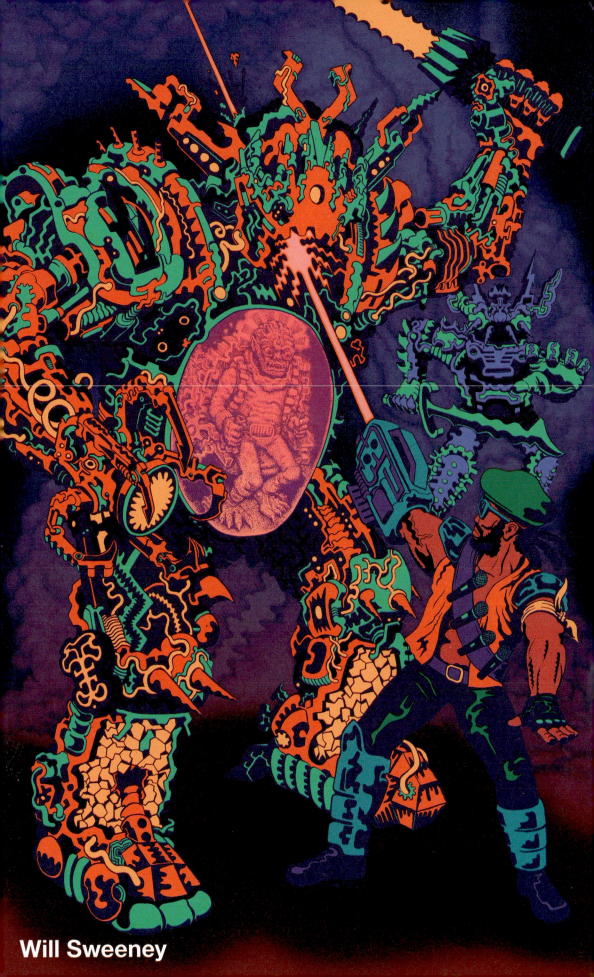

Will Sweeney

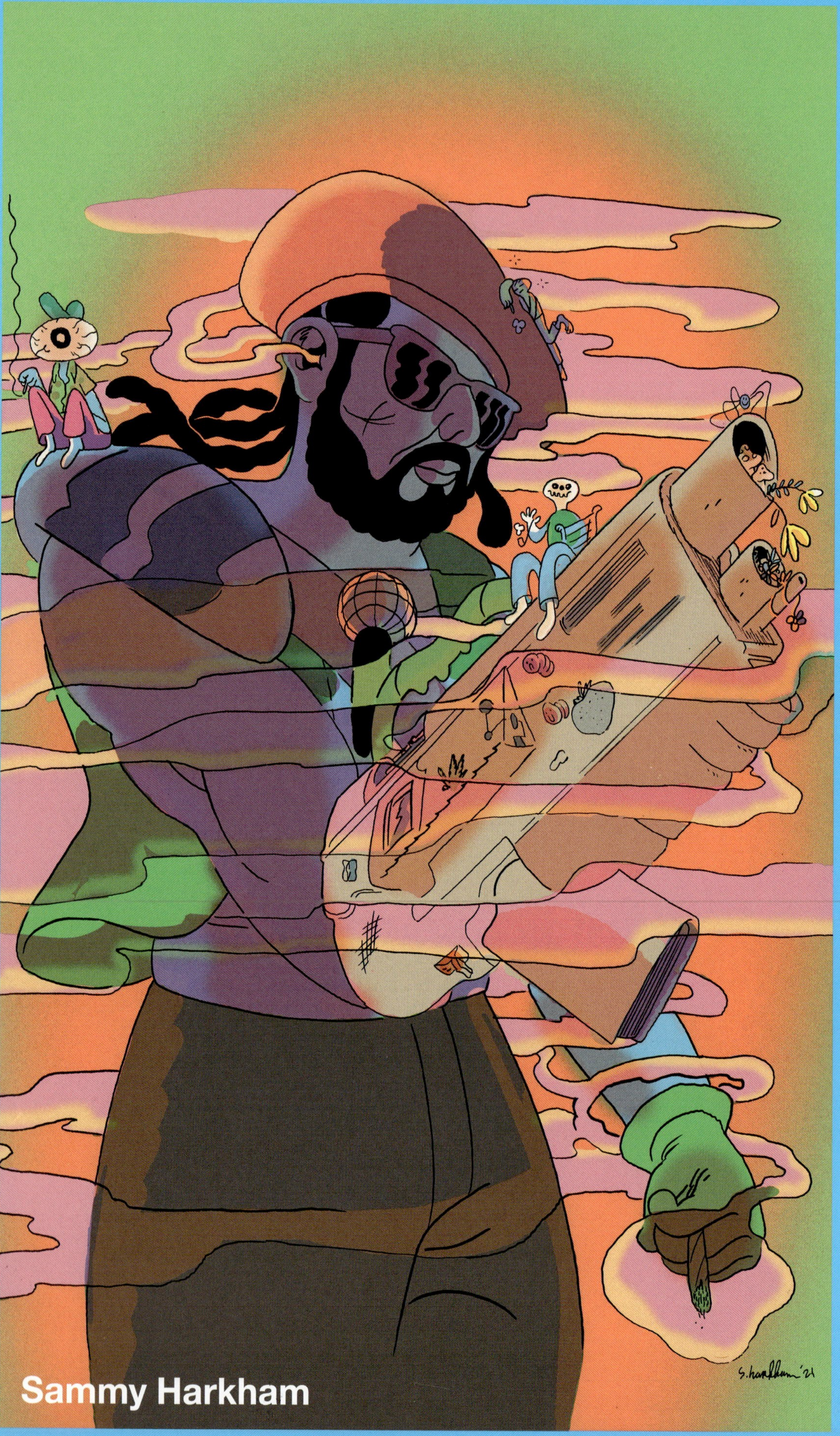
S. harkham '21

Sammy Harkham